The Administration of Imperialism:
Joseph Chamberlain at the
Colonial Office

The Administration of Imperialism: Joseph Chamberlain at the Colonial Office

Robert V. Kubicek

Number 37 in a series published for the

Duke University Commonwealth Studies Center

Duke University Press, Durham, N.C.

1969

© 1969, Duke University Press
Library of Congress Catalogue Card Number 72–89874
S.B.N. 8223–0216–0

Printed in the United States of America
by Kingsport Press, Inc., Kingsport, Tenn.

To M,

Foreword

The Center for Commonwealth Studies at Duke University began its book publishing in 1956 with Professor Frank H. Underhill's *The British Commonwealth: An Experiment in Cooperation among Nations*, which consisted of lectures with which Underhill had inaugurated the formal public operations of the Center. It was what might be called trunk-line history of the old Commonwealth, as interpreted by a wise and witty Canadian liberal. (As used here, in A.D. 1969 by one well over thirty, that last word is not in the least intended to be defamatory.) In the years between, the Duke group has published further monographs, symposia, and lectures on the old Dominions, but it also plunged zestfully into the multiracial Commonwealth, into the themes of Asian and African affairs that were just becoming fashionable when the Center was born. It has busied itself with Pakistani, Ceylonese and Malaysian bureaucracy, with African political and educational problems, with both economic and political development in underdeveloped states. The Center now proposes to add to its empire studies in the political and cultural expansion of parts of Western Europe other than Great Britain.

For its thirty-seventh volume, however, the Center returns from its restless flitting about in the social science of other continents to the fountainhead, with a book about one of the most noted figures in British imperial history, Joseph Chamberlain as secretary of state for the colonies. Associate Professor R. V. Kubicek of the Department of History in the University of British Columbia scrutinizes Chamberlain from a historian's viewpoint, but he does so with full knowledge that an interdisciplinary approach is increasingly necessary for sound social science. He treats

Chamberlain's tenure at the C. O. as a case study in administration. The book therefore befits a Center that has always combined and sometimes fused the work of economists, historians, and political scientists.

The most inspiring, and perhaps in the end the most useful, enterprise of the Center for Commonwealth Studies has been to draw in students from the Commonwealth for graduate training in the three disciplines. They have come from many members, but in Australia, Canada, and New Zealand the Center has formed selection committees to screen applicants for fellowships. Canada, because of its proximity and the Center's especial interest in the Dominion, has furnished more students than any other member. Dr. Kubicek represents the process admirably. He came to Duke from Alberta, performed his graduate work, did his research in the capital of the Commonwealth, and returned to Canada with his Ph.D. degree.

The Duke University Center for Commonwealth Studies must not pass up an opportunity to thank its benefactors. It was launched by the support of the Carnegie Corporation of New York and later nurtured by the international-studies programs of the Ford Foundation. It has been encouraged also by the Rockefeller Foundation.

W. B. HAMILTON

COMMONWEALTH HOUSE, DUKE UNIVERSITY
MAY 12, 1969

Preface

Through strident appeals to sentiment and dynamic political leadership, Joseph Chamberlain gave great impetus to British imperialism. The nation's leading exponent of expansion and consolidation also made an immense effort to improve the instruments of imperial power and wealth. He labored to strengthen his own department and reform the colonial civil service. He tried to set up development programs for tropical dependencies and fashion schemes for new tariff arrangements with the white settlement empire. He sought co-operation from the War and Foreign Offices and his cabinet colleagues to save British hegemony in South Africa. He grappled with the formidable problem of controlling activist governors. He also sought to strike productive alliances with sectors of the commercial community. These personal initiatives plunged institutions of imperial administration into much more activity than that to which they had been accustomed.

Because these structures were extensive and complex, the range of Chamberlain's activities immense, and administrative studies require a detailed approach, the following examination is selective. While the case studies chosen are intended to reassess Chamberlain's reputation as an administrator and further understanding of the operation of imperial power, they are also concerned with the role and function of public administration. It distinguished sharply between political and bureaucratic structure. Its bureaucracy featured an ordered staff hierarchy with its own values, rules, methods and duties, recruited by an impartial exam, promoted by a system based on seniority and achievement, and capable of a high degree of efficiency through the division of labor and specialization. Yet there were significant departures from the ideal. The Colonial Office failed to achieve efficiency. Treasury officials, who played a major role in blocking Chamberlain's innovations, engaged in political activity quite removed from their administrative function; so did the governor holding down the most important post in the colonial civil service. More important was the attitude, generally shared by Whitehall officials, that their function was to preserve existing practices and policies. Earlier in the century the Treasury may well have substituted "a dynamic for a static concept of administration." But by the 1890's it had become the watchful guardian of the status quo. Chamberlain's department also remained static. His efforts to make imperialism more efficient, responsive, and adventuresome were contrary to the attitude and function of administration. Its institutions resisted many of his reforms and frustrated his policies and programs. Inadvertently, he weakened its structure when he imposed burdens upon it which it was not designed to take. The confrontation between the colonial secretary and the men in the institutions whom he sought to direct or influence in the task of empire building and the results of that conflict are the major concern of this book.

Acknowledgments

In the course of writing this book, which evolved out of a Ph.D. thesis submitted to Duke University, I have received much assistance from many sources. Quotations from Crown-copyright records in the Public Record Office appear by permission of the Controller of H. M. Stationery Office. My thanks are due to Dr. K. W. Humphreys, chief librarian of Birmingham University, on behalf of the Chamberlain family, for permission to quote from the Chamberlain Papers. The Bodleian; Christ Church and New College, Oxford; and the British Museum have been good enough, as has Lord St. Aldwyn, to let me use documents in their possession. For much help in obtaining access to research materials I would like to thank officials of the Institute of Historical Research, University of London (particularly Mr. A. Taylor Milne), and the National Register of Archives, London.

For generous financial assistance I am indebted to the Duke University Center for Commonwealth Studies, the Canada Council, and the University of British Columbia.

Several historians have helped immeasurably. For encouragement, stimulation, and training in the beginning I am grateful to Professor Donald M. L. Farr, Professor Leonard M. Thompson, and Professor Harold T. Parker. For advice and criticism along the way I must thank Dr. John W. Cell, Dr. William Roger Louis, Professor John M. Norris, and Professor Kenneth E. Robinson. I particularly want to express my gratitude to Professor William B. Hamilton, without whose many kindnesses and incisive comments my work would have been much more difficult and far less worthwhile.

R. V. K.

London, December, 1968

Contents

Tables

The Administration of Imperialism:
Joseph Chamberlain at the
Colonial Office

The Colonial Secretary: Political Style and Imperial Ideals

Many men of mark in action have gone to school to books, and taken care, in the midst of minor business, to live in hours of leisure with the immortals of a library, for refreshment, edification, stimulus. That is true. But after all, the influence of his time, whether it finds a willing or unwilling, an assenting or reluctant subject, is the educating as well as the stimulating force, and Chamberlain's school was affairs and the demands of circumstance and event. In short, though not of the politicians who are forced into action by an idea, he was quick to associate ideas with his actions.

John, Viscount Morley,
Recollections (2 vols.;
New York, 1917), I, 152.

When Lord Rosebery's Liberal government fell in June, 1895, Lord Salisbury formed his third administration. He combined the Foreign Office with the prime ministership and his nephew, Arthur Balfour, became first lord of the Treasury and leader of the House of Commons. Also from the Conservative party came the chancellor of the exchequer, Sir Michael Hicks Beach. Other cabinet posts went to Liberal Unionists who, following their break with Gladstone on Home Rule for Ireland in 1886, had allied themselves with the Conservatives. George Goschen went to the Admiralty and Lord Lansdowne to the War Office. The Duke of Devonshire, leader of the Whig faction, became president of the Council and maintained titular control over the education department; and Joseph Chamberlain, leader of the radical wing of the Liberal Unionists, opted for the Colonial Office. These men were to be key figures in the coalition government for the next several years.

Once he had formed his administration Salisbury sought public approval. The Unionists won the election in convincing fashion, achieving a majority of 152 seats over the combined number of Liberal and Irish members. Chamberlain was a particularly conspicuous figure in the campaign and perhaps the most successful as evidenced by a Unionist sweep of the Midlands, the center of his political power. He was soon to gain the reputation as well of being at least on a par with Salisbury in terms of influence in the Unionist cabinet.

Chamberlain became colonial secretary on June 29, 1895. On the eighth of the following month he marked his sixtieth birthday; but despite his years he gave an impression to all who knew him of remarkably youthful vigor. Thin, erect body; assertive chin and prominent upturned nose; jet-black hair and a clean-shaven face when beard and moustache were the fashion; and piercing, alert eyes all gave credence to this impression. An ever-present monocle on his eye and a fresh orchid in his lapel delighted cartoonists, impressed the man on the street, and amused his political peers. Admired by all for his formidable will, diligent effort and oratorical skills, he was, nonetheless, disliked and distrusted by many upper-class Englishmen for his abrasive style and poor taste. For "he was not," as one of them remarked, "born, bred or educated in the ways which alone secure the necessary tact and behaviour of a real gentleman." [1] Others like Balfour and Salisbury were not inclined to judge Chamberlain harshly for his crudeness. They were, however, much concerned about his impulsive nature.[2] His own immediate followers, men like Jesse Collings, a Birmingham member of Parliament, and Lord Selborne, Salisbury's son-in-law and Colonial Office parliamentary under-secretary (1895–1900), although they might be aware of Chamberlain's instability,[3] were attracted to him for his loyalty

1. Diary entry by Sir Edward Hamilton, financial secretary of the Treasury, Dec. 3, 1899, Hamilton MSS, British Museum, Add. MS 48675.
2. Lady Frances Balfour, *Ne Obliviscaris* (2 vols.; London, 1930), II, 270, 332.
3. See for example Selborne to Salisbury, April 7, 1895, Salisbury MSS, Christ Church, Oxford; and Selborne to Balfour, Oct. 16, 1900, Balfour MSS, British Museum, Add. MS 49707.

and kindness and his decisive and confident manner. His confidence and style had been forged in his career as a successful self-made businessman and the cut and thrust of municipal politics. He had also performed on the amateur stage well into his thirties, an experience which helped him as a politician to hold an audience, to play a part, to convey an impression or to hide a feeling.

Chamberlain entered national political life in 1875 as a member of Parliament for Birmingham. In 1877 he created the National Liberal Federation, a political machine that effectively delivered to the Liberal party the votes of the recently enfranchised and politically uncommitted in the Midland ridings. This agency, rather than birth, education or connection, was the key to his rapid rise to political prominence. After only four years in the House he became president of the Board of Trade. Here he was introduced to the subtleties and frustration of British cabinet government and the nation's economic problems. At the outset, he later told a Birmingham audience, he found himself "face to face with a hundred questions, many of them involving many technical details of which I humbly confess I was profoundly ignorant; and if I was saved from making mistakes which would have been humiliating, I owe it to the care and knowledge and intelligence of the permanent officials of my department."[4] One of those officials, Sir Thomas Farrer, the board's permanent secretary, "was surprised to find how ignorant . . . Chamberlain was of all economic questions. At the same time he was struck by [Chamberlain's] adroitness in assimilating and reproducing arguments which he did not understand."[5]

While at the Board of Trade, Chamberlain engaged in a sharp contest with one of the most influential sections of the nation's business community—the shipowners. Taking up the crusade of Samuel Plimsoll, the owners' most vehement critic, he helped bring to public attention abuses in the industry which brought hardship and death to merchant seamen. Particularly abhorrent was the practice of sending undermanned, overloaded, poorly

4. Quoted in J. L. Garvin and J. Amery, *The Life of Joseph Chamberlain* (4 vols.; London 1932–51), I, 410.
5. Sir Algernon West, *Contemporary Portraits* (New York, 1920), pp. 68–69.

fitted and overinsured ships to sea. If a ship made it to port a profit would be realized; but even more could be had if it sank. As Chamberlain put it, "I know absolutely no trade except that of shipowners, in which it is possible for a man to lose his property and make a profit by it." [6] Set off by Plimsoll's charges, he launched his own investigation, assembled facts to frame sweeping legislation, and spoke out to arouse public feeling and flail the offenders. In what was to become a familiar pattern of reaction by his adversaries, the shipping interests were stung into rebuttal by Chamberlain's strong accusations. His aggressive tactics and his attempt to impose government regulation on the industry aroused both Conservative and Liberal hostility. The cabinet and the prime minister, preoccupied with other matters, found it expedient to avoid giving Chamberlain support. Stiff opposition and calculated indifferences greatly annoyed the impatient reformer. Characteristically, he was inclined to defeat rather than conciliate his adversary, to win a victory rather than seek a compromise. His Merchant Shipping Bill had to be withdrawn in 1884, but the prime minister was able to dissuade him from quitting the cabinet. While Chamberlain was unable to carry through his reforms in what was to become a familiar pattern of the aftereffects of his efforts, subsequent administrations legislated against the more glaring abuses in the shipping industry.

From his vantage point at the Board of Trade, a chief function of which was to compile trade statistics, Chamberlain could hardly avoid becoming engrossed in the leading economic problems of the times. The boom of prosperity which had coincided with Chamberlain's years in business and municipal politics had petered out.[7] Although trade and industry revived after slumps in the late 70's and early 80's, overproduction, declining prices, and decreasing profit margins harassed commercial Britain for the next 20 years.

6. Quoted in Garvin, *Life*, I, 424.
7. C. Gill and A. Briggs, *History of Birmingham* (2 vols.; London, 1952), II, 30–33; G. C. Allen, *The Industrial Development of Birmingham and the Black Country* (London, 1st edition, 1929; reprinted with corrections, 1966), pp. 175–243; W. Ashworth, *An Economic History of England, 1870–1939* (London, 1960), pp. 25–45.

Disgruntled businessmen and agriculturists began to question the validity of free-trade dogma as deepening depression led to protectionist ferment. "Very early, however, the discussion of protective tariffs broadened into a discussion of imperial tariff preferences." [8] Canada had been forced to erect tariff barriers in 1879 against the United States in particular, and certain of its leaders indicated a willingness to use these to work out a preference arrangement with Britain. Tariff reform groups which sprouted freely in the mother country responded encouragingly to the Canadian suggestions. The National Fair Trade League, established in 1881, was a leading example. Its founders included representatives primarily from the Midlands (Bradford, Liverpool, Dewsbury, Birmingham) but even from Manchester. They advocated the adoption of imperial preference and modest retaliatory tariffs.

Salisbury's short-lived government of 1885 felt called upon, in the face of this agitation, to investigate the depressed condition of the nation. The complaints made by the Birmingham Chamber of Commerce before the government inquiry are instructive: "The Board of Trade returns . . . show, with regard to Birmingham, the exports of the manufactures of the district . . . a very large falling off of late. . . . Not only the volume has fallen off, but the . . . profits also reduced." The gun trade had "very much declined"; staple trades such as wire and nails were "falling off"; demand for silver-plate was declining; the jewelry trade was "one of the most depressed"; great stocks of unsold steam engines, pumps, lathes and lamps were accumulating. Questioned as to the reasons for the slump, delegates replied that "many trades that formerly had their centre in Birmingham solely for the world's supply are now distributed for competition between four or five different countries." They said they had "suffered a good deal from continental competition in the trade to India and the Colonies, and China." As for solutions, the chamber was divided sharply on the merits of retaliatory tariffs against the products of protectionist countries in the home markets. But its

8. B. H. Brown, *The Tariff Reform Movement in Great Britain, 1881–1895* (New York, 1943), pp. 12–13.

members agreed on the desirability of creating an imperial *zoll-verein*—one which would "give free entrance of colonial produce into this country, and . . . obtain free, or at least preferential entry to the colonies of our goods, in return for their protection . . . by England." [9] The Sheffield Chamber of Commerce expressed similar misgivings and solutions.

Despite a strong ground swell of protectionist feeling in Birmingham, Chamberlain fought against it in the election campaign of 1885.[10] Having, however, to delve into the question of tariffs in his work and seeing how protection had caught on in Birmingham, he turned himself to asking searching questions of fiscal orthodoxy. His investigation even led the permanent secretary of the Board of Trade to think he was "not a sound Free-Trader." [11]

Chamberlain's radicalism was also tested in the 1880's. Essentially his radical program was designed to force the haves to justify their rights and privileges by assuming new duties and obligations towards the have-nots. He "sought to remedy, not replace, the *laissez-faire* system." [12] It included a demand for non-sectarian, compulsory and free education; land reform to increase the number of landowners; fiscal changes to place more of the tax burden on those who could better afford it; and strengthening local government to deal with social problems. It was further contrived to exploit the immediate situation: agitation by nonconformists, unrest among rural laborers, demands for the extension of the franchise, in order to widen and strengthen the base of his political support. Chamberlain used the program in appeals to the country as a cabinet minister even though several of his Whig and Liberal colleagues were against it. This challenge to constitutional practice, perhaps even more than the radical nature of the program itself, drew the criticism of men like Devonshire and Gladstone. Indeed, not only did Gladstone and the Whigs block his efforts to legislate social reform, but middle-

9. Great Britain, *Parliamentary Papers, 1886* [C. 4715], XXI, 257–71.
10. Garvin, *Life*, II, 121–22.
11. *Ibid.*, p. 122.
12. P. Fraser, *Joseph Chamberlain, Radicalism and Empire, 1868–1914* (London, 1966), p. 49.

class concerns at home and imperial problems abroad under-
mined the effect of his radical program in the 1885 election. His
platform helped to sweep the counties for the Liberals, but his
campaign had limited appeal in the boroughs, where the Tories,
who sniped at Gladstone's imperial policies (in the Sudan, the
Transvaal and Ireland) and supported Fair Trade schemes, ran
well. "The failure to secure a [Liberal] majority dependent on the
Radical section, but independent of the Irish vote, was amongst
the heaviest disappointments of Chamberlain's whole career." [13]

He suffered a further setback in his confrontation with Gladstone over Ireland. He was prepared to grant that troubled land
local self-government, but Irish members would continue to be
elected to the imperial Parliament. Gladstone determined to pursue another course. His Home Rule Bill of 1886, which was designed to remove the Irish contingent from Parliament, ignored
Chamberlain's suggestions, and his political strength. Chamberlain resigned office, launched a sharp attack on Gladstone's bill,
and marshalled opposition within the Liberal ranks to defeat it.
He did; but also helped split the Liberal party, which lost the
next election. [14]

Out of office in 1886, he escaped the pressures and accusations
of the political turmoil he had helped create by going abroad.
He toured the Middle East. In Turkey he drew up and submitted to the Sultan a scheme for railroad development. The
next year Salisbury found it convenient to appoint him to head
up a British delegation to Washington to settle a fishing dispute
between Canada and the United States. While in North America
he travelled to Toronto, and, as the occasion demanded, he spoke
of the British empire and race. He was, he said, impressed by the
idea of "the greatness and importance of the distinction reserved
for the Anglo-Saxon race—for that proud, persistent, self-assert-
ing, and resolute stock, which no change of climate or condition
can alter, and which is infallibly bound to be the predominant
force in the future history and civilisation of the world." Another

---

13. Garvin, *Life,* II, 125.
14. See Fraser, *Chamberlain,* pp. 81–111, for a recent interpretation in which
Gladstone appears to have "manipulated, slighted, and humbugged" Chamberlain
into implacable opposition to Home Rule.

idea, he said, attracted him: "It may yet be that the federation of Canada may be the lamp lighting our path to the federation of the British Empire. If it is a dream—it may be only the imagination of an enthusiast—it is a grand idea. It is one to stimulate the patriotism and statesmanship of every man who loves his country; and whether it be destined or not to perfect realisation, at least let us all cherish the sentiment it inspires."

He might indulge in and be warmed himself by the social Darwinism and patriotic rhetoric of pro-imperialist contemporary intellectuals. Yet he was responding to the toast of "The Commercial Interests of the Empire" before a dinner sponsored by the Toronto Board of Trade. And imbedded in imperial sentiment were other considerations reflecting Chamberlain's interest in imperial trade. He felt called upon to deny reports in the Canadian press that he came as a representative of British exporters or that he once declared that the interests of Canada should be subordinated to those of Britain. "I can assure," he continued, "that, except as far as the interest of Birmingham and Manchester are identical with yours, you may trust me to lay them aside on the present occasion." Yet he urged Canadians to consider reducing their tariffs and hoped Americans would do the same; and he added: "I am in favour of the widest possible commercial union and intercourse, not only with the United States but with all the world. That is the true, unrestricted reciprocity." [15] Still a free-trade advocate, he had nonetheless, been vague and suggestive enough to have his speech well received in Canada; but it was one that would be acceptable in Birmingham too.[16]

In 1889 Chamberlain visited Egypt where he attempted to study firsthand the effects of British rule, and where he took it upon himself to write to Sir Evelyn Baring (later Lord Cromer), the British chief administrator, advising him on how that rule might be improved.[17] The next year Chamberlain struck up an acquaintance with Sir Ambrose Shea, governor of the Bahamas.

15. Speech of Dec. 12, 1887, quoted in W. Maycock, *With Mr. Chamberlain in the United States and Canada, 1887–88* (Toronto, 1914), pp. 104–11.
16. The speech was extensively reported in *The Times*, Jan. 2, 1887.
17. Chamberlain to Baring, Jan., 1890, printed in C. H. D. Howard, ed., *A Political Memoir, 1880–92, by Joseph Chamberlain* (London, 1953), pp. 314–20.

Shea convinced him of handsome profits to be gained from investing in the cultivation of sisal in the islands. He took an option on 20,000 acres and sent out his youngest son, Neville, to oversee operations. This transaction was an attempt to offset substantial losses Chamberlain had just incurred through the failure in South America of British business ventures in which he had invested. More than 6,000 acres were planted and up to 800 laborers employed. But the plantation did not prosper. By mid-1896 (Chamberlain was then colonial secretary), the decision was made to abandon the operation at a loss of £50,000.[18] He was later forced to raise capital to cover expenses by selling shares held in the Canadian Pacific Railway. Unfortunately, these subsequently rose in value and he was thus prevented from recouping his finances. As an imperial investor Chamberlain had limited success; yet his setback, curiously enough, did not prevent him from encouraging others to put capital into the empire.

By 1895 Chamberlain had spent nine years out of political office. During that period his activities appeared to be in marked contrast to those of his earlier career. The Birmingham social reformer had become more interested in imperial affairs than domestic issues. He had visited the Middle East, shown an interest in affairs in Egypt, negotiated for Canadian fishing rights, spoken optimistically of imperial federation, and invested in a plantation in the West Indies. He also expressed a wish to serve at the Colonial Office.[19] His imperial activities coincided with and no doubt drew succor from a growing concern in Britain with the fate of the empire. That concern had evolved from nationalist challenge in Africa and Ireland and colonial expansion on the part of continental powers, developments which had disturbed successive British governments. These trends and events drew Chamberlain's attention at a time when he and his Midland constituents had come to view empire as a means to solve economic problems. As he told a Walsall audience following his appointment as colonial secretary:

Old markets are getting exhausted, some of them are being closed to

18. K. Feiling, *The Life of Neville Chamberlain* (London, 1947), p. 29.
19. In 1888. Garvin, *Life*, II, 347.

us by hostile tariffs, and unless we can find new countries which will be free to take our goods you may be quite satisfied that lack of employment will continue to be one of the greatest of social evils, and it's because I believe this that I have accepted the office which I have the honour to hold (loud and prolonged cheering). It is because I desire to see whether there may not be room for still developing our resources in these countries and for opening up British markets.[20]

In other words Chamberlain was arguing that social reform, difficult enough to introduce in time of prosperity, would be impossible to pursue effectively in time of distress; and increased imperial trade was the solution. As always, Chamberlain was offering what appeared to be a simple and attractive solution for a complex problem which required more sophisticated remedies. Ironically enough his own remedy was to be much more difficult to implement than its sanguine exponent imagined.

Yet Chamberlain once more had a cause to which he could divert his boundless energies and aggressive political style—a cause not for city redevelopment or national social reform, but rather for empire building. If his task seemed more grandiose he now possessed more political power than he hitherto enjoyed. Political success and the wisdom that comes with age and experience could conceivably smooth his abrasiveness and bridle his impulsiveness on his return to public affairs.

20. *The Times,* July 16, 1895.

2

The Colonial Office: Its
Staff and Problems

They say—I do not know whether it is true, but I have heard it more than once—that [Mr. Chamberlain] made his office the only Government Office whence one could get a reply to a letter by return post. At all events, he brought a business spirit into that office which it has never since lost.

> Theodore Taylor, M.P., July 28, 1914, *Hansard,*
> 5th series, LXV, 117.

During the last seven years it has been impossible to discharge the work of the Colonial Office promptly and thoroughly. . . . Indeed it may be said that in 1896 the work fell in arrear[s] from which it has never recovered.

> Frederick Graham, Colonial Office assistant
> under-secretary, March, 1903, CO 885/8/154.

I

"Within a few weeks" after Chamberlain began actual work at the Colonial Office in August, 1895, "the organism roused to new life, felt his quickening influence in every vein"; so asserts Chamberlain's biographer. "Like all the greatest administrators," continues Garvin, "he had the secret of daring delegation, giving a play to his staff that brought out all ideas and abilities." "Not content with changing the spirit of the Colonial Office he improved its aspects, apparatus and procedure." [1] Garvin relied on the recollections of the colonial secretary's staff. One claimed, for example, that in 1895 the office "was dimly lighted by candles in candlesticks of antique design" and that Chamberlain promptly

1. Garvin, *Life,* III, 10–14.

had electric light "installed throughout the building." [2] Garvin thought this story symbolic: "We may say that in many things concerning the relations of the Colonial Office with the Empire he superseded candles by electric light." [3]

However, a poorly maintained gas system, not candles, lit the office. In 1888 and again in 1894 the staff complained of eye strain to the Office of Works. It was reluctant to make improvements "in view of the possible early introduction of electric lighting." [4] Chamberlain had his staff prod the works department again in November, 1895. His office was immediately connected to an electrical system installed recently next door in the Foreign Office. But the Treasury refused a supplementary estimate to illuminate the whole department. It "returned to the charge," as one official put it, in the fall of 1896, sufficiently cowed by departmental intransigence to be content with new gas burners. However, the works department and the Treasury finally relented. The ground and first floors of the office received electricity by the fall of 1898, the second floor the following year. The third floor continued for sometime thereafter to be lit by gas. [5] The change in the office lighting system was not as dramatic or immediately effective as faulty memories recalled. Indeed, Garvin's assessment of Chamberlain's administrative ability and success, like his exaggerated story about the lights, is distorted. [6]

Since 1876 the Colonial Office had occupied quarters on the corner of Whitehall and Downing Street. Casual visitors were impressed with the spacious and decorative stairwell off the department's main entrance, and even more taken with the colonial secretary's immense office on the first floor, with its huge globe, handsome map cases and eighteenth-century fireplace. The per-

2. Sir Harry Wilson, former private secretary and legal assistant under-secretary, "Joseph Chamberlain as I Knew Him," *United Empire*, n.s., VII (February, 1917), 104.
3. Garvin, *Life*, III, 15.
4. CO 323/399/22127.
5. *Ibid.*, CO 323/410/11064; CO 323/438/28323.
6. For examples of the acceptance of Garvin's interpretation see R. H. Wilde, "Joseph Chamberlain and the South African Republic, 1895–1899," *Archives Year Book for South African History*, I (1956), xii; and A. F. Madden, "Changing Attitudes and Widening Responsibilities [in the Empire-Commonwealth], 1895–1914," *Cambridge History of the British Empire* (9 vols. in 8; Cambridge, 1929–1963), III, 383.

manent under-secretary's room was admirable too, and the library, originally intended to serve the needs of several departments, functional and large. Only if the visitor had occasion to see a lesser official would he discover the labyrinth within which most of the staff worked. Rooms were laid out indiscriminately on five levels about three sides of a dark court—rooms too small or too large for particular office needs, rooms tucked round corners or off stairwells, rooms poorly lighted and of curious shape, their dimensions dictated by architectural effect or the limitations of heating by open hearth. Poor maintenance in the thirty-year old building left the staff to complain of unpleasant smells in several rooms, dirty windows, smoking chimneys, and an unreliable elevator.[7]

Number 12 Downing Street in 1895 functioned with a staff of 83 men and women. Office keepers, messengers, maids and charwomen engaged in menial tasks about the building. Most of the 48 staff clerks were attached to one of five departments. Each department dealt with a geographically defined area of the empire. An exception, the general department, dealt with office procedure as well as business which affected the colonies as a whole, such as trade and defense. A secretariat of three assistant under-secretaries and the permanent under-secretary topped the staff pyramid. It was responsible for the operation of the office establishment and advised the department's political heads—the colonial secretary and the parliamentary under-secretary—on policy.

The geographical departments included one for the West Indies; a second for North America and Australasia (and Gibraltar and Cyprus as well); a third for West Africa (and Mauritius, Malta and St. Helena too); a fourth for South Africa and the Far East. Each of these departments was staffed by two or three junior or second-class clerks, one senior or first-class clerk, and a principal clerk who acted as head of a department. These clerks belonged to what had come to be known since 1876 as the first or upper division of the civil service. Most of them were univer-

7. R. V. Kubicek, "Joseph Chamberlain and the Colonial Office: A Study in Imperial Administration," (Unpublished Ph.D. dissertation, Duke University, 1964), pp. 32–33.

sity men who had obtained positions in the office through open exams set by the civil service commissioners—a practice which had been introduced in 1870.

Typical representatives of the experienced upper-division staff who worked for Chamberlain were Charles Lucas and Reginald Antrobus. Lucas, a son of a doctor, and Antrobus, a son of a vicar, had been contemporaries and friendly rivals at public school. Both attended Winchester and obtained scholarships to Oxford; Lucas to Balliol, Antrobus to New College. At Balliol, Lucas, a diffident but industrious student, was a contemporary of Alfred Milner, who was to become Chamberlain's chief administrator in South Africa.

They were among sixty-odd candidates who competed in the civil service examinations of March, 1877, for two vacancies in the Colonial Office. The exams were calculated to test those kinds of knowledge and ability fostered by the great public schools and universities. As such they were weighted in favor of the student of the classics. Lucas, who placed first in the competition, amassed more than one-half of his point total through his performance on Greek and Latin tests. Antrobus, second in the competition, did the same.[8]

The variety of work promised and the comparatively high salary offered by the Colonial Office made it a prestige department able to recruit from among the top candidates.[9] But were these the kind of men it needed? As one of Chamberlain's staff contended, "tact, manners, and *savior faire* if combined with good average abilities, are likely to be of as much importance in the discharge of a great part of [a clerk's] duties as mere capacity for piling up marks at an examination."[10] Nonetheless, the examinations insured that successful candidates were diligent and conditioned by an experience common to Great Britain's adminis-

8. *Parl. Pap.*, *1877* [C. 1867], XXVIII, 5–6; *1878* [C. 2178], XXVII, 185.
9. B. L. Blakeley, "The Colonial Office: 1870–1890," (Unpublished Ph.D. dissertation, Duke University, 1966), p. 143; J. A. Cross, "The Colonial Office and the Dominions Before 1914," *Journal of Commonwealth Political Studies*, IV (July, 1966), 140.
10. Sir William Baillie Hamilton, "Forty-Four Years at the Colonial Office," *The Nineteenth Century and After*, LXV (April, 1909), 608. With a public school and legal background he entered the office before the civil service competition had been established.

trative and political elite; almost all were public school and Oxbridge graduates. Certainly Lucas and Antrobus did not lack for
tact and manners, as their minutes in office records reveal. They
were also model civil servants who identified with the cautious
and dilatory atmosphere of Whitehall, but who managed, nonetheless, to adapt to Chamberlain's dynamic personality and administrative style.

Antrobus, as did many upper-division clerks beginning their
work in the office, served as a private secretary to successive
colonial secretaries and permanent under-secretaries. And, as did
several, he obtained some on-the-spot experience in the empire,
as an acting governor of St. Helena. He was promoted to senior
clerk in the West African department in 1894. As head of that
department and after 1898 as an assistant under-secretary Chamberlain found him indispensable in embarking on an aggressive
West African policy. Antrobus, Chamberlain told the prime minister, "has worked like a horse during the recent negotiations
[with the French] and . . . I feel immensely indebted" to him.[11]
Antrobus also acted as a useful intermediary when a clash of policy and personality between Chamberlain and Frederick Lugard
threatened to prevent the office from obtaining the latter for
service in West Africa.[12]

Lucas became an under-secretary in 1897. He acquired an immense knowledge of the colonies and, continuing the scholarly
inclinations displayed at Oxford, he wrote extensively on the
empire.[13] An expert on the West Indies, an advocate of preferential tariffs, with a strong commitment to the concept of imperial
unity, he provided memorandums and despatches particularly
relevant to Chamberlain's schemes for empire. Though masterful
with the pen he was diffident with people.[14] He was twice passed

11. Chamberlain to Salisbury, June 23, 1898, Salisbury MSS. Antrobus received
a knighthood in 1898.
12. Margery Perham and Mary Bull, eds., *The Diaries of Lord Lugard* (4 vols.;
London, 1959–63), IV, 333, 353.
13. His major work prior to 1903 was *A Historical Geography of the British
Colonies,* a multi-volume work which he projected and to which he contributed an
Introduction (1887) and volumes I to V, Part I (1888–1901). His later works
included: *A History of Canada, 1763–1812* (1909); *The Partition and Coloniza-
tion of Africa* (1922); and *Religion, Colonizing and Trade* (1930).
14. *The Times,* May 8, 1931; and *United Empire,* n.s., XXII (June, 1931),
309–12.

over for the permanent under-secretaryship and retired at fifty-eight in 1911.

Lucas and Antrobus were, in their middle-class backgrounds, classical Oxbridge education and tactful and devoted service, typical of the upper-division British civil servant at the turn of the century. But several were atypical. Francis Round, head of the general department, joined the office in 1869 before the civil service exam was instituted. He was noted at Balliol more for his cricket ability than for his scholarship. His advancement was slow—he did not become a principal clerk until 1896—because of his reputation for procrastination and indecision. "If a file repelled him, he merely removed it to his home, and there it rested. Among his effects when he died, there was a large tin box crammed with official files which he had hidden there." [15] Chamberlain complained on a docket "that this important paper which might and ought to have been answered at once has been kept by Mr. Round from July, 1898, to May, 1899. Such a delay is most unsatisfactory and brings great discredit on the C[olonial] Office. I hope it will not happen again while I am S[ecretary] of S[tate]." [16] This reprimand had little effect on Round's work habits. Since his department was responsible for such business as trade and defense as well as the office establishment, Round's tardiness hindered not only office reform, but also its labors in two facets of empire with which Chamberlain was vitally concerned. Furthermore, Round was such a convinced free trader that Chamberlain thought it necessary to disagree sharply with him on the tariff question.[17]

Frederick Graham, a graduate of the University of Edinburgh, entered the office under the old system, the last to do so, in 1870. More blunt than, but as diligent in his minuting habits as Lucas and Antrobus, he held the most demanding posts in the office. He became head of the South African department in 1896 and the following year succeeded Assistant Under-secretary Edward Fair-

15. Sir Cosmo Parkinson, *The Colonial Office from Within, 1909–1945* (London, 1947), p. 42. Parkinson does not refer to Round by name but see CO 323/470/23974 and CO 323/479/29164.
16. May 13, 1899, CO 323/434/15229. Round retired in 1905.
17. CO 323/407/25374.

field, one of the office's most talented and valued members. Fair-field collapsed under the strain of the Jameson Raid crisis and died in the spring of 1897.[18] Though also of delicate health and suffering from poor eyesight,[19] Graham drafted increasing numbers of despatches and telegrams in the years of further crises, war and reconstruction which followed. He also dealt with office routine and procedure. Little wonder that his room became a bottleneck in the circulation of papers. "Found in Mr. Graham's room," was a minute often seen on "lost" or delayed correspondence during Chamberlain's administration.

Sydney Olivier conformed to no pattern but his own. Though a rector's son and an Oxford graduate in the classics, he developed heterodox political notions. Like Sydney Webb who joined the office a year before he did in 1881, he became a Fabian socialist. His department head, who held that civil servants should not participate in politics, reprimanded him for speaking at a socialist congress on the continent in 1893.[20] If his political activities were anathema to his colleagues, so too were Olivier's character traits. Indiscreet, intolerant of others' inadequacies, and self-assertive, he caustically criticized Round and the Foreign Office when they delayed consideration of his plans for accounting reforms in the colonies and protectorates.[21] He also seems to have been the only member of the office who would not back down from a confrontation with Chamberlain. In apologizing to the colonial secretary for Olivier's belligerence, Lucas wrote: "He has the type of mind which is aggressively independent. His work is good and able in spite of his tone, which no one personally objects to more strongly than I do."[22] If Olivier's attitude prevented his advancement in the office, it did not hinder his promotion in the colonial service. He went on several missions to the West Indies to sort out chaotic accounting systems, served as secretary to a royal commission appointed by Chamberlain to

18. R. B. Pugh, "The Colonial Office, 1801–1925," *CHBE*, III, 745.
19. *The Times*, February 23, 1923. See also Chap. 5, n. 68.
20. BM Add. MS 43553, ff. 128–29; Margaret Olivier, *Sydney Olivier, Letters and Selected Writings* (New York, 1948), p. 9.
21. CO 323/443/7487; CO 323/445/9081.
22. Minute of Aug. 5, 1902, JC 14/3.

inquire into the islands' economic condition, and acted as Jamaica's colonial secretary (1900–1904) and governor (1907–1913).

Herbert Read's education, as well as his career in the Colonial Office, was unusual. The son of a drapery store owner, he distinguished himself in mathematics at Brasenose. He was one of five of the 43 members of the department's upper division in 1903 who had been educated in the sciences,[23] a background which he turned to good account. As Chamberlain's private secretary (1896–1898) he stimulated his chief's interest in tropical medicine and served on committees instrumental in its development. Shy and reticent in public, effusive and genial in private, he possessed "a veritable genius for committee work, not only setting them up, but for seeing there was work for them to do and that they got on with it." [24] His promotion was rapid and he later served in turn as head of the East and West African departments and as governor of Mauritius (1924–1930).

Uniformity of background and education was clearly evident in the Colonial Office's upper division at the turn of the century. Its members were drawn from the professional ranks of the country's middle class and usually educated in the classics at a renowned public school and at Oxford. Despite these similarities, differences were evident in temperament and ability as well as in background and education. While Chamberlain encouraged initiative, ability and imagination, he tolerated tardiness, ineptitude and diffidence. Although an official might be passed over for promotion his job was secure. As one staff member put it, even though an official might be inefficient and lack ability, "so long as you conduct yourself well you will not be dismissed." [25] Office tradition also contributed to caution, delay, and the status quo. New territorial acquisitions had been viewed by its senior secretariat—the under-secretaries—as burdens, not challenges. New organizations such as the Royal Colonial Institute and the Imperial

23. Derived from various numbers of the *Colonial Office Lists, The Oxford Magazine,* and *The Times.*

24. P. Manson-Bahr, *History of the School of Tropical Medicine in London, 1899–1949* (London, 1956), p. 128. See also Chap. 7 below.

25. Sir Robert Meade speaking before the Ridley inquiry into the civil service, *Parl. Pap.,* 1888 [C. 5545], XXVII, 154.

Federation League designed to activate interest in empire were unwelcome. Internal office reform had come about because of general changes in the civil service and the sheer necessity of coping with increased work.[26] Indeed, Chamberlain was to lose, permanently or temporarily, the services of some of his most talented and ambitious officials who found posts within the empire more of a challenge than administrative work in the office. Olivier, who spent a substantial part of the period 1895–1903 in the West Indies, was one of these. Four others followed Milner to South Africa. They included George Fiddes, a first-class clerk, who only returned to the office as a consequence of friction on Milner's staff and later (1916–1921) became its permanent under-secretary; Harry Wilson, the legal assistant under-secretary; and John Perry and Geoffrey Robinson, both second-class clerks. Robinson later changed his name to Dawson and became editor of *The Times*.[27] The upper-division staff, though with few exceptions diligent and conscientious, lacked through temperament and experience the capacity for innovation and experiment.

Lower or second-division clerks, of whom there were twenty in 1896, were part of a class introduced into the civil service in 1876, and filled through open competition. Their pre-job training qualified them for slightly higher paying but less secure clerical posts in the City. Examinations encompassed the elementary branches of an English education: geography, penmanship, rudimentary bookkeeping, vulgar fractions and English composition. These clerks were attached to the various branches of the general department: the registry, the library, and the printing, correspondence, financial and copying divisions. They were eligible for promotion to the higher division, but none was elevated before or during Chamberlain's administration, a situation which reflected a sharp dichotomy between the two divisions.

Usually junior members of the upper division served as a minister's private secretary. They knew office routine and could be employed on departmental business. But three of Chamber-

26. Blakeley, "Colonial Office," pp. 298–316.
27. Chamberlain to Milner, April 9, 1902, JC 13/3; J. E. Wrench, *Geoffrey Dawson and Our Times* (London, 1955), pp. 31–34.

lain's four secretaries in 1896 were from outside the office. His engagements and correspondence were so many and varied that by 1900 he needed six. But they could not assist much his direction of office business, not only because several were not staff members but also because they often changed. For example, his principal private secretary, always from outside the office, was Wilson until 1897, Lord Ampthill to 1900, and Lord Monk Bretton until his resignation.[28]

II

Clerks, whether employed in "mechanical" or "intellectual" work, or both, performed their duties at some stage of an elaborate paper-circulating system. Usually each despatch, letter or telegram received in the office was docketed, numbered and keyed to related correspondence by lower-division clerks in the registry. "Gradually files grew, as docket was added to docket. . . . A single docket [was often] extracted from its file and sent on with another file, to which it [had] relevance; and as this is an imperfect world, [would] in all probability be missing when wanted." [29] From the registry a new paper usually went to a second-class upper-division clerk. He minuted it (deciphered it if a telegram), linked it with related papers pulled from the files, and sent it on to a first-class clerk or his department head for further comment. Then if not stopped by an official qualified to dispose of it, the paper passed by way of the senior secretariat to the secretary of state. Draft replies based on the minutes were usually composed by second-class clerks. But first-class clerks, department heads and even the under-secretaries, any one of whom might approve drafts, often wrote them as well. Approved drafts usually went to a third-floor room to be copied by women typists, first introduced into the office in 1893.[30] Victorian

28. Both Wilson and Monk Bretton were contemporaries and friends of Chamberlain's eldest son.
29. Parkinson, *"The Colonial Office,"* pp. 28–29.
30. Six female typists were employed in 1896 but by 1902 seventeen were found inadequate to meet copying needs. CO 323/417/8852 and minute by the head of the copying branch, Oct. 15, 1902, CO 878/10.

conventions permitted only two of the male staff to take work to the typing cloister. Finished copies went back to the departments or under-secretaries for signature and were then indexed and made up for the mails by second-class clerks. This system of "registration and consideration and submission to the higher authority by minute . . . and drafting and copying and signature and dispatch" took time and caused inevitable delay.[31]

In 1896, Chamberlain's first full year in office, 26,800 despatches and letters reached the department; 25,000 originated there. Of the total, between 16,000 and 25,000 items did not go beyond the departments.[32] The remainder were seen by the three under-secretaries so that each had to deal with several thousand papers. The permanent under-secretary handled somewhat more, though he did not draft as many letters or write as many instructions as any one assistant under-secretary. Chamberlain likely handled two or three thousand papers. These statistics in their immensity, coupled with the involved procedure used to dispose of correspondence, indicate that at all levels of the office hierarchy, the staff was hard pressed to get through the paperwork promptly and effectively. And it did not.

Chamberlain entered an office which had felt the strain of increased work and pressures for many years. Whereas the office had dealt with 42,700 papers in 1881 and 46,300 in 1891, it handled 48,000 in 1895. Statistics, however, revealed only a part of the increase in work. During the decade prior to 1895, problems related to some fifty different communities within the empire became more important, complex, and time-consuming. Self-governing colonies drew the office more frequently into foreign relations and international arrangements which covered such subjects as telegraph cables, postal regulations, health problems and trade exhibitions. Appointed colonial representatives and others with imperial interests took up more office time in interviews. The political and economic growth of the crown colonies and the multiplication of questions affecting their defense, necessitated by the imperial aspirations of other world

31. Parkinson, *"The Colonial Office,"* p. 39.
32. Derived from figures cited by Graham, CO 885/8/154, p. 4.

powers, contributed to the changing nature of the work. Above all, however, the office business was greatly expanded by the development of jurisdiction and responsibility in the colonies of South-east Asia and in territories adjacent to colonies in South and West Africa. Administrative problems connected with trade, communications and public works, which previously had little place in office deliberations, rivalled political questions in complexity. Finally, the question of French and German colonies in proximity to British spheres of influence brought to the office such tasks as the exchange of information about common problems, the extradition of criminals and the delimitation of international boundaries. Yet since 1881 the staff had remained at almost the same strength.[33] To meet the increased burden of work a little more responsibility was delegated to second-division clerks;[34] upper-division staff worked longer hours, forfeited portions of their leave, attended the office on Sundays and took more papers home.

Trends apparent in the office business in the decade before 1895 became more pronounced as Chamberlain embarked on his forward policies. Attempts to develop and expand the crown estates, draw the self-governing colonies closer to Britain, increase imperial trade, and, above all, to save British hegemony in South Africa, launched the office into a period of unprecedented activity. Correspondence totalled 56,000 items in 1896, about 75,000 in 1899 and reached more than 116,000 in 1902, before it dropped to 101,000 in 1903.[35] Telegrams too increased in length and number. The office received and sent more than 2,000 cables in 1895, 4,700 in 1899, 9,000 in 1902 (the last year of the Boer War), and 6,000 in 1903.

Heavy pressure on the South African department caused by the Jameson Raid prompted Chamberlain, in the early months of

33. CO 323/407/14272. Two first-division clerks had been added in 1881–82 when the Colonial Office assumed responsibility for Cyprus. When one of them left the office in 1891 two lower-division clerks were appointed.

34. For the first time in 1891 some lower-division clerks were allowed to prepare simple drafts, fill up forms and address despatches, but not minute. CO 431/116/36925; Add. MS 43558, f. 4.

35. These figures include an approximate estimate of non-registered routine papers disposed of by the registries.

1896, to instruct his staff to expand and reorganize the office establishment. Work had, in fact, begun to fall into arrears in other departments as well. The senior assistant under-secretary, John Bramston, was entrusted with the task. His plan called for the detachment of Eastern business (that from Ceylon, the Straits Settlements and Hong Kong) from the over-strained South African section and the creation of a new department to handle it. A separate sub-registry for North American and West African work was called for and was designed to remove from these departments the tasks of making up the mails and drafting simple letters of acknowledgment. Bramston, fearing the office would have "difficulty in getting all this through the Treasury," tried to be as economical as possible. He would add only two clerks to each of the divisions and institute a few promotions in the lower one to placate its staff who would now have more to do in the new registry.[36] Chamberlain thought Bramston had "erred on the side of moderation," but he did not interfere. "I emphasize [he minuted], the absolute necessity of making further provision for the constantly increasing work. What that provision is to be must be settled by the permanent officials who know the inner work of the Office. The proposals seem to me very moderate."[37] The Treasury first opposed then finally accepted the proposals; but, much to the consternation of the staff members concerned, it whittled down the increased salaries recommended to go with the promotions to be carried out in the second division.[38]

Within two years of the implementation of the Bramston plan the office had to expand again. This time Chamberlain himself had to take a prominent part in drafting letters for Treasury consideration. More sub-registries were to be set up, more second-division clerks employed and others promoted. This time the Treasury gave prompt approval to the scheme which was designed to build up the lower division. A sixth geographical section, a second West African department, was to be created. An

36. Minute by Bramston, May 4, 1896, CO 323/407/14272.
37. Minutes by Chamberlain, May 19 and June 21, 1896, *ibid*.
38. Treasury to CO, June 4, 1896, CO 323/407/18024.

assistant under-secretary, one principal, four first-class and two second-class clerks were to be added to the upper division at a maximum cost of £6,400 annually. This figure represented a 15 per cent increase on establishment costs. The plan was supported by immediate and long-range arguments. The office was still behind in its work and concern was expressed for the health of its overworked staff. If something were not done immediately, this predicament would be compounded by contemplated new responsibilities in Africa: the take-over of the territories of the Royal Niger Company, more controls to be exerted over the British South Africa Company, and new work incurred sooner or later by the transfer from the Foreign Office of the administration of territories north of the Zambezi including the British Central Africa protectorate. Chamberlain also wanted one or two "spare" first-division clerks available to send on missions within the empire.[39]

Previous Treasury policy ran completely counter to this plan, designed as it was to expand so markedly the upper division. Treasury officials had long considered that the Colonial Office staff was top heavy, that either the heads of departments or the assistant under-secretaries were redundant, and that the upper-division clerks performed duties that could be just as well accomplished at much less expense in the lower division.[40] However, the Colonial Office arguments, coupled with direct consultation between Chamberlain and the chancellor of the exchequer, overcame these strong reservations. Except for a quibble over the number of first-class clerks, the scheme was promptly sanctioned.

Yet once again the staff increase proved inadequate; even though the contemplated take-over of the Niger protectorate was delayed a year until January 1, 1900, and that of the British Central Africa protectorate until after Chamberlain left office. The work load brought on by the outbreak of war in South Africa in the fall of 1899 made the reforms of the previous year obsolete. The office had to continue to increase its staff and ex-

39. CO 323/431/19966; CO 323/431/20304.
40. Blakeley, "Colonial Office," p. 139.

pand its departments. But after 1898 these reforms were done in piecemeal fashion. At the beginning of 1900 a second and a third sub-registry were set up, the latter to handle South African and West Indian work; but again this addition proved unsatisfactory. For in 1902 a fifth sub-registry was inaugurated to deal exclusively with West Indian work. Colonies, such as St. Helena, Mauritius, Cyprus and Bermuda, which did not fit conveniently into any department's work, were shuttled from one section to another in an attempt to relieve work pressure. In the lower division six new clerks were brought into the office in 1899, four in 1900, eight in 1901, four in 1902 and one in 1903. In the upper division two clerks were added in 1899, three in 1900, three in 1901, two in 1902 and one in 1903. In that year the Colonial Office staff totalled 113.[41] These measures represented too little and materialized too late, for they did not solve serious difficulties which frustrated effective office reform and efficiency.

First, in time of office crisis in which arrears mounted, papers were mislaid, parliamentary questions increased and novel business arose, new, untrained staff could be more of a hindrance than a help. As one senior official put it:

It is not that the *nature* of the work demands especial qualifications. It is the *amount* of it which demands from at least three fourths of the present staff experience which is only gained by years in one particular department. We get through the work because each man carries in his mind more or less information on particular subjects, obtained gradually and slowly, and imprinted on his mind by repeated reference, and correction by those of larger experience. With it he is in a position to give the Secretary of State a useful opinion, or to furnish, with little trouble, a memorandum or minutes on which an opinion can safely be formed. Without it, there are traps and pitfalls at every turn. An outsider of intelligence can obtain the same information, on certain specific subjects, at the cost of going through volumes of printed matter or reams of manuscript.[42]

A third of the upper-division clerks had only a year's experience at the beginning of 1900. A similar situation was evident in the second division and was aggravated by certain frictions caused

41. CO 323/469/4190; CO 323/487/1740; *Colonial Office Lists.*
42. Memo by Graham, July 25, 1899, CO 885/7/123.

by delegating more work to its clerks. Their salaries were much lower than those in the upper division and they complained strongly about assuming such tasks as coding telegrams and drafting simple letters, work once exclusively dealt with in the upper division.[43] These complaints coupled with a reluctance on the part of some of the senior officials to entrust lower-division staff with new tasks seem to have resulted in limited and uneven delegation of responsibility.[44] Second, the office staff sanguinely expected the war to be a short one and did not, on its termination, want to be found in the position of having to admit redundancies. So, as Round put it, "a good deal of overtime work has been temporarily sanctioned in the hopes that each fresh accession of work might not prove to be permanent." [45]

Finally, there was simply no room in which to put more help. As early as 1898, William Baillie Hamilton, the chief clerk, complained, "we are absolutely at the end of our resources . . . and no amount of ingenuity could devise any means of cramming any more into this already overcrowded building." [46] So crowded was the office that it could not find space either to store or weed a vast accumulation of records dating back to 1875, documents estimated to weigh fifty tons, accruing at the rate of three tons a year and occupying half a mile of shelf space. These records, in loose bundles, were even left to lie on floors of the office corridors. Although it was realized as early as the beginning of Chamberlain's administration that something must be done, weeding and binding did not begin until 1904.[47]

To obtain more space, the Crown Agents, who occupied twenty-four rooms on the basement and ground floors of the building, were asked to vacate part of their premises. They refused, but agreed to vacate completely within eighteen months to two years. At the same time, the Foreign Office, next door and

43. Strongly worded petitions were submitted by the second-division clerks to the permanent heads of the office in 1896 and 1902 and a third went to the Treasury in 1898 along with similar protests from clerks in other government offices.
44. CO 431/116/36925.
45. March 9, 1901, CO 323/469/4190.
46. Sept. 28, 1898, CO 323/438/19986.
47. CO 885/8/155; CO 323/488/18532.

also overcrowded, refused the use of some of its space.[48] Selborne suggested that one of the less important office departments should move out of the building until the Crown Agents left. Chamberlain agreed that this was "the best solution of the temporary difficulty"; the permanent staff did not, thinking it would lead to great inconvenience and set a dangerous precedent. Chamberlain offered to vacate his own office for a smaller room.[49] Instead, however, the under-secretaries decided to convert the living quarters of the resident clerks into work rooms in which to squeeze part of the new West African department. The clerks went to digs nearby. When in fact the Crown Agents made final preparations to leave in the fall of 1903, two years later than originally planned, it was discovered that "like the rest of the building their rooms do not appear to have been arranged upon any particular system . . . and are by no means well adapted to our departmental arrangements." It is a case, confessed Hamilton, "of putting thirteen horses in twelve stalls." [50]

When Graham finally found time in 1903 to compose a memorandum about the office establishment, he summarized concisely the difficulties under which the office staff had labored for so long:

During the last seven years it has been impossible to discharge the work of the Colonial Office promptly and thoroughly. This is primarily due to the fact that while . . . the volume of work has increased steadily and rapidly, the increase of the staff has always been behind it. Indeed it may be said that in 1896 the work fell in arrear[s] from which it has never recovered. The difficulties have been increased by the want of space to accommodate conveniently the additional numbers of men and papers.[51]

---

48. Lack of space in the Colonial Office was "one of the chief impediments" which delayed the Niger protectorate take-over. J. E. Flint, *Sir George Goldie* (London, 1960), pp. 306–07.

49. CO 323/434/28581.

50. June 13, 1903, CO 323/488/15645.

51. CO 885/7/154, p. 4. Neither Graham nor the permanent under-secretary, Sir Montague Ommanney, who also commented on office organization, foresaw the creation of the dominions department five years later. Cf. with *Parl. Pap., 1908* [Cd. 3795], LXX, 621–27.

III

Technological innovation in communications did not change imperial administration significantly in the 1890's either in gathering and disseminating information, formulating and implementing policy, or modifying organization and procedure. London had been linked by submarine cable in the 1870's to the most important overseas territories, to Canada, to India by way of Gibraltar, Malta and Aden, to Singapore, Adelaide, Wellington and Cape Town. But for some time after the actual installation of cables, overseas telegrams served as an expensive and undependable adjunct of, rather than as an alternative to, shipborne messages. The impact of the telegraph was limited by its cost and unreliability and by significant innovations in ship communication (steam turbines, fast mail ships, reliable schedules) which reduced the time messages spent in transit from months to weeks.[52] During the 1880's, however, cables were duplicated or triplicated and better constructed, although as late as 1899 communication with South Africa was subject to disruption and delay.[53] Improved service was provided by the development of such combines as the Eastern Telegraph Company and its associates, which operated cables on the direct route to India. Transmission was much improved through new instruments which, for example, introduced the system of duplex telegraphy that permitted simultaneous sending of messages in both directions from each end of a conducting line. Initial high costs, which made all but brief messages prohibitive, were substantially reduced by increased volume and the introduction between 1875 and 1880 of codes and ciphers. As late as 1890 messages to Cape Town cost 8s 9d per word (the charge was reduced to 5s in 1896), but by then the Atlantic could be bridged for a shilling a word, Bombay reached for four. Finally offshoots were added to main trunk lines. East African ports such as Zanzibar (1879) and West African places such as Lagos (1885–1886) were connected to the Eastern Telegraph Company's grid which in turn hooked up with

52. See H. Robinson, *Carrying British Mails Overseas* (London, 1964), Chaps. xiii, xxii.
53. CO 323/413/24723; CO 323/444/3047.

all major European capitals.[54] What Charles Bright called "the world's system of electrical nerves" consisted by the mid-1890's of 170,000 nautical miles of ocean cables, 662,000 miles of aerial wire and buried land cable and carried an average of 15,000 messages a day.[55]

The Colonial Office used the telegraph with increasing frequency but as late as the 1890's, though it accelerated the pace of some aspects of decision making, it had not supplanted the mailed despatch as the chief focus of office business. By 1893 it handled an average of 6 telegrams an official day compared to 138 letters and despatches. A decade later the figures were 20 and 315 respectively.[56] Cables from abroad were received in the offices of telegraph companies located in the City. Messengers delivered them to the office. If, as was often the case, they arrived at night, they were placed in a box which was cleared by the resident clerks before midnight. They would decode them in preparation for consideration when the office opened next day. Telegrams which arrived during the early morning or office hours were sent to the departments to be decoded.

Once deciphered, the telegram, if of special urgency, was sent directly to the permanent or political head. Usually, however, cables were registered, attached to minute papers, and went the rounds of despatches and letters. Telegrams originating in the office were also handled much like correspondence. The methods of delivery, decoding, and disposal clearly showed the office provided no special provisions for handling telegrams. Chamberlain himself showed up late one evening in the offices of the Eastern Telegraph Company demanding to know what had happened to an important cable expected from South Africa. Thereafter, the anomalous telegraph box disappeared and cables were taken directly to the resident clerks who after 1899 lived off the

---

54. CO 323/458/8207.

55. C. Bright, *Submarine Telegraphs: Their History, Construction and Working* (London, 1898), p. 167. As Kipling put it:

> On the great grey level plains of ooze, where the
>   shell-burred cables creep.
> Here in the womb of the world—here on the tie-
>   ribs of earth
> Words, and the words of men, flicker and flutter
>   and beat.

56. CO 323/447/1249; CO 323/497/1321.

premises. And Lord Selborne, the parliamentary under-secretary, could complain to Milner that he had spent two hours decoding a message, a remark which reflected the absence of a formal deciphering system.[57]

While improved cable facilities reduced from hours to minutes the time cables took in transit, there was no corresponding attempt in the office to cut the time involved in handling them. This omission might be explained by administrative inertia, but it probably fed on the knowledge that no matter how rapidly telegrams were received or sent, effective control of the local situation did not increase. As one harassed colonial secretary attempting to stop his South African governor from provoking war with the Zulu complained the year before the Cape was linked with London by cable, he could not control Sir Bartle Frere "without a telegraph—(I don't know that I could with one)."[58] Nor had the extension of the telegraph to Malaya permitted the office to curb the activist inclinations of successive governors.[59] If anything the telegraph gave the local administrators the opportunity to create a sense of the immediacy and urgency of a problem or crisis with an intensity that despatches, which took weeks or months to reach London, could not. The telegraph as a medium of communication in this stage of development made the office more acutely aware of the need to support rather than curb or direct the actions of the man on the spot. It is significant that in each year from 1895 to 1903 the office received many more telegrams than it sent although in most of these years it mailed out slightly less or even more despatches than it received. Furthermore, the most important trouble spot, South Africa, generated by far the most telegrams and was the least amenable to office control.[60]

If the office reacted passively to the telegraph (as if it were a

57. CO 323/422/10010; Wilson, *United Empire*, n.s., II, 103–04; Sir John Bramston, "The Colonial Office from Within," *The Empire Review*, I (April, 1901), 281–82.

58. Hicks Beach to Lord Beaconsfield, Nov. 3, 1878, quoted in Lady Victoria Hicks Beach, *Life of Sir Michael Hicks Beach*, (2 vols.; London, 1932), I, 103.

59. C. D. Cowan, *Nineteenth-Century Malaya: The Origins of British Political Control* (London, 1961), pp. 266–67.

60. CO 323/487/1740; and Chap. 5 below.

variation of writing and printing rather than a new medium)[61] it responded hostilely to two other more recently developed communication devices, the typewriter and the telephone. Ernest Darnley, one of the younger, experimentally inclined second-class clerks, obtained a typewriter cast off by the copying branch and used it to draft letters. He found it very helpful to decode telegrams and provide finished copies of despatches which had to be done after office hours. But he was discouraged from using the machine and refused a new one by the permanent undersecretary, Sir Montague Ommanney, who thought typing was too noisy and would encourage overlengthy minutes.[62]

By 1895 all Whitehall offices were connected by telephone. The Colonial Office possessed one instrument (located in a public corridor) on the government exchange. The staff found the system "troublesome and inefficient."[63] By 1897 Chamberlain's private secretaries had telephones in their room connected to both government and private networks through which they called the colonial secretary when he was at the House of Commons, in his London residence or at Highbury, his estate near Birmingham. But the telephone was little used by the regular staff. Only two under-secretaries had instruments in their rooms, and one was a cumbersome extension installed in 1901. Disuse was partly explained by the occasional unreliability of the invention at this stage of its development, but senior members of the staff were reluctant even to try it. Hamilton admitted he never used the telephone. Charles Alexander Harris, a first-class clerk, considered it an "awful nuisance." Others would not trust it for anything which might be considered confidential. Finally, within the office itself communication was somewhat improved by the installation, in 1896, of one speaking tube between a

61. The printing branch did not have its own facilities but depended on the overtaxed and out-dated presses at the FO to turn out CO confidential prints and cabinet memoranda and HMSO to produce blue books.

62. CO 323/489/36366.

63. CO 323/475/9132. In 1894 the private National Telephone Company, with more than 73,000 exchange lines and private wires, controlled the entire telephone service of the country except 1,233 subscribers served by the General Post Office. By 1901 the two systems provided free interconnections and in 1911 the government took over the private network. A. Hazlewood, "The Origin of the State Telephone Service in Great Britain," *Oxford Economic Papers*, n.s., V (March, 1953), 13–25.

geographical department and the main registry. A plan for a twenty-phone, interroom system was put forward in 1901, but was shelved by the staff pending the office reshuffle that was to take place after the Crown Agents left.[64]

IV

If the communication system frustrated Colonial Office efforts to impose specific policies on colonial governments, it was also inadequate as a vehicle for changing European attitudes towards indigenous people. Although office minutes and Chamberlain's own speeches voiced the strident clichés of social Darwinism they also contained the familiar rhetoric of nineteenth-century humanitarianism. Whatever the strength, however, of the Colonial Office's collective conscience, its vitality was sapped by indifferent officials, authoritarian governors and the clash of cultures in the colonial setting. Chamberlain himself questioned whether any society should use corporal punishment.

Flogging [he wrote] is neither more nor less than the application of torture as a punitive proceeding. . . . Still, in a European country, where there is an active public opinion and a vigilant press, it may be desirable avowedly to employ torture to a certain extent [as under the English penal code] as an effective means of repressing particular crimes, and as preferable in some cases to imprisonment for lengthened periods and the moral contamination which is sometimes incidental to imprisonment.

But if its abuse had been checked in Europe, such was not the case in crown colonies

where there is no proper public opinion, and where the persons to be flogged are of a different race and colour to the persons who desire to flog them. All experience shows that the European authority is only too ready to inflict a punishment of this kind, which costs nothing, causes him no trouble or compunction, and gratifies his sense of personal power and superiority. The liability to abuse in these cases, therefore, is very great, and actual abuse has been in our Colonies,

64. CO 323/469/10398; CO 323/476/17366; CO 323/479/25941 /29811.

and still more in the Belgian and German possessions, neither more nor less than a gross and discreditable scandal.

He wanted to stop any new provision in colonial laws extending punishment by flogging and limit existing practices by making the governor review each sentence before it was imposed and report annually the number and nature of floggings to the Colonial Office.[65]

Accordingly, on May 25, 1897,[66] the office issued a circular despatch containing a version of Chamberlain's remonstrations, asking for statistics, and including a model set of prison regulations. These stated the lash was to be used only on the order of a magistrate and the approval of the governor for mutiny, destruction of property or "extraordinary" acts of insubordination. Strokes with a government-approved instrument should not exceed twenty-four for adults, twelve with a birch rod in the case of juveniles. A medical officer must determine if the prisoner was fit for punishment and attend the whipping.

Answers, as usual with circular despatches, slowly trickled into the office. They were collated by a senior second-division clerk, Charles Niblett, who drafted, on instructions from Lucas, a circular reminder issued on August 1, 1898, to ten delinquent colonies. By early 1899 they had received returns from all the crown colonies. Several failed to record floggings for crimes other than prison offenses. Some governors, as in the case of Jamaica and Barbados, were reluctant to reduce the maximum number of strokes. In some instances communications were so difficult (i.e., Northern Nigeria and Cyprus) that governors could not review each case before punishment was administered. Local officials also argued convincingly that flogging was absolutely necessary to combat certain offenses they felt endemic in local society. In the Bechuanaland protectorate "malingering" was an offense punishable by flogging as was petty theft among juveniles in Jamaica. The office thought floggings were excessive in Ceylon's prisons and administered for offenses of too minor a nature (such as "committing nuisances") in the Gold Coast.[67]

---

65. Minute for all departments, April 27, 1897, CO 67/106/9614.
66. CO 854/33.   67. CO 885/7/112, *passim*.

Another circular was issued on August 13, 1902, asking that all floggings be reported. On something as specific and tangible as a number (twenty-four lashes or twelve strokes) or a regulation, the office could be insistent. Colonies had to provide ordinances setting out the penalty as prescribed by the office. But it could only urge and not demand what offenses should be punished. Commented Chamberlain, "the Aborigines P[rotection] Socy. and their friends will never be satisfied but I think I have done as much as I am inclined to think wise for the present." [68]

Whether the office ever articulated and imposed an effective "native policy," it did not do so in Chamberlain's time. Such groups as the Aborigines Protection Society failed to enjoy the same degree of support in Westminster and Whitehall they had had at mid-century, and so they could not apply pressure to the Colonial Office. They still submitted briefs and petitions, but the interventions of H. R. Fox Bourne, the society's secretary, on behalf of Africans in the Transvaal were ignored. "It seems undesirable," minuted Ommanney, "to trouble Lord Milner for reports and returns merely to satisfy this busybody." [69] Such groups as the Protection Society, the South African Native Races Committee and the British and Foreign Anti-Slavery Society were concerned that in the aftermath of war the British administrations to be established in the former Boer republics would feature the ignorance and injustices in native policy that were found in the Cape and Natal. To support their contentions they drew on findings of the Anthropological Institute of Great Britain and members of the British Association for the Advancement of Science.[70] They argued that South African natives had tribal organizations, religious institutions and a morality of their own which contact with Europeans shattered and failed to rebuild. Disturbances and suffering followed. No judicious native administration or legislation could be achieved without a thorough study of native society. They could point out, for example, that even experienced European magistrates in Natal

68. Minute of Aug. 9, 1902, CO 147/161/18453.
69. April 19, 1902, CO 417/366/11767.
70. For briefs from these groups see CO 417/313/26300 /26561; CO 417/314/31852; CO 417/315/40367.

and the Cape had failed to understand that *lobola* was not a sale but an integral part of African marriage custom. Not only such native customs, but questions of land tenure, overcrowding on locations, education, labor recruitment, pass laws and liquor traffic should be thoroughly investigated in the Cape and Natal as well as the Transvaal. These memorials generated little response in the Colonial Office. It was pointed out that the office had no authority to implement an inquiry in the self-governing Cape and Natal, that Milner could not be expected to initiate such an immense study in the Transvaal with other problems more pressing, that Chamberlain had already agreed to a tax in Southern Rhodesia as an inducement to labor, that it was probably necessary to allow an "unoppressive" compound system in the Transvaal. As Ommanney summed it up, "the native question in the new colonies can only be dealt with on the same general lines as in the Cape and Natal." [71] New anthropological insights about tribal societies made no impact on an establishment conditioned to prevent abuses in the existing order and leave unchanged fundamental colonial attitudes towards race and corporal punishment.

V

Chamberlain's eight-year term of office was unusually long for a colonial secretary; the terms of his permanent under-secretaries, however, were remarkably short. From 1854 (when separate secretaries of state for war and the colonies were appointed) to 1895 no colonial secretary held office for more than six consecutive years, and the average tenure was less than two. The average length of service for permanent under-secretaries was ten years, but four took turns working under Chamberlain. Their comings and goings reflect critical problems in office administration and reveal some of Chamberlain's methods and successes as an administrator.

Sir Robert Meade became permanent under-secretary in 1892 succeeding Sir Robert Herbert who retired after twenty-two

71. Minute of Jan. 12, 1901, CO 417/315/36651.

years at the post. Both Oxford men, they were, by birth and experience, socially superior to other Colonial Office civil servants.
Herbert, a cousin of Lord Carnarvon, had been premier of
Queensland and had served at the Board of Trade before going to
the Colonial Office in 1870. Meade, the second son of the third
earl of Clanwilliam, served on several diplomatic missions and at
the Foreign Office before joining the Colonial Office in 1871 as an
assistant under-secretary. Both men were noted for their tact,
charm and knowledge of colonial affairs.

Because his health was poor, Meade had wanted to retire when
Chamberlain's predecessor, Lord Ripon, left office. Chamberlain
persuaded him to stay, but one evening in mid-December, 1896,
Meade slipped and broke his leg as he was leaving the office.
After a period of convalescence he planned to return, but successive attacks of gout forced him to submit his resignation, to take
effect on the appointment of his successor.[72] Meade did not share
Chamberlain's schemes for empire. He was a Liberal free trader,
an advocate of fiscal economy in imperial administration and
opposed to new territorial acquisitions. Yet he found Chamberlain considerate and open to criticism. As a loyal civil servant
he acquainted Chamberlain with office procedure, helped secure
co-operation from other departments and pointed out the con-
sequences of rash actions in South African affairs.[73]

Meade's abilities were sorely missed, particularly as Fairfield,
Meade's likely successor, was lost to the office about the same
time, and Richard Ebden, the able head of the general department, died of diphtheria in February, 1896. Chamberlain, much
troubled, took his staff problem to the prime minister. The
Colonial Office, he wrote to Lord Salisbury, "has gone to pieces
altogether. . . . I must look outside the present staff, and the
post [of permanent under-secretary] is really so important that a
very good man is required." [74] Salisbury could sympathize with

72. CO 323/421/4497. Meade died in 1898.
73. Pugh, *CHBE*, III, 745; Ann N. Burton, "Treasury Control and Colonial
Policy in the Late Nineteenth Century," *Public Administration*, XLIV (Summer,
1966), 171; memo by Meade, Dec. 13, JC 9/6 and Chamberlain to Meade, Dec.
14, 1895, University of Birmingham, Austen Chamberlain MSS, AC 2/1; Hamilton Diary, Add. MS 48671, f. 11; Chap. 5 below.
74. Jan. 8, 1897, Salisbury MSS.

his colleague, for at the Foreign Office he depended on the indispensable services of its able permanent under-secretary, Sir Thomas Sanderson.[75] Several names were canvassed and Chamberlain finally sent for George Murray, a promising principal clerk in the Treasury. Murray wanted the promotion but he suggested that Chamberlain should secure the approval of the chancellor. After much wrangling Hicks Beach agreed to let Murray go to the Colonial Office. While his transfer was pending Chamberlain again raided the Treasury. Milner, then chairman of the board of inland revenue, gladly accepted the opportunity extended to him by the colonial secretary to become governor of Cape Colony and high commissioner of South Africa.[76] When the surprised chancellor learned of Chamberlain's second coup, "a violent explosion by Beach and much lurid language" followed. The controversy had to be resolved by Salisbury, who decided that Milner would go to South Africa and a "rather disappointed" Murray remain with the Treasury.[77]

This incident had several repercussions. It sent a strong-willed autocrat to South Africa. It exacerbated relations between the Colonial Office and the Treasury. It caused ill feeling in the civil service.[78] It disturbed the Colonial Office secretariat, as they preferred to see the permanent under-secretary come from within the office, thereby creating opportunity for promotions.[79] It left Chamberlain without an office head for more than three months.

Eventually Chamberlain picked Sir Edward Wingfield, the second senior assistant under-secretary, who assumed the highest post in the office on March 1, 1897. His senior, Bramston, was passed over because he was about to retire. The son of a justice of the peace, Wingfield had been educated at Winchester and New College. He was admitted to the bar and practiced on the

75. Zara Steiner, "The Last Years of the Old Foreign Office, 1898–1905," *Historical Journal,* VI (1963), 63–66.
76. Milner initially declined an offer for the permanent under-secretaryship. C. Headlam, ed., *The Milner Papers* (2 vols.; London, 1931–33), I, 28. He was told to keep his acceptance of the second offer a secret. Milner to Chamberlain, Feb. 3, 1897, JC 10/9.
77. Murray to Garvin, Nov. 3, 193[4], JC 11/5. Murray took Milner's place at the board of inland revenue and later became the Treasury's permanent administrative secretary.
78. Add. MS 48670, ff. 122–23; Meade to Chamberlain, Feb. 6, 1897, JC 9/7.
79. Selborne to Chamberlain, Jan. 21, 1897, JC 9/7.

home circuit before joining the Colonial Office as a legal assistant under-secretary in 1878. He was noted for his unselfishness and hard work, but his promotion was considered both temporary and inauspicious.[80] However, when he reached the compulsory retirement age of sixty-five in March, 1899, the office had to seek Treasury approval so he could carry on.

Their Lordships are aware that the last few years have been a period of exceptional difficulty and pressure in the Colonial Office. The Department has lost through sickness and death the services of some of its ablest and most experienced members. . . . Thus the labours and responsibilities of the Permanent Under Secretary, at all times great, are . . . at present unusually severe. . . . Moreover, the administrative development in the West Indies, West Africa and elsewhere which Her Majesty's Government have recently decided on are only just initiated, and in their first stage.[81]

Although an extension of two years to Wingfield's appointment was promptly granted, he never finished the extra term. The burden of work was too great. He suffered a stroke on the eve of the South African War and had to leave the office. Although Wingfield lost the ability to write with his right hand he still minuted documents with his left and his resignation was not officially accepted until January 31, 1900.[82]

With war imminent Chamberlain filled the critical gap in the office staff by calling Herbert out of retirement on October 10, 1899. More tactful than decisive in temperament [83] and now sixty-eight, he was not suited to respond successfully to the challenge of pressure and complexity in office work. He stayed on only six months, leaving on March 31, 1900.

Meanwhile the civil service was again canvassed for a replacement. Sir Reginald Brett (shortly to become Viscount Esher), secretary of the Office of Works and a friend of the colonial secretary, was offered the post. By this time, it was common knowledge in the civil service that Chamberlain thoroughly dominated Colonial Office policy. For a man of independent disposition the under-secretaryship was to be avoided:

80. Ripon MSS, BM Add. MS 43555, f. 68.
81. CO to Treasury, Feb. 14, 1899, CO 323/443/4690.
82. CO 323/442/29442; CO 323/452/11542; CO 323/454/400.
83. Blakeley, "Colonial Office," pp. 60–68.

I took 23 hours [wrote Brett to Lady Ripon], to consider and then decide. I cannot face a couple of years with Chamberlain. I should have no influence with him, and should be merely his 'devil', not an enviable position. There seemed to me no call of public duty, as there are several civil servants who could do the work *under Joe* just as well, or better.[84]

But another outside civil servant was not found. Again Chamberlain turned to men under his own jurisdiction, this time to the Crown Agents. Sir Montague Ommanney, the head agent, assumed the duties on June 7, 1900.

Unlike his predecessors Ommanney was not an Oxford graduate nor did he possess their range of knowledge on colonial affairs and office practice. Yet his connections and particular experience well suited him to assist Chamberlain in implementing one facet of his colonial policy. The son of a banker and naval agent, Ommanney went from a public school to the Royal Military Academy. With a commission in the royal engineers he served the War Office and Admiralty as an architect before entering the Colonial Office as a private secretary to Lord Carnarvon in 1874. He had been a Crown Agent since 1877. His education and professional work made him an expert in the financial position and material needs of the crown colonies. His expertise, as much as Chamberlain's vision, made colonial railway development possible. Furthermore, he could hold his own in dealings with other government departments and private financiers. The Treasury's financial expert, who worked with Ommanney to persuade the City to loan money for reconstruction in South Africa, thought the permanent under-secretary had "got into the Colonial Office saddle very well." [85] His contribution to office reform or other aspects of colonial policy was not so effective.

Illness and accident denied Chamberlain the continuous service of a permanent under-secretary. His attempts to find a man outside the office showed he wanted a permanent head of stature and obvious ability: someone to reorganize effectively the office staff to meet the onslaught of increasing business, someone who would be respected and heeded by civil servants in other depart-

84. Dec. 18, 1899, Add. MS 43544.
85. Add. MS 48677, ff. 74–75.

ments, someone not thoroughly identified with the office's traditions. The search was hindered if not thwarted by Chamberlain's own tactics and reputation.

Because of necessity and inclination Chamberlain attempted to reform the Colonial Office establishment. Formidable, if not insoluble, difficulties intervened. He could only encourage reform; actual changes had to be made by the staff. Yet unimaginative and harassed senior officials lacked the ability and opportunity to devise such needed experiments as delegating further responsibility to lower-echelon clerks, securing work space outside the overcrowded office, or using technological innovations to improve administrative procedure. Indeed, they found it difficult to fulfill their main function—to provide Chamberlain with sound advice. Their task was made difficult by the intransigence of other government departments, ingrained office tradition, staff losses through illness, and the mounting burden of work. The Colonial Office was not up to the tasks Chamberlain set it.

3

The Colonial Office and
the Colonial Service

Here is this colonial service of ours, which is known and admired throughout the world for its absolute integrity, its freedom from corruption, its ability, its humanity. It is only by these extraordinary qualities that what I may call the daily miracle of the successful administration of the British Empire is continuously carried on. But for them, how would it be possible for these two small islands of ours to administer so large a portion of the earth's surface and with so much distinction and general satisfaction.

Joseph Chamberlain, March 21, 1906, *Hansard*, 4th series, CLIV, 486.

I

So varied were the geographical characteristics and human relationships extant in different parts of the empire that each presented a unique socio-economic problem. Downing Street had attempted to control each problem by encouraging the development of various political forms, each hopefully designed to meet local needs and necessities while insuring imperial economy and convenience. In contrast, for example, to the tropical island of Mauritius with 370,000 people of different races and a plantation economy governed as a crown colony, there was Canada, part of a vast continent, a "white" self-governing dominion of 4,850,000 inhabitants with an economy founded on fish, grain, and timber. As one thoughtful office staff member put it,

the enormous difference in the popular basis of [colonial] societies vitiates any comparison. In Ceylon you have established organic societies on which you have imposed a machinery of administration: the people really look after themselves. In the West Indies you have an artificial population, which has modified rapidly in a few generations, and is now at a very critical stage: a much more childish people and one with which you can do more for good and evil than you can with the people of Ceylon or the Malay peninsula. This is why the close personal knowledge and attention of [the] Governor is of so much more importance here, and why as a fact, there are so many more calls on a Governor's attention.[1]

In the crown colonies, political systems, as well as social and economic characteristics, varied considerably. Some possessed elected or partly elected legislatures which might or might not exercise a degree of control on a colony's purse strings; others had no assemblies.

Reflecting the heterogeneity of the empire, the colonial service, in contrast to the uniformity of the home and Indian civil services, displayed marked diversification in recruitment and function. As one Colonial Office clerk remarked, "the whole tradition of this department for at least this century has been to govern the Colonies, not as a whole, but as separate local entities, each with a separate Governor, Executive Council, and separate local legislatures; and many Civil Service questions have been dealt with by these Legislatures in all sorts of ways. . . ."[2] Self-governing colonies possessed their own public services and the Colonial Office, with the exception of the appointment of the governor, took no part in their selection. In the case of the West Indian crown colonies, government staff was largely drawn from local candidates appointed or recommended by the governor, a practice designed to please interests represented in the island legislatures. The secretary of state, however, appointed directly an occasional colonial secretary or chief justice. In the eastern colonies (Ceylon, Straits Settlements and Hong Kong), a civil service modelled after the Indian pattern was in effect. After 1896 higher administrative openings were filled by cadets recruited through the same examination taken by candidates for the home and Indian service. In the West African protectorates,

1. Minute by Olivier, March 13, 1899, CO 318/298/4072A.
2. Minute by Round, Nov. 15, 1898, CO 885/7/123.

governors, in the absence of effective local legislatures, exercised their widest powers. Here too the secretary of state's patronage had its greatest latitude, for when Europeans possessing particular professional qualifications were needed, he appointed harbor masters, military officers, district commissioners and medical staff as well as civil personnel. In the light of the diversity of the empire's colonies and the eclectic patterns of recruitment and jurisdiction, a colonial service, in the sense of a unified administrative entity, did not exist.[3]

Not only did the service lack unity, but the Colonial Office view was that it lacked talent and ability too. Governors, with a few exceptions, were "very inferior Personages,"[4] prone to disregard instructions,[5] to indulge in financial extravagance,[6] and public indiscretions.[7] In comparison to their counterparts in the Indian service, they were for the most part second-rate.[8] In addition to the inadequacies of governors, the occasional colonial secretary was found to be incompetent or a source of embarrassment,[9] the odd chief justice to be indiscreet,[10] and several minor

3. For brief historical treatments of the service before 1914 see C. Jeffries, *The Colonial Empire and Its Civil Service* (London, 1938), pp. 3–29; and R. Heussler, *Yesterday's Rulers, The Making of the British Colonial Service* (Syracuse, N.Y., 1963), Chapter i.

4. The judgment of Meade, Dec. 8, 1892, Add. MS 43556. William Hamilton was more emphatic, noting a "prevalence of a regrettable mediocrity in the higher ranks of the Colonial Service." Minute of Dec. 19, 1898, CO 885/7/123.

5. South African governors such as Sir Henry Loch and Sir Alfred Milner were particular offenders. See Meade to Ripon, April 3, 1893, Add. MS 43556; and Chapter 5 below.

6. This charge was levelled at Sir W. Haynes-Smith, governor of the Bahamas (1895–97). See Ripon to Sir Reginald Brett, Nov. 20, 1897, Add. MS 43544. And Sir Henry Blake, governor of Jamaica (1889–97), failed to curb the free-spending ways of the legislature of that colony. See Sir W. Thiselton-Dyer, director of Kew Gardens, to Chamberlain, Feb. 19, 1899, JC 14/3.

7. Sir Gilbert Carter, governor of Lagos (1891–96), and Sir Gerard Smith, governor of Western Australia (1895–1900), drew sharp strictures from Chamberlain for writing controversial letters to newspapers. Chamberlain minute on Carter to the colonial secretary, Nov. 22, 1896, JC 9/5; and Smith to Chamberlain, March 7, 1901, JC 14/1. Sir William MacGregor, governor of Lagos (1899–1904), was reprimanded when he allowed E. Morel to publish his critical assessment of the Crown Agents in *The Affairs of West Africa*. R. B. Joyce, "Sir William MacGregor—A Colonial Governor," *Historical Studies: Australia and New Zealand,* XI (November, 1963), 30.

8. There was a general and often-expressed opinion in the Colonial Office that the Indian service was far superior to the colonial service and that it would be desirable to emulate it.

9. Chamberlain considered Frederick Evans, colonial secretary of Jamaica (1895–1900), "weak" and "unequal" to his task. Chamberlain to Lansdowne, Aug. 18, 1899, JC 5/4. Sir Graham Bower, imperial secretary in South Africa

officials dishonest [11] or intemperate—intemperance was particularly a problem in West Africa.[12] Only the exam-recruited university graduates in the eastern service were thought to be "thoroughly sound." [13] Some indication of the low regard in which the office held the service may be gathered from the fact that Chamberlain found it necessary on several occasions to modify the language of drafts to governors which were "too peremptory in their terms." Furthermore, he instructed the staff to avoid censoring, snubbing or overruling governors in official communications.[14]

Since many colonial administrators had not the Oxbridge stamp upon them it might be argued that this disdain on the part of the office clerks and secretaries reflected an antipathy toward men of lower station and less education, but not necessarily of less ability. However, Chamberlain too, expressed privately the opinion that he felt the service was "lamentably weak." [15] And there is no evidence to suggest that he and the office staff were not in agreement when it came to enumerating those qualities which typified the ablest administrators. On the contrary, their ideas coincided. Hamilton expressed the office view when he minuted:

(1884–97) was party to the Jameson conspiracy and as such caused the office considerable concern. See J. G. Lockhart and C. M. Woodhouse, *Cecil Rhodes* (New York, 1963), pp. 287–91.

10. For example Roger Yelverton, chief justice of the Bahamas (1890–95). See Buxton to Ripon, Dec. 29, 1892, Add. MS 43553.

11. As in the case of officials in Sierra Leone. See C. Fyfe, *A History of Sierra Leone* (London, 1962), pp. 532–33. A junior clerk in the receiver general's office in British Bechuanaland was sentenced in 1895 to three years for stealing £430 in public funds. An accountant of the public works department in Cyprus embezzled £272, another in the Hong Kong Treasury almost $65,000 between 1888 and 1892, and a stamp clerk in the Selangor treasury took $16,000 during 1897–98. See T 7/29, ff. 902, 956; T 7/30, f. 651; CO 273/261/17613.

12. See for example MacGregor to Chamberlain, Aug. 11, 1899, JC 9/5, in which the former deprecates the excessive drinking habits of three of his Lagos staff; and Lord Ampthill's minute of April 25, 1898, CO 429/17/6617 citing the intemperance of another official. An official in St. Kitts-Nevis was also obliged to retire because of "indulgence in drink." T 7/30, f. 978.

13. Minute by Hartmann Just, principal clerk in the South African Department, Nov. 29, 1898, CO 885/7/123.

14. Minute by Chamberlain addressed to all departments, April 27, 1898, CO 878/9. Lord Elgin, one of Chamberlain's successors, criticized the office staff for the same habits. R. Hyam, *Elgin and Churchill at the Colonial Office, 1905–1908* (London, 1968), pp. 483–86.

15. In a conversation with the Treasury official, Edward Hamilton, recorded in the latter's diary, June 28, 1896, Add. MS 48669.

These qualifications are somewhat difficult to describe but it will, I think, be found that the best Governors have almost invariably been those, who, without being exceptionally brilliant in any one particular respect, have combined fair administrative ability with some common sense, tact, decision, knowledge of the world and of 'men and things', and above all, with the power of exercising personal influence.[16]

Two other officials, Antrobus and Round, agreed that these necessary attributes were to be found more in the ex-military man than in the experienced colonial secretary.[17] Chamberlain's description of the able governor, less subtle than but not inconsistent with the opinions of his staff, was one who could combine "with great success the iron hand and the velvet glove." [18]

Chamberlain and his staff were referring in particular to the crown colony governor who had often to deal with obstreperous legislatures, sudden crop failures or human strife. There was of course a need for a different stamp of man for governorships in Australasia and Canada. Here, where the paramount concern was to avoid offending the easily slighted sensibilities of both emerging nationalists and imperial federationists, the need was for a distinguished and diplomatic peer, rather than an autocratic military officer.[19]

As long as no major policy change need be implemented or serious local crisis attended to, the inadequacies of colonial administrators, although a source of annoyance, could be tolerated

16. Dec. 19, 1898, CO 885/7/123.
17. Minutes of Nov. 15, 1898, *ibid.*
18. Chamberlain to Milner, Nov. 5, 1900, Milner MSS, XXV. He alluded in this instance to the abilities of Lieut-General Sir Francis Grenfell, governor of Malta (1899–1903).
19. Not perhaps untypical of the petty local disputes in the self-governing colonies which embarrassed the governor and perplexed Downing Street was that of a squabble over precedence in New Zealand. By the terms of his royal commission, the island's chief justice, Sir Robert Stout, took precedence at government house functions over the prime minister, Richard Seddon. When, however, the social-conscious wives of politicians attempted to reverse this order, Lady Stout, not inclined to be superseded by the wife of a former gold miner, stirred up a furore. Lord Ranfurly, the governor, beleagured by both factions, found it expedient to curtail entertainment and press the Colonial Office for a decision which he could use to support one side or the other. Ordered by Chamberlain to "proceed very cautiously in this delicate matter" (Minute of Nov. 21, 1901, CO 323/462/32396), the office wobbled for several weeks, belatedly obtained the ruling of the law officers that Stout's commission should be upheld, and hesitated before informing the New Zealand government of these findings, one which would "bring joy to hearts of the supporters of Lady Stout and mortification to the Seddonites." Minute by Hamilton, Nov. 4, 1901, CO 323/464/38124.

in the Colonial Office. But, in time of stress and expansion, the insufficiency of the service could not be ignored. Lord Selborne's argument submitted to Chamberlain in this regard is compelling:

> Whenever any special emergency has arisen, you have had to seek for a suitable man to appoint from outside the ranks of the Colonial Service. When, in a critical and important state of affairs in British Guiana, you had to find a new Governor, you had to come to the Colonial Office. When you wanted a British Agent for Pretoria, you had to go to the Foreign Office. If you wanted a new High Commissioner for South Africa, could you find one in the ranks of the Colonial Service? When you sent a fresh Governor to Newfoundland, to deal with the very remarkable state of affairs that had there arisen, you had to have recourse to a retired officer of the British Civil Service. Therefore the Colonial Service cannot be said to be self-sufficing in the way that the Indian Civil Service may be said to be.[20]

Chamberlain, already aware of the problem, had, as early as November 1895, instructed Selborne to sound the office staff on means to reform and expand the service.[21]

Preliminary reports raised, but did not resolve, the possibility of creating a unified service, with standard entrance requirements and an integrated program of transfer and promotion. West Africa, then the scene of increasing imperial activity, was in great need of staff. But with its deadly climate it offered no attraction for an experienced member of the eastern administration or for a promising young man contemplating a career in the service. Recruitment standards must be less demanding and more flexible than elsewhere, for, as Antrobus put it, "the difficulty of getting candidates is so great that we must get them as best we can." [22] In addition, the necessity to transfer officers having served time in West Africa to healthier climates tended to foster ineptitude in the service. For those who survived were often "men whose physical [were] stronger than their administrative or social qualifications," men who were "sometimes pushed up into positions in other Colonies for which they were not fitted." [23]

20. Minute of Nov. 5, 1896, CO 885/7/123.
21. *Ibid.* Selborne did not take up Chamberlain's instructions until a year later, a delay which reflected the office's own administrative difficulties.
22. *Ibid.*
23. Minute by Arthur Pearson, head of the West Indian Department (Dec. 4, 1898, *ibid.*) which also prompted agreement from Antrobus and Wingfield.

The West Indies, Mauritius and Malta, where climatic conditions were more amenable, offered opportunities for at least senior officials recruited by examinations. But difficulties arose from the claims of colonists.

They look to the Colonial Civil Service as the career for their children, who could only in very rare instances compete in an open examination with home candidates. To separate the service in these Colonies into a higher division filled by competitive examinations in England, and a lower division filled by nomination or examination in the Colonies, would create great bitterness. . . .[24]

So diverse then were conditions in various groups of colonies that administrative experience in one would not necessarily be helpful, and perhaps even harmful, in another. Some offered attractive positions for the able, but local pressures excluded them from these posts. Other colonies found it difficult to recruit anyone. In August, 1899, almost four years after the office began its study of the subject, Chamberlain, echoing the words of Hamilton and Wingfield, agreed that objections to a general closed civil service for the colonies were "insuperable." [25]

Nonetheless, a significant number of the colonial governors were, by 1903, experienced professionals, university educated or possessing other useful training. Not including the chief administrators of the "fortress" colonies (Gibraltar, Malta and Bermuda), who were invariably serving generals, there were twenty-nine crown colony governors, of whom fifteen began their careers in the colonial service.[26] Three had joined as Eastern cadets, five had begun in the West Indies. Four had legal training, another medical experience. Some six of fourteen whose first employment was outside the service had been army officers, one a naval officer. Five came from the home civil service (three from the Colonial Office, one each from the Treasury and Post Office); another had been a magistrate in Ireland. Ten had been to university, six to Oxbridge. In 1903 there were also eleven governors

---

24. Minute by Wingfield, July 20, 1899, *ibid.*
25. Minute of Aug. 9, 1899, *ibid.* The service was not unified until the 1930's.
26. These figures exclude resident administrators or commissioners in such minor postings as Basutoland or St. Lucia. Compiled from *Colonial Office Lists.*

holding positions in the responsible government colonies.[27] Two
were peers. Five had served lengthy periods in the colonial service. Five were army officers, two naval officers. Five had been
to university, all at Cambridge. Chamberlain supported various
modest steps suggested by his staff to strengthen the service and
improve relations between it and the office. To enlarge the source
of new talent, efforts were to be made to borrow men on a temporary basis from the home service for West African work. Unsuccessful candidates in the open examinations for home, Indian
and eastern service posts were to be encouraged to attempt a
less rigorous competition designed to recruit for a cadetship program on the Gold Coast. Chamberlain heartily endorsed a plan,
already in operation, which called for the exchange of Downing Street and colonial personnel; and another which proposed
to improve the office's unwieldy system by which the secretary
of state's patronage was handled. He particularly supported a
scheme whereby colonial salaries would be raised and pensions
revised. He hoped, through the latter measure, to be able to rid
the service of its more notorious bunglers by retiring them before
they reached the accepted pensionable age. Finally, a departmental committee was to be established to consider, report and
act on these suggestions.[28]

The immediate results of these proposals were not auspicious.
For they were either not implemented, implemented so modest-
ly, or encountered such formidable difficulties as to be largely
ineffectual. The principle of seconding men from the home service for temporary work abroad had already been approved by
the Treasury. But it would appear that few civil servants availed
themselves of this opportunity. Recruiting candidates from among
unsuccessful competitors in open examinations was tried "without success." [29] An obvious reason for the failure to expand the
source of talent was the Boer War, for it laid claim to the abilities and energies of many men who might otherwise have been
attracted to the colonial service. Not until war's end in 1902 did

27. This figure excludes lieutenant-governors in Australia and Canada, but in-
cludes state governors in the former.
28. CO 885/7/123.
29. See minute by Lord Ampthill, March 24, 1899, *ibid.*

demobilization provide a spate of officers, administrators and adventurers which the office might obtain for colonial work.

The lack of confidence in the men on the spot which Chamberlain had noted to be evident in the office was reciprocated by colonial administrators. Sir Charles Bruce, governor of Mauritius (1897–1904), Sir Frederick Lugard, high commissioner in Northern Nigeria (1900–1906), Sir William MacGregor, governor of Lagos (1899–1904), and Milner, high commissioner and governor of the Cape (1897–1901), were some of the governors who at one time or another complained of the office's deliberate intransigence or the incapacity of its staff.[30] Contrasting social backgrounds, personality clashes, ability or lack of it, differences on basic policy, all these contributed to misunderstanding and contention; so did the different contexts in which the office and the governors operated in pursuit of the power and prosperity of the empire. The office was sensitive to and under the aegis of national priorities and perspectives which did not always coincide with colonial needs and realities. Governors were absorbed with the problems of specific intractable colonial societies and economies in which administrative fiat often had little impact. Neither could ever fully appreciate the other's position. Although Chamberlain might not realize that the credibility gap was unbridgeable, he keenly felt its existence and sought to close it. He encouraged governors to write to him privately about their difficulties and aspirations and would have their letters referred to the under-secretaries for comment. He also hoped that temporary exchanges between Downing Street and the service would be of "great advantage in giving to the service abroad an insight into methods of the Office—and to the Office some knowledge of the practical difficulties and local conditions of administrators abroad."[31] Consequently, in 1897, a program of exchange had

30. See Sir Charles Bruce, *The Broad Stone of Empire* (2 vols.; London, 1910), I, 181–202; Margery Perham, *Lugard* (2 vols.; London, 1956–60), II, 187–95; Joyce, "MacGregor." *Historical Studies,* XI, 31; Chap. 5 below. See also R. Oliver, *Sir Harry Johnston and the Scramble for Africa* (London, 1957), pp. 245–86, for similar complaints by another colonial administrator made this time against the Foreign Office.

31. Minute of Aug. 28, 1899, CO 885/7/123. Chamberlain also gave dinner parties for office staff and colonial administrators on leave at which he would sound the latter on their grievances. R. Furse, *Aucuparius* (London, 1962), p. 26.

begun with the colonial secretary of British Honduras, Ernest Sweet-Escott, acting as a first-class clerk in the Colonial Office in the place of George Fiddes who joined Milner's staff in South Africa.[32] By the end of 1903, eight members of the colonial service, six of whom subsequently returned to posts abroad, had served for short periods in the office.[33] At the same time a like number of the office staff, of whom only four were to resume their careers in Downing Street, served in the colonies.[34]

During these six years (1898–1903), difficulties arose which limited the exchange program's usefulness and caused the office staff to lose interest in it. Apart from the keenly felt permanent loss of four staff members as a result of it, the program exerted further hardships as the untrained colonial servicemen were introduced into the office at a time when it was in a period of considerable turmoil because of illness and a tremendous work burden. Even if the office had been in a more settled state it would have been found difficult to expand the program. Salary and pension adjustments became a particularly complicating factor. In order to fill posts in the office which might be open to them, colonial officials usually had to take a decrease in salary, and, as the Treasury was not inclined to make up the difference, suitable candidates for temporary office work were difficult to obtain.[35] Then too, the Treasury, despite repeated protests from Wingfield, and later Ommanney, ruled that office staff could not count time spent working abroad for increments and pensions. This ruling, which the Colonial Office did not have rescinded, fell particularly hard on the income of second-division clerks, and only three of them served overseas.[36] Since the exchange plan, because of its

32. CO to Treasury, Dec. 31, 1897; CO 323/417/25569.
33. These men included: Sweet-Escott, who later became governor of British Honduras; Everard im Thurn, later colonial secretary of Ceylon; John Udal, later acting chief justice of the Leewards; Sir Henry Hocking; Frederick Evans, later colonial secretary of Gibraltar; Henry Bovell, later chief justice of British Guiana; Lieutenant Ernest Roupell; and Hugh Bourne, later colonial secretary of Jamaica.
34. These included: Harry Wilson, George Perry, Geoffrey Robinson and C. W. Appleyard, all of whom did not return to the office; and George Fiddes, Sydney Olivier, Matthew Drayson and E. B. Burley, who did. In 1896 the office lost Sir Augustus Hemming to the colonial services as well.
35. See minute by Ommanney, May 7, 1902, CO 323/479/19135.
36. They were Appleyard, Burley and Drayson. After Chamberlain agreed with his staff that the "Treasury decision must be resisted" (minute of March 8,

limited scope and disruptive effect, did not serve to any marked degree to alleviate friction between the office and the service,[37] it was allowed to lapse. Chamberlain, who had put considerable faith in the plan, seems to have made no effort to keep it in operation.

Although reforms in the civil service had markedly reduced the scope of ministerial patronage in Great Britain, it could prove to be a troublesome matter for a secretary of state for the colonies who still had posts to fill and promotions to make in the colonial service. Pestered by applicants complete with impressive testimonials, Chamberlain, at the outset of his administration, remarked that patronage would become "the curse of my existence." He continued, "I am rather prejudiced against applicants who fancy that official appointments go by favour, and that a letter from a nobleman or member of Parliament who knew their wife's aunt's cousin three times removed, will materially assist their chances of promotion." He might be annoyed at such job seekers, but he could not afford to snub them. He therefore told the permanent heads of the office that he would "be mainly guided by their advice," although it would "be necessary that I should have a good answer to the applicant and his sponsors if I am obliged to refuse him." [38] While he did thus delegate part of the distasteful chore to his staff, Chamberlain did not sacrifice the advantages to be derived from finding an occasional place in

---

1900, CO 323/454/7398), and Ommanney met with Treasury officials and finally obtained their grudging consent to make provisions for maintaining increments and pension rights (see his minute of June 16, 1902, CO 323/481/52780), the matter was not pursued to a successful conclusion but was allowed to be dropped. See unsent and undated draft from Colonial Office to Treasury and minute by first-division clerk Robert Geike of Dec. 27, 1902, *ibid.*

Under the Pensions (Colonial Service) Act of 1887 no payment could be made from imperial funds for employment in the permanent civil service of a colony. So, the Treasury argued, the colony should pay that part of a Whitehall official's pension applicable to his period of service there. Treasury to CO, Nov. 26, 1897, T 7/30.

37. It was subsequently revived for a time by L. S. Amery, secretary of state for the colonies (1924–29), but evidently without success. See Heussler, *Yesterday's Rulers*, p. 31 and n.10 (where it is suggested Amery originated the exchange program).

38. Minute of July 23, 1895, Monk Bretton MSS. For an example of the type of testimonial which annoyed Chamberlain and which was dealt with in the manner suggested above see Lord Russell of Killowen, the lord chief justice of England, to Chamberlain, Dec. 28, 1899, and accompanying minutes. JC 9/6.

the colonial service for candidates foisted upon him by members of the cabinet and political acquaintances. At Salisbury's request he appointed Sir Joseph West Ridgeway governor of Ceylon,[39] although he would do nothing for Sir Harry Johnston or Lord Hertford when they were pressed on him by the prime minister.[40] He obtained posts for two of Devonshire's nominees, and promised another for an individual sponsored by Lord Cadogan, lord-lieutenant of Ireland and a member of the cabinet.[41] A letter from Sir Michael Hicks Beach helped another applicant obtain a post.[42] And Sir William Harcourt was in Chamberlain's debt for placing his former private secretary in the service.[43]

Chamberlain, of course, preferred to exercise his patronage unfettered by the need to give favors or to regard the wishes of his cabinet colleagues. But, at the same time, he showed no radical inclination to tap other than traditional reservoirs of recruitment—the home civil service and the military—to strengthen his colonial administration. Two cases in point were his choice of men to serve in the empire's major trouble spots—Milner for South Africa and Lugard for West Africa. Both, of eminently suitable background and experience, seemed also to be the potential self-willed autocrats towards whom the office was favorably disposed.[44]

39. See Salisbury to Balfour, July 31, 1895, Add. MS 49690, which indicates Chamberlain would be sounded on finding a post for Ridgeway who shortly thereafter went to Ceylon and served there from 1896 to 1903.

40. See Chamberlain to Salisbury, Jan. 8, 1897, JC 11/6, in which the former scotches the latter's suggestion that Johnston, a former foreign service administrator in West and East Africa, be made high commissioner in South Africa. Also see R. Oliver, *Johnston*, pp. 276–77.

Chamberlain indicated he was unable to find a place for Lord Hertford who, as a financially embarrassed member of the landed gentry in need of employment, had gotten Salisbury to write in his behalf. See Salisbury to Chamberlain, Nov. 23, 1897, JC 9/7; and Chamberlain to Salisbury, Nov. 25, 1897, Salisbury MSS.

41. See Devonshire to Chamberlain, Dec. 21, 1896, JC 9/7; Devonshire to Chamberlain, July 19, 1901, enclosed in CO 429/20/19822, and accompanying minutes; and Lord Cadogan to Chamberlain, Nov. 30, 1898, JC 9/7.

42. See minute by Arthur Collins, a first-division clerk, Feb. 6, 1899, CO 429/18/3095.

43. See Harcourt to Chamberlain, Dec. 19, 1897, JC 9/7: "The appointment of little Rees Davies [as attorney-general of the Bahamas], has been received . . . as Xmas tidings of great joy. . . . Your kindness will save him from a position of real distress. Thanking you again personally for your considerate regard to my request. . . ."

44. Chamberlain had recruited these two men against the wishes of his cabinet colleagues. Milner, an Oxford contemporary of Lucas and Antrobus, who was an

Major appointments in connection with thirty-odd governors could be managed directly by Chamberlain with assistance from the permanent heads and his private secretaries. He was unable, however, to concern himself, except very cursorily, with some 250 to 300 lesser officials whose selection and promotion depended on his patronage. Including professional (legal, medical, engineering) and "civilian" personnel, there were 1,696 officers in the colonial service in 1898. But the number appointed directly from the Colonial Office was small. For example, of 414 chief civilian officers, 102 had been recruited by impersonal examination for eastern work and some 150 selected locally. In that same year, the office had before it the claims for appointment, transfer or promotion of applicants for twenty-three governorships, three colonial secretaryships and twenty-one lesser posts such as assistant chief collectorships of customs.[45] This branch of the appointments and promotions Chamberlain delegated to his private secretaries in keeping with traditional office practice. Although they worked in the office, most of them were brought in from outside and they were constantly changing. The resulting . lack of continuity, coupled after 1898 with a sharp increase in the patronage business, with which the secretaries were unprepared to deal, permitted recruitment standards and practices to suffer. Obviously, as Antrobus commented in tactful understatement, "in order to secure the selection of the best men some alteration is required in our arrangements as to 'patronage.'"[46]

Antrobus advocated that promotions, as distinct from first appointments, should be dealt with by the permanent office staff and in particular by the general department. Earlier, Wilson, Chamberlain's principal private secretary (1895–1897), had found that no provisions had been made for keeping individual records of officers in the service. He revived a scheme set up by Antrobus

---

admirer of Lord Cromer, for whom he had once worked in Egypt, had been taken by Chamberlain from the Treasury, much to the displeasure of the chancellor. Lugard was a successful explorer and military officer selected by Chamberlain to lead expeditions to thwart the French and to later administer Northern Nigeria. Lugard, a *bête noire* to the French, received his first appointment at a time when Salisbury was attempting to placate them.

45. CO 885/7/123; and minute by Wilson, Jan. 12, 1898, Monk Bretton MSS.
46. Minute of Jan. 11, 1899, CO 885/7/123.

in the 1870's that had fallen into disuse, by which governors were to submit annual confidential reports on men deserving of promotion.[47] These too were to go to the general department. Wilson's successor, Lord Ampthill (who was himself to leave the office in 1900), concurred with the changes. Noting the necessity "to secure accuracy of information and continuity of policy," Chamberlain also agreed with the suggestions,[48] thereby indicating he was not averse to delegating some of his patronage to the permanent staff to promote efficiency.

These reforms, however, were vitiated from the start. Governors seldom responded fully or promptly to printed circulars, and those requesting them to provide reports on their staffs found no exception.[49] Matters were not helped by the notorious inefficiency of the general department. Consequently each geographical department fell to keeping an *ad hoc* record of personnel; and promotions continued to be made by the private secretaries as well as by the permanent staff. Some idea of the resulting confusion may be gained from one incident in which the West African department seconded an officer for work on the Gold Coast while he was still in the employ of the West Indian branch of the service.[50] Meanwhile, a rapid turnover and depletion of the private secretaries, coupled with a more than doubling of the patronage work between 1899 and 1900, resulted in their inability to cope properly with the appointments business.[51] The job was left to a young first-division office clerk, Edward Marsh, who acted as one of Chamberlain's junior assistant private secretaries. He, in his own words, "sat in a back room with an unpaid colleague [recruited from outside the office] of about his own age, and made

47. See circular to governors of Dec. 18, 1897, enclosed in CO 323/424/233. The initiative for this reform has been ascribed erroneously to Wilson's successor. See Jeffries, *Civil Service*, p. 13.

48. Minute of Aug. 28, 1899, CO 885/7/123.

49. For example in 1899 six colonies did not complete reports and one, Hong Kong, ignored three reminders to do so. See CO 323/424/233. For a belated personnel report by one of the Empire's most diligent governors see MacGregor to Chamberlain, March 24, 1902 CO 147/160/14572, which reveals more about the author than his subjects.

50. See minutes by Harris and Ampthill, June 14, 1900, CO 429/19/17690.

51. Minute by Lord Monk Bretton, May 29, 19[01], Monk Bretton MSS.

(subject to the Minister's assent, which was seldom withheld) all the new appointments to the Colonial Service."[52]

The new permanent under-secretary, Ommanney, looked askance at this practice and wanted to put an end to it. He would have preferred to have taken most of the patronage work, including technical appointments, away from the private secretaries and transfer it to the geographical departments.[53] However, at the insistence of Lord Monk Bretton, the principal private secretary after 1900, all appointment work was retained by the secretaries, for the time being at least.[54] And the departments, overcrowded and understaffed, could not even undertake the work of promotions. At this critical juncture one of the clerks, Harris, was employed on special duties which for the moment were not of a pressing nature. So Ommanney used him temporarily along with several assistants from the second division, to deal with promotions and transfers in such a way that the work could be readily passed on to the departments a year hence.

When the burden on the departments did not dissipate, the promotions post had to be retained. By mid-June, 1902, Harris was dealing with all applications for transfer, promotion, reemployment; encroaching on the private secretaries' work by handling the occasional first appointment application from the colonies; and keeping the personnel records which once had been lodged in the departments.[55] When in 1904, for example, the governor of Lagos telegraphed that he urgently needed an assistant colonial treasurer, the West African department referred the matter to Harris. He asked the departments to submit a list of candidates already in the service and Marsh to provide another of likely

---

52. Edward Marsh, *A Number of People* (London, 1939), pp. 123–24. Marsh gives a misleading account of his responsibilities. As the patronage records (CO series 429) show, it was seldom that an assistant under-secretary or principal clerk did not scrutinize or advise on selection. In addition his primary task was to interview candidates for professional and minor civilian posts in West Africa, a somewhat more humble occupation than his memoirs suggest. Nonetheless, his position was anomalous.

53. Minute of Nov. 16, 1901, Monk Bretton MSS.

54. See Monk Bretton's minute for Chamberlain of Nov. 19, 1901, *ibid.*, which, however, Chamberlain did not comment on.

55. See minute by Harris to all departments of Dec. 2, 1901, and minute by Ommanney to all departments of June 10, 1902, CO 878/10.

prospects seeking employment in it. In-service candidates were available from the West Indies but governors objected to them, especially if they were colored. "My anxiety," minuted Harris, "has been not to send too many West Indian Candidates to West Africa unless they compared sufficiently favourably with the 'Private Secretary's men,' hence I have to some extent poached on the Private Secretary's preserve. . . ."[56] Finally, one of Marsh's prospects, strongly supported by the testimonial of an official from the exchequer and audit department of the Treasury, was recommended by Harris, approved by Antrobus, but later rejected when he failed to pass examination by the office's medical adviser. The outlines of what was to become a separate appointments branch headed by a permanent official were now discernible. The origins of that branch lay less in any preconceived design than in accident or at least what was thought at the time to be temporary expediency. The branch came too late to be of any significance in the office's efforts under Chamberlain to reform the colonial service and to secure the best selection of candidates as Antrobus had hoped.[57]

If the system which dealt with patronage was haphazard and diffuse, so too were the devices and criteria used in the actual selection of personnel. For the staffing problem was a formidable one lending itself to no easy solutions. As noted previously, the lesser patronage work focused chiefly on West Africa. Some idea of the increasing extent of this work is gained from the fact that, with the creation in 1900 of the Northern Nigeria protectorate, a staff of 104 civil officers was added to the service. By 1903–04, the number had increased to 231.[58] These officers had to be obtained, it should be remembered, in time of war and for a region notorious for its unhealthy climate.

56. Dec. 8, 1904, CO 147/172/38963. Despite acute staff shortages Afro-West Indians and Africans were deliberately excluded from the colonial service of West Africa. Segregation practiced to prevent disease (see Chap. 7 below), the prejudices of particular governors, and the pervasive contemporary racist ethos contributed to the trend which began in the 1890's. See R. Symonds, *The British and Their Successors* (London, 1966), Chap. vi.

57. For the subsequent establishment and development of the appointments branch see Heussler, *Yesterday's Rulers*, and Furse, *Aucuparius*, Chaps. i and ii.

58. Perham, *Lugard*, II, 144. Military personnel in 1900–01 numbered 200 and 186 in 1903–04.

As a first step in obtaining candidates the office relied partly on periodic advertisements and informal contacts with legal, medical, military, university and home civil service representatives. Organizations such as the Council of the Bar of Ireland, the Oxford University Appointments Committee and the Cambridge Appointments Association, and such individuals as Dr. J. Hawtrey Benson, medical adviser for Ireland to the Colonial Office, and Sir Richard Webster, the attorney-general, would be asked to steer toward the office men suitable to fill vacancies. Interested applicants would be requested to complete rudimentary forms giving information as to their background and education and provide testimonials from acquaintances as to their ability, character and health. They would then be asked to present themselves at the Colonial Office for a short interview, usually conducted by a private secretary. On the recommendation of the secretary and the concurrence of a permanent head, the acceptable candidates would be appointed for service. On very rare occasions Chamberlain's approval would be sought.

This particular scheme of screening, however, was by no means a satisfactory one. The office had come to regret taking the advice of impersonal bodies or distinguished personages, for far too often a candidate with impressive references had turned out to be a failure. Wingfield probably reflected office opinion when he noted that he had come to "have absolutely no faith in testimonials." [59] And, if their innocuous minutes are any indication, the staff were aware of the limitations of evaluating a man's worth in a short interview.[60]

59. Minute by Wingfield, May 5, 1898, Monk Bretton MSS.
60. A few selected minutes are revealing:
"Mr. Rowland called today and seemed to me an energetic keen little chap, though he is not beautiful to look at (rather like a cheese-maggot) and drops his H's. He has made several trips to the Coast . . . likes what he has seen of W. Africa and is not afraid of the climate. On the whole I am inclined to think that he is a useful man. . . ." Minute by Ampthill, Aug. 9, 1898, CO 429/17/17924.
"Mr. Robinson called here on the 4th inst. and seemed to me to have his head screwed on the right way." Minute by Ampthill, July 5, 1898, *ibid.*, /14981.
"Mr. Castor called today. He is certainly not a pure European, but his colour is not pronounced—he might almost be a well tanned West Indian planter. I do not feel at all sure that his foreign ancestor was an African—I see his father was in the Indian marines, and he was born in Cochin China. . . ." (Minute by Gilbert Grindle, July 4, 1900). "*Mr. Harris:* I think, if you agree, that Dr. Castor

Consequently the selection process was supplemented by an *ad hoc* exploitation of contacts from outside the office which achieved mixed results. A candidate recommended to the office by an individual who was known and respected by a member of the staff was preferred to others no matter how impressive their testimonials. Another technique employed is suggested by Wingfield in connection with obtaining men for legal appointments: ". . . it used to be and I think still is the practice to inquire privately of some leading Counsel on the Circuit to which an applicant belongs before recommending him. I have in this way weeded out from time to time several candidates who upon their testimonials looked good enough." [61] Oxbridge men were of course always preferred, although they were not always available; but even they were not infallible and private letters passed between officials and former esteemed tutors for information. When a governor was home on leave his advice and recommendation on men for work in his colony were always well received.[62] In the case of Milner, the office went a step further. He was actually permitted to appoint men from England, without recourse to the office, for reconstruction posts in South Africa. When, however, he deputed members of his own staff to make appointments, the office regretted this dispersion of patronage:

I fear [minuted Graham] . . . that the Civil Service of the Transvaal at least is crowded with people selected not because of their ability and integrity, but because of their acquaintance—sometimes only through third parties—with heads of the Departments. . . . The situation is one to cause great anxiety, and we should do all we can to put an end to the system of patronage hitherto followed. It is not I think a case for an official despatch but rather for a private letter to Lord Milner, drawing his personal attention to the serious dangers of the case.[63]

---

might be offered the appointment as a Gold Coast medical officer without troubling the S[ecretary] of S[tate]." Minute by Ampthill, July 12, 1900. "I agree. . . ." (Minute by Harris, July 13, 1900, CO 429/19/20172.)

61. Minute of May 5, 1898, Monk Bretton MSS.

62. Lugard, in fact, "took the lead" in the choice of men for Nigeria. Marsh, *A Number of People*, p. 124.

63. Minute of Dec. 29, 1902, CO 429/21/31678. Graham also expressed his regret for overlooking the matter until "most of the mischief [had been] done."

Questionable methods of selection, rapid turnover of personnel who handled the office patronage work, and the unpopularity of the West African service made for minimum standards in appointments. As Ampthill succinctly put it, "we have cast all rules to the wind." [64] Consequently Chamberlain, usually a stickler on morals, agreed to the appointment of a divorcee to a district commissionership in Lagos and gave an intemperate assistant colonial secretary a second chance for employment. Military police were usually recruited from the ranks of officers who could not afford to remain with their regiments, but one who had lost his commission as a result of a canteen brawl joined the Gold Coast constabulary; another who went absent without leave with regimental funds ended up collecting customs in British Guiana. [65] And an hitherto accepted rule that married men were not to be placed in West African work was ignored as were age limits.

Less obvious, but no less significant than office inefficiency, climatic hazards and war as factors which made successful recruitment and promotion impossible, were problems of pensions and salaries. Existing regulations on pensions discouraged the removal of incapable officers and encouraged the promotion of officials in the twilight of their careers. An officer was expected to serve, in usual cases, for forty years; and, unless proof of mental or physical incapacity was forthcoming, he would not be eligible for pension earlier even though he might be totally unsuited for his work. "We put a round peg in a square hole," Lucas stated candidly, "and he spends the best years of his life vainly trying his best to fit it, but without success, and we cannot get rid of him without harshness." [66] At the same time, pensions were based on the salary earned by officials in their last three years in the service. There was thus a "great inducement to intrigue for promotion towards the close of a career, frequently at a time when the officer's powers have deteriorated, and a not unnatural desire on the part of his superiors to assist him in this attempt." [67] Perhaps the decisive factor in determining the quality of the average

64. Minute of May 30, 1900, CO 429/19/16933.
65. Minute by Chamberlain, Jan. 12, 1900, *ibid.*, /31856.
66. Minute of Nov. 9, 1899, CO 885/7/123.
67. Minute by William Mercer, Sept. 5, 1899, CO 323/448/23839.

colonial administrator was low salaries.[68] Even West African emoluments, set specially large to compensate for the unhealthy climate, were "miserably small as compared with the Indian salaries." [69]

Chamberlain, following the pension plans outlined by his staff, set forth a scheme whereby a central fund, tapping imperial coffers as well as officers' salaries and colonial funds, would be established. Through it the incompetent might be pensioned off before the official pensionable age; retirement pay would be based on total years of service rather than on emoluments earned at the end of a career. In addition, Chamberlain advocated a substantial and general increase in colonial salaries.

These pension and salary reforms, along with the various other suggestions raised by the office staff in its study of the colonial service, were allowed to languish. They were to have been further investigated and where possible expanded and implemented by a departmental committee. But it never met. The minutes and proposals had gone untouched for six years when they happened to cross the desk of the permanent under-secretary. In instructing that they be "put by" again, Ommanney commented, "These papers were left by the late Sir R. Herbert in June 1900. Nothing had then been done as to the appointment of the proposed Committee and owing to the pressure of the War and changes in the Office, the question has not since been re-opened." [70]

II

A vital link in colonial administration which also arrested Chamberlain's attention, and which he investigated, was the Crown Agents for the Colonies. This agency was both an appendage of the office and a tool of colonial administrators. It acted as an economic and technical adviser to the office and as a banker, broker, buyer, shipper and contract negotiator for the crown

68. Lucas asserted that "bad pay is at the root of defects in the Colonial Service." Minute of Feb. 28, 1899, CO 885/7/123.
69. Minute by Wingfield, n.d., *ibid.*
70. Minute of March 28, 1906, CO 323/448/23839.

colonies. The agents, with their dual status and varied functions, were, confusingly enough, neither a true government department nor a commercial firm. For, although under the supervision of the secretary of state (he appointed the agents and fixed their salaries), the agents, by charging commissions for work done and levying fixed contributions on the colonies, were financially independent of the imperial government. The agents hired and fired their own staff, recruited from outside the civil service and, in conducting financial transactions, had come to be granted wide latitude by the Colonial Office. Supposedly the servants of the colonies, they inclined also to make decisions, particularly in purchase of stores and plant, which ignored colonial wishes and then fell back on the office for sanction of these acts. Thus the agents were an anomalous establishment, but an important one too, as underscored by Chamberlain's appointment of the head crown agent, Ommanney, as his permanent under-secretary in 1900.[71]

The agents—there were three of them after 1895—and their staff (fifty-nine clerks in 1898) were caught up in the whirl of economic activity triggered by Chamberlain's efforts at developing the crown estates and accelerated by the reconstruction necessitated by war's devastation in South Africa. Between 1895 and 1902, for example, business valued at £2,107,000 in connection with West African railway construction passed through the agents' hands. That business, for which the agents earned a commission of £13,340, included the employment of consulting engineers, and consultation with the office and colonial governments on all phases of construction including decisions on policy.[72] The agents drew up all contracts, placed all orders for plant and stores, supervised the execution of the contracts and inspection, arranged through shipping agents for the shipment

71. For the beginnings of the agency see Lillian Penson, "The Origin of the Crown Agency Office," *EHR*, XL (April, 1925), 196–206; for its functions and status see *Parl. Pap., 1881* [C. 3075], LXIV, 589–600; for a brief history see A. W. Abbott, *A Short History of The Crown Agents and Their Office* (printed privately, London, 1959).

72. See minutes enclosed in CO 323/483/6134 and evidence before a commission of inquiry into the agent's status. *Parl. Pap., 1909* [Cd. 4774], XVI, 403–628.

of goods, and even recruited engineers for colonial construction projects. They negotiated with the Treasury and City financiers in raising some £30,000,000 in loans for South Africa, then handled the details of issuing the loans and provided for their use and repayment. Also, even before the Colonial Office assumed jurisdiction from the Foreign Office for British territories in Central and East Africa, the Crown Agents had taken over buying, banking and contracting services for these areas. The agency staff, consequently, soon doubled and subsequently tripled. They too found their Downing Street quarters inadequate, and had to construct a temporary hut (dubbed the "tin tabernacle") in the Colonial Office courtyard before moving to new quarters in the fall of 1903.[73]

The anomalous position and increasing activities of the Crown Agents seemed to focus colonial and parliamentary attention on their establishment and mode of operation. The colonies complained strongly of the agents' alleged high-handedness and inefficiency, and the innuendo of corruption was not absent from these strictures.[74] At the same time some members of the office staff were disturbed about the agents' financial maneuvers.[75] Chamberlain himself levied what amounted to a fine on the agents when an engineering consultant hired by them exceeded estimates in supplying locomotives for a Jamaican railway.[76] Disturbed by scandals then being unearthed in the War Office, questions directed at him in the House of Commons,[77] and complaints from governors, Chamberlain, wishing to nip in the bud any embarrassing accusation about departments under his own jurisdiction, ordered that the colonies should be given an opportunity to put their criticism of the agents in writing. The

73. CO 323/483/37853.
74. See for example evidence of Sir Robert Llewelyn, governor of the Gambia (1891–1900), and of the Windwards (1900–06). *Parl. Pap., 1909* [Cd. 4474], XVI, 452–54; and Joyce, "MacGregor," *Historical Studies*, XI, 30.
75. See critical minutes by Round, March 31, 1899, CO 323/441/5729; and Dec. 7, 1899, and by Graham, Dec. 8, 1899, CO 323/442/32675; and Round again, Jan. 22, 1900, with Chamberlain's concurrence, Feb. 6, 1900, *ibid.,* /34697.
76. *Parl. Pap., 1909* [Cd. 4474], XVI, 408, 414. Sir Ernest Blake, who succeeded Ommanney as head crown agent, thought Chamberlain's "fine," which amounted to £600, "monstrous" and "outrageous."
77. See *Hansard*, 4th ser. LXXX, 384, and LXXXIII, 33, 238, 405.

agents would be given an opportunity for rebuttal and the information thus gathered presented to Parliament.

In June, 1901, the colonies were circularized and requested to substantiate charges against the agents.[78] This investigation reflected, significantly enough, the administrative weakness of the Colonial Office more than it did any inadequacies or irregularities on the part of the Crown Agents. The colonial reports were tabulated, submitted to the agents for comment and to Chamberlain for consideration. Following what even an official of the office noted was a period of considerable delay,[79] and more than two years after the study had begun, a further circular was sent to the colonies informing them that Chamberlain was satisfied with the agents' commercial work.[80] Only minor changes in business practice were suggested to circumvent delay in the filling of orders—the only criticism by the colonies which was judged pertinent. It was left to Chamberlain's successor on the initiative of the office staff to present the papers to Parliament.[81]

The superficial investigation which avoided consideration of the root cause of colonial dissatisfaction and office concern—the agents' anomalous position—did not stem the tide of criticism. Five years later (in 1908), a parliamentary inquiry had to be instituted to retrace the steps of the Chamberlain-inspired study in more thorough fashion. It suggested more sweeping reforms designed to make the agents more clearly an arm of government, more subject to the control of the Colonial Office and more receptive to the wishes of the colonies.[82]

78. Circular to governors of June 1, 1901, based on a draft by Ommanney of Jan. 22, 1901, and enclosed in CO 323/470/19132.
79. Minute by Lucas, Aug. 13, 1903, *ibid.*
80. Circular to governors of Aug. 25, 1903, CO 885/8/161. Had not Chamberlain heard further harsh criticism of the agents while on tour of South Africa in early 1903 he might not have bothered to have had the circular sent. See *Parl. Pap., 1909* [Cd. 4474], XVI, 458, Q. 1108.
81. See *Parl. Pap., 1904* [Cd. 1944], LIX, 659–66.
82. See *Parl. Pap., 1909* [Cd. 4473], XVI, 377–402. Pertinent specific recommendations were that the agents should be organized on the lines of a department of the home civil service with the same recruitment, salary and pension plans; that the agents be more receptive to the tenders of local firms to fill colonial government requirements; that the agents make a more concerted attempt to meet with colonial representatives while they were in London; and that the operations of the agents should be the subject of annual reports submitted to Parliament and the colonies—a measure that would insure that the Colonial Office would concern itself more with the agents' activities.

Administrative anomalies and weaknesses in the colonial service, the crown agents and the office itself, were cogently enumerated by the clerks and under-secretaries. These criticisms, elicited by Chamberlain, formed the basis for reforms which he encouraged the office to undertake. Yet, despite Chamberlain's initial leadership and the staff's encouraging response to it, efforts at reform soon foundered. A large part of a colonial service reform program, enunciated over a period of four years, was allowed to gather dust; it was not used as a blueprint for concerted action. Mediocrity remained entrenched in parts of the service as pensions and salaries remained largely unchanged.[83] Patronage work was expediently but not uniformly handled. The Crown Agents were investigated but more to allay criticism than to clarify or remove the source of dissatisfaction—their questionable position in relation to the office and the colonies.

In part, reform failed because of the formidable nature of the difficulties to be overcome: the diversity of the existing colonial service, the hazardous West African climate, vested and sensitive colonial interests, and the vagaries of war. The incapacity of the office, preoccupied with its own administrative problems produced by illness, overcrowding, understaffing and overwork, vitiated efforts at reform from the start. Finally, after the first flush of activity, Chamberlain's enthusiasm and leadership tapered off noticeably. By 1900 his original pervasive presence in office administration was not as readily apparent. Issues, if they were decided at all, were decided after that date by the under-secretaries. Fewer directives emanated from his room; the office committee on colonial service reform never met; modifications in the patronage system after 1900 were carried out by the permanent staff without his intervention; and the Crown Agents' study languished.

After a workmanlike start in coming to terms with the most important but weakened link in the imperial administrative chain

83. When Sir Walter Hely-Hutchinson replaced Milner as governor of the Cape in 1901, Chamberlain had to make a private arrangement with him which "would not appear on any estimate and would have to be kept absolutely secret," whereby he would receive £3,000 in addition to his official salary—a highly irregular procedure but indicative of the low emoluments in the service. See draft of telegram by Graham of July 13, 1900, to Milner, JC 13/1.

—the colonial service—the office staff and their chief lapsed first into procrastination and then indifference as the immensity of the task of reform became more apparent.

If administrative reform was minimal, this is not to say that the *esprit de corps* and ability of the colonial service languished. On the contrary, they probably improved. Certainly several able governors, though they censured the permanent establishment, were attracted into the service by Chamberlain's enthusiastic commitment to empire and appreciation of his calculated effort to make himself accessible.[84] His personal political talents, rather than the administrative reforms he advocated, served to improve the workings of the imperial factor.

84. Garvin, *Life*, III, 15–16.

4

Treasury Control and the Fate
of Imperial Development [1]

The Treasury has obtained a position in regard to the rest
of the departments of the Government that the House of
Commons obtained in the time of the Stuart dynasty. It has
the power of the purse, and by exercising the power of the
purse it claims a voice in all decisions of administrative
authority and policy. I think that much delay and many
doubtful resolutions have been the result of the peculiar
position which, through many generations, the Treasury
has occupied.

Lord Salisbury, January 30, 1900, *Hansard,*
4th series, LXXVIII, 32.

I

Shortly before becoming colonial secretary in 1895 Chamberlain told a Birmingham audience that it was

not enough to occupy certain great spaces of the world's surface unless
you can make the best of them, unless you are willing to develop
them. We are landlords of a great estate; it is the duty of the landlord
to develop his estate. . . . In my opinion [he continued], it would be
the wisest course for the Government of this country to use British
capital and British credit in order to create an instrument of trade
[i.e., railways] in all . . . new important countries. I firmly believe that
not only would they in so doing give an immediate impetus to British
trade and industry in the manufacture of the machinery that is necessary for the purpose, but that in the long run . . . they would sooner
or later earn a large reward either directly or indirectly.[2]

1. This chapter is a revision of my article "Joseph Chamberlain, The Treasury
and Imperial Development, 1895–1903," *Canadian Historical Association Report,*
1965, pp. 105–16.

2. He spoke to the annual banquet of the Birmingham Jewellers and Silver-
smiths. *The Times,* April 1, 1895.

In office he developed his "imperial estates" program in more detail. He wanted the imperial government to provide capital and credit for railways and improved harbors in the under-developed colonies of tropical Africa, and an irrigation system and railways in Cyprus. He also advocated that imperial tariff arrangements be made, as well as direct grants and loans, to help the depressed West Indian sugar islands. State aid, he predicted, would promote the economic and political viability of these re-gions, attract private investors and provide ultimately lucrative markets and raw materials for British industry.[3] The imperial government had been accustomed to award aid for administra-tors' salaries, to supplement declining revenues, provide ne-glected public works, and offset crop devastation.[4] But there was no precedent for the scale on which Chamberlain proposed to grant such aid, or for his efforts to transform *ad hoc* measures of assistance into formal arrangements for long-range development.

Trends in world trade, political developments and disturbances in the colonies and elsewhere, changing private investment patterns economic growth or decline at home—all these fac-tors would in some measure facilitate or curtail Chamberlain's schemes. His relations with his colleagues in the cabinet and the abilities and capacities of his own staff at the Colonial Office would help or hinder programs. Yet in the efforts of himself and his officials to adjust a tariff, to aid an ailing colonial industry, or to launch a public works project, the attitude and workings of the British Treasury were decisive. Traditionally its officials and the chancellor of the exchequer were important participants in the formulation of imperial policy.[5]

3. Chamberlain's objectives were set out in public speeches and memoranda to his cabinet colleagues. See *ibid.*, Aug. 24, 1895; *Hansard*, 4th ser., XXXVI, 642. Memoranda of Nov. 25, 1895, and Jan. 8, 1896, Salisbury MSS (Colonial Office, private); and Chamberlain to Hicks Beach, Sept. 26, 1895, Hicks Beach MSS, Williamstrip Park, Cirencester, Glos., PCC/86.

4. Parliament, for example, authorized a guaranteed loan of £600,000 for Mauritius in 1892 for public works and hurricane damage. T. 7/28, f. 316. Between 1869 and 1880 it authorized nineteen grants-in-aid for new charges which exceeded £5,000 totalling close to £400,000. Ann M. Burton, "Treasury Control and Colonial Policy in the Late Nineteenth Century," *Public Administra-tion* (Summer, 1966), XLIV, 169–92.

5. See C. W. de Kiewiet, *The Imperial Factor in South Africa* (Cambridge, 1937), pp. 8–11, 229–30; D. M. L. Farr, *The Colonial Office and Canada, 1867–1887* (Toronto, 1955), pp. 64–106; and J. C. Galbraith, *Reluctant Empire*

The Treasury's role in the control of expenditure was presumably subsidiary to that of Parliament. Yet departmental estimates could not be submitted to the political arena until approved by one of the Treasury's control divisions.[6] The spending departments had to accept Treasury decisions on proposed new expenditure, subject only to reversal by the cabinet. An auxiliary branch, the comptroller and auditor-general's department, examined the manner in which funds allocated to departments were spent. At the same time no other office intervened in its own bailiwick—the raising and collection of revenues. The Treasury knew far more about other departments, which often complained without full knowledge of its parsimony and obstruction, than departments knew of it. By the very nature of his function, the chancellor became the butt of many strictures. He had to defend expenditure before a continuously questioning opposition in Parliament and justify new measures to an unsympathetic public so he habitually responded negatively to new demands of the spending departments. This habit was reinforced by the traditions of economy established by Gladstone. Even after his political opponent's departure from political life, Salisbury could deprecate the "Gladstonian garrison" still entrenched at the Treasury.[7] This stronghold was commanded by Salisbury's chancellor, Sir Michael Hicks Beach. His lieutenants were two experienced officials in the department, Sir Francis Mowatt, the permanent secretary, and Sir Edward Hamilton, the permanent assistant secretary in charge of finance.[8]

Hicks Beach, a reserved but blunt Conservative landowner, had himself been a colonial secretary and president of the Board of Trade. He served in the former capacity in a Disraeli ministry in 1878–80, as successor to Lord Carnarvon.[9] Knowledgeable in

(Los Angeles, 1963), pp. 22–23. For a contrary view see Burton, "Treasury Control," *Public Administration*, XLIV, 169–92.

6. The Treasury also presented the estimates of all civil departments to Parliament.

7. Salisbury to Chamberlain, Dec. 13, 1896, Chamberlain MSS, JC 5/7; and *Hansard*, 4th ser., LXXVIII, 32, 237–40.

8. An administrative change in 1902 made Mowatt and Hamilton joint secretaries; the former became administrative head, the latter financial head of the Treasury.

9. Hicks Beach's period at the Colonial Office was dominated by South African

colonial affairs, he also had a reputation for sound but unimaginative business acumen. Mowatt had served with distinction in the Treasury since 1856. Appointed permanent secretary in 1894, he began a series of administrative reforms which were successful in reducing the Treasury's notoriety. A standing Whitehall complaint which he minimized was the Treasury's habit of issuing tardy and offensive letters to other departments. Hamilton, not brilliant but extremely conscientious and thorough, was liked and trusted among the ruling elite, many of whom he knew intimately. He joined the Treasury in 1870, subsequently served as Gladstone's private secretary, and specialized in finance. All three were free traders and conceived the role of government to be passive rather than active in the economic and social structure of the country. All three by temperament were inclined to be satisfied with what was, rather than contemplate what might be. Experience in the vortex of power and influence reinforced their conservatism, for it enmeshed them in a wide variety of administrative procedures and expertise which could be used to block innovations. But at the same time experience taught them a degree of practical flexibility.

Treasury officials viewed Chamberlain's demands for funds within the context of the government's general financial position. Although Hamilton expected a near-record surplus for the fiscal year 1895–96, he feared that "unless the brake is applied to the present spending propensities of the state," the government might "find themselves confronted with great difficulties." He thought the chancellor would "have his work cut out for him in resisting some of the demands which Chamberlain and Co. are sure to press, and are beginning to press—like development of Crown Colonies and the further support of voluntary schools." [10] Hicks Beach, himself, expected a "battle royal" with his col-

---

developments. He attempted to pursue a policy of caution and consolidation following the annexation of the Transvaal by his predecessor. Though he did not actively support, he did countenance the expansionist policy of his man on the spot, Sir Bartle Frere, governor of the Cape and high commissioner of South Africa. Hicks Beach was working for a South African confederation when his party was defeated at the polls in 1880. See Lady Victoria Hicks Beach, *Life of Sir Michael Hicks Beach* (2 vols.; London, 1932), I, 63–179.

10. Hamilton Diary, July 30 and Oct. 15, 1895, BM Add. MS 48667.

league, George Goschen, at the Admiralty who wanted the surplus for the navy.[11] Also Salisbury needed funds for building the
strategically important Uganda railway in an imperial estate
under his own jurisdiction at the Foreign Office.[12] Seeing his chief
"badgered by his colleagues for more and more money," Hamilton
remarked on Hicks Beach's unenviable position: "Members of the
Cabinet press proposals on the Chancellor of the Exchequer from
which they derive or hope to derive credit for the expenditure
involved thereby and never take into account the discredit which
he may get for having to provide the money." [13] What concerned
Hamilton, and Hicks Beach as well, was that present taxation
would not keep pace with growing expenditure. Neither, however, wanted to ask the British taxpayer for more money. Existing taxes would have to satisfy the departments, including the
Colonial Office.

During 1895 and 1896 Chamberlain pushed forward with specific development programs for Cyprus which local authorities
had long urged. That island's administration paid the Ottoman
emperor an annual tribute of £92,800 as part of the agreement
through which Turkey relinquished control of the colony to Great
Britain in 1878. The British government usually provided part of
the cost but the remainder fell on the island's meager, fluctuating
revenues. Curiously enough, the tribute never reached the Sultan
as it was transferred to an account of the British Treasury. It
used these funds to help pay off an Ottoman loan, guaranteed
jointly by France and Great Britain, upon which the Sultan had
defaulted. Chamberlain proposed what the Colonial Office had
twice before (in 1883 and 1892) advocated, that the entire
burdensome tribute be cancelled or met out of imperial funds.
He also wanted an annual grant for five to seven years of £40,000
to help cover normal administrative costs and improve roads,
bridges and public buildings; and loans or grants up to £300,000
to construct railways and irrigation systems.

11. Hicks Beach to Balfour, Oct. 31, 1895, Balfour MSS, BM Add. MS 49695.
12. Salisbury was not much concerned with the economic potential of Uganda.
He wanted a railway to facilitate control of the region as part of his policy to
secure Britain's position in the Nile valley. Robinson and Gallagher, *Victorians,*
pp. 350–51.
13. Jan. 9, 1896, Add. MS 48668.

These proposals were put formally to the Treasury by the office in early September, 1895, reiterated to Hicks Beach by Chamberlain in private correspondence later that month, and answered officially in early December.[14] Then and in later negotiations Hicks Beach and Hamilton refused to make up the tribute from imperial funds, but they made an effort to terminate it. However, with the French government party to the arrangement, Salisbury unwilling to activate the question, and the Sultan's ambassador hoping to capitalize on any adjustment, the issue proved too delicate to untangle.[15] Hicks Beach would not commit the Treasury to a fixed annual grant; but he agreed to continue to assist the island's administration to meet expenditures when revenues declined. He was also prepared to ask Parliament for a loan of £60,000 to commence irrigation works recommended by a survey team that Chamberlain had sent out to the island. The loan would be charged against the island's revenue and was not to be taken as a pledge of future assistance which would only be forthcoming if the island's tax system could stand the charge and the project proved successful.[16]

The finances of impoverished Dominica also demanded immediate attention. The Colonial Office calculated a £15,000 grant was needed to repay the island's floating debt and repair neglected public works. It further suggested Britain should loan the colony £100,000 for construction of new roads, wharves and a light railway.[17] Hicks Beach agreed to the grant but turned down the loan, arguing that not only would the colony be unable to repay a loan but that it was a worthless possession.[18] The Treasury's official communiqué was based on practically the same sources used by the Colonial Office in putting the case for aid. The island could not, the Treasury concluded, afford the loan

14. Chamberlain to Hicks Beach, Sept. 26, 1895, Hicks Beach MSS, PCC/86; Treasury to CO, Dec. 10, 1895, T 7/29.
15. Hicks Beach to Salisbury, Sept. 22 and Oct. 5, 1895, Salisbury MSS; Hamilton to Chamberlain, Jan. 31, 1898, JC 9/3. See also Sir George Hill, *A History of Cyprus* (4 vols.; Cambridge, 1952), IV, 474–75.
16. Treasury to CO, Dec. 10, 1895, T 7/29. In 1906 the Treasury finally agreed to fix the annual grant to Cyprus at £50,000.
17. Based on an on-the-spot study made in 1894 of the island's problems. See *Parl. Pap., 1894* [C. 7477], LVII, 145 ff.
18. Hicks Beach to Chamberlain, Dec. 19, 1895, JC 14/3.

because its tiny, dwindling population (27,030 including only 330 Europeans) was composed mostly of small peasant proprietors engaged in subsistence agriculture who provided annual public revenues of only seventeen shillings a head. It further argued that any future imperial aid could not be considered until the island adopted a rigorous program of fiscal retrenchment, and this could be best achieved by denying its legislature any say in the collection and expenditure of funds.[19]

Concessions obtained from the Treasury by the Colonial Office for Cyprus and Dominica were indeed modest in comparison to the success of other departments. Hicks Beach, for example, assured the prime minister that the Treasury was prepared to ask Parliament to finance the Uganda railway although it might take £2,000,000 to £4,000,000 to complete and although he probably shared Hamilton's view that the project would end in a financial "fiasco." [20] Goschen secured most of the £4,210,000 surplus for the navy as well as an increase in the naval vote of £3,122,000. That estimate was part of the chancellor's first budget presented in April, 1896, which forecast expenditure of £100,047,000, an increase of some £4,000,000 over 1895–1896. The total colonial service appropriation, including supplementaries, was only £129,700, a reduction of £27,400 on the previous vote.[21]

During the first months of his administration, Chamberlain made no specific appeal to the Treasury or Parliament for aid to West Africa. He did, however, towards the end of 1895, instruct the administrations of Sierra Leone and Lagos to begin construction on the first sections of railways recommended in surveys ordered by his predecessors. He also had a survey begun so that the harbor at Lagos might be improved.[22]

Meanwhile Chamberlain produced an ingenious scheme to establish a reliable source of money for these projects. The government was obtaining almost £700,000 a year in dividends from

19. Treasury to CO, Dec. 21, 1895, T 7/29.
20. Hamilton Diary, Aug. 9, 1895, Add. MS 48667. In fact the railway, which was completed in 1905, cost more than £5,550,000.
21. B. Mallet, *British Budgets* (London, 1913), pp. 103–106; *Parl. Pap.*, 1896 (H of C 7), LV, 458–64; (H of C 53), LV, 720, 730.
22. *Parl. Pap.*, 1905 [Cd. 2325], LVI, 393–96; 1906 [Cd. 2787], LXXVIII, 29–52.

Suez Canal shares it owned as a result of Disraeli's purchase in 1875. He proposed in July and August, 1895, to set aside this income in a special loan fund to be used exclusively for imperial development. He suggested to Salisbury that it could be used to finance the Uganda railway and sought his aid to obtain Hicks Beach's approval. Salisbury reported that the chancellor "seemed quite favourable" to the proposal and he, himself, "heartily concur[red]" in it, especially if its use was confined to tropical and subtropical countries. Arthur Balfour, the leader of the House of Commons, approved too, although he wanted to use part of the fund for public works at home.[23] Hamilton was less encouraging. Following an interview with him Chamberlain reported, "I fear the opposition of the permanent officials of the Treasury who hate anything new." [24] Admittedly Hamilton disliked innovation but he had sound reasons for blocking the scheme. It would, he wrote,

complicate our financial system, it would be undoing what has recently been done, it would be withdrawing public charges from the control of the House of Commons, it would be giving legitimate cause of complaint to the taxpayers, especially the income taxpayers, a truer allocation of this special receipt is to Naval expenditure than to Colonial expenditure.[25]

More specifically he pointed out that the cost of the shares had not been fully repaid to the exchequer (£1,700,000 was still outstanding), and dividends could hardly be set aside for development purposes until they paid for the purchase. Furthermore, the government, faced with rising expenditure, could not afford to write off the debt, nor was it advisable, he argued, to sell shares (13,000 would be needed) to meet it, as a diminished stake in the canal company would be objectionable politically.[26] These figure-studded arguments persuaded Chamberlain's colleagues, despite their initial approval in 1895, to withdraw support from

23. Salisbury to Chamberlain, July 31 and Sept. 27, 1895, JC 5/7; Balfour to Chamberlain, Sept. 27, 1895, JC 5/5.
24. To Balfour, Nov. 26, 1895, Add. MS 49973.
25. Dec. 6, 1895, Add. MS 48668.
26. Cabinet memoranda on the Suez Canal shares scheme by Hamilton, Hicks Beach and Chamberlain, Jan. 8, 1896; and further memo by Hamilton, March 5, 1896, Cab. 37/41.

his scheme in early 1896. He later asserted, because increasing revenues could have been used to pay off the canal debt, that Hamilton's claim was "fallacious"; and Salisbury agreed, adding that the "Gladstonian garrison" of the Treasury had a "very disastrous effect on the chancellor's mind." [27]

Hamilton also persuaded Chamberlain not to pursue another scheme designed to entice the self-governing colonies to contribute to the cost of the navy. The colonial secretary suggested that the imperial government borrow money raised at low interest through the issue of securities to be called "Colonial Consols." Money, thus raised, would be lent to the colonies at a rate higher than at which it had been obtained. Half of the difference between the two rates would go to the navy, the rest to imperial communications and colonial exchequers. However, as Hamilton explained, the margin between the two rates would be extremely small. In addition, colonies with poor credit would be inclined to use the arrangement more than the financially sound. What would happen if a colony defaulted? "Should we," he asked facetiously, "be prepared to land a Naval force at (say) Sydney and impound the receipts in the Custom House, when, owing to some terrible drought, or some abnormal fall in the price of wool, New South Wales was reduced to financial straits?" [28]

Dominica's financial crisis emphasized the general state of economic decline of the West Indian sugar islands and prompted Chamberlain to obtain relief for them. He first suggested in cabinet that an attempt be made to end the export bounties on beet sugar produced in the various European countries by negotiating with those countries and to back the negotiations with the threat of retaliatory tariffs.[29] Hicks Beach and the permanent officials at the Treasury opposed this proposal on the ground that it violated free trade principles and, more specifically, because it would increase the cost of sugar to the consumers. As the chancellor put it to Salisbury, "Whatever the strength of the sentiment on behalf

27. Chamberlain to Salisbury, Dec. 11, 1896, Salisbury MSS; Salisbury to Chamberlain, December 13, 1896, JC 5/7.
28. Memo by Hamilton, Nov. 30, 1895, T 168/34; Hamilton Diary, Nov. 28 and Dec. 6, 1895, Add. MSS 48668.
29. Cabinet Memo, Nov. 8, 1897, Cab. 37/45.

of our Colonies, it will not weigh much against the interest of the pocket. And I would sooner see the West Indies ruined than the Unionist party." [30] Chamberlain then suggested to Hicks Beach that direct relief be tried as recommended by the Norman commission (which he had sent out to the islands in 1896) to improve steamship communication, create a department of agriculture, establish more peasants on the land, build sugar factories, and alleviate growing debts. This aid, to be effective, he said, would cost considerably more than the "totally inadequate" sum of £580,000 (£460,000 in grants spread over ten years and loans of £120,000) estimated by the commission.

If [he told the chancellor] we decide not to fight the bounties we must reckon with large Imperial expenditures. . . . These colonies cannot be left to repudiate their debts and relapse into anarchy. For myself, I am not prepared to be responsible for the administration of colonies which the mother country will neither save from ruin nor regenerate when ruined. [31]

Hicks Beach, because he was afraid that his colleagues might indeed adopt the retaliatory duties, [32] accepted this substitute, and it was adopted in principle by the cabinet.

Hamilton and Hicks Beach reluctantly accepted what was to them an unfortunate precedent that government should aid depressed industry. They were, therefore, especially concerned with how and in what amount aid would be allocated. A simple parliamentary grant had to be spent by a department within the fiscal year, accounted for in detail, and any unused portion of it returned to the Treasury. Such an arrangement was difficult to operate in a colonial context given the vagaries of local revenues and delays occasioned by distance in forwarding records. A more appropriate device was the grant-in-aid. The recipient could account for it merely by a receipt, need not spend it exclusively on items enumerated in estimates, and could retain its unspent portions. Although not recognized by statute and a departure from general financial practice, it had been used before, particularly

30. Nov. 24, 1897, Salisbury MSS.
31. Chamberlain memo for Hicks Beach, Nov. 26, 1897, JC 14/3.
32. He told Hamilton afterwards that he "fully expected to be beaten" on the tariff issue. Dec. 9, 1897, Add. MS 48672.

when the costs involved could not immediately be determined.[33] The Colonial Office wanted to use the grant-in-aid device to obtain a lump sum of £500,000 to begin implementation of the Norman report as well as proposals it had devised. These included £300,000 to be made available for remission of import duties on American produce so as to negotiate a reciprocity agreement with the United States, and £36,000 to aid in bringing coolies to work on sugar plantations. Hamilton objected.

The responsibility [for a grant-in-aid to relieve the distressed West Indies, he wrote], must directly or indirectly rest with H. M. Government [a difficult matter], when some of the purposes on which the money is to be expended do not admit of being ascertained or explained; and when other purposes involve recurring grants and consequently an outlay spread over some years. The Colonial Office would in course have to account for the Vote. So in short, it would be giving the Secretary of State a blank cheque.

I think the Government might be seriously taken to task for asking Parliament to part with so large a sum of money under such circumstances.[34]

After what a Treasury letter called "repeated communications between the Chancellor of the Exchequer and Mr. Secretary Chamberlain," the Colonial Office's proposal was dropped. Instead it was to make requests for grants and subsidies on an annual basis in yearly estimates.[35] Under an agreement made between the two departments in the 1870's, the annual estimates of a colony receiving imperial assistance to offset expenditure must be sanctioned by the Treasury.[36] It could thus review the financial position of aid-receiving colonies, make the Colonial Office justify in detail each additional request for aid, and, on the basis of this information, trim or even refuse to consider an estimate before presenting it to Parliament. To cite an example of the thoroughness with which the Treasury used these powers, it approved the

33. The procedure was used to provide the Egyptian government with £892,000 to help conduct the Sudan military expedition. Notes by Hamilton on information received from A. Milner and C. Dawkins, Dec. 19, 1896, T 168/38; and Hamilton to Hicks Beach, Feb. 9, 1898, T 168/39.
34. *Ibid.*
35. Treasury to CO, March 8, 1898, T 7/30.
36. T 7/33, f. 737; and Blakeley, "Colonial Office," p. 252.

expenditure of £454 10s. on fitting the government of Antigua's launch with a new boiler and condenser instead of £275 originally authorized for equipment renewal, but only because the colony's revenues had improved.[37] More significant to colonial development was the Treasury's insistence that the annual estimate of one of the most constructive efforts to come out of the Norman commission recommendations—the West Indian agriculture department—should not exceed the commission's financial projections.[38] Only when Chamberlain pleaded its absolute necessity if Jamaica was to be kept from bankruptcy did Hicks Beach overrule a Treasury decision not to provide a steamship subsidy.[39]

II

The chancellor preferred to provide loans rather than grants-in-aid to the West Indies because he discovered that for once a colonial need could alleviate a government financial difficulty. If the Treasury would not tamper with the Suez account, it did see an advantage in using another entrusted to it for imperial loans. Hamilton could not find a safe outlet for investing large amounts of money deposited in post-office and trustee savings banks. Two outlets he customarily exploited—national securities and municipal loans—proved inadequate. Since the Treasury had to pay depositors interest on their savings and since it could not invest all this money at a profit, the account showed a deficit. In 1895 Hamilton predicted that over the next eight years £100 million would come into the savings-banks account and only one half that amount could be invested in government securities.[40] Hicks Beach thought that a portion of this unemployed capital—some of the money returned to the account by municipal bor-

37. Treasury to CO, June 19, 1903, T 7/33.
38. See Treasury to CO, March 31, 1901, T 7/32; and Table 2.
39. Hicks Beach to Chamberlain, Jan. 15, 1900, JC 14/3.
40. Hamilton Diary, Aug. 4, 1895, Add. MS 48667. An increase in the limit on deposits and a general cheapness of money attracted exceptionally large sums to savings banks between 1890 and 1898. Between 1894 and 1897 deposits exceeded withdrawals by an annual average of £7,187,000. *Parl. Pap.*, 1902 (H of C 282), IX, 4.

rowers—might be lent to the Colonies "at rates of investment that would pay very well." [41] In other words, interest charged on the loans would be higher than that paid to savings-banks depositors. This situation explains Hicks Beach's willingness to consider loans for Cyprus and the West Indies.

By 1897 Hamilton was very concerned about the lack of opportunity for investment.[42] In May he, Hicks Beach and other Treasury officials discussed a draft of a bill for establishing a colonial loans fund from money in the savings-banks account.[43] The chancellor introduced the bill in the House of Commons in July, 1898. But he withdrew it when a few critics pointed out that it did not provide an opportunity for Parliament to review proposed loans before they were sanctioned by the departments.[44] This omission was rectified in a bill presented the following year. But it was delayed in committee when a small faction of the opposition proposed various disabling amendments and asked for a list of the loans to be made under the act for that year.[45]

Meanwhile the delay had placed the Colonial Office in an extremely awkward position. It had proceeded on the assumption that the bill would provide the needed funds to promote several colonial development programs. By mid-1899 the Crown Agents, who acted as financial advisers and brokers to the crown dependencies, reported that they had advanced £1,877,370 to colonies for various public works projects Chamberlain had sanctioned in the West Indies, West Africa, Cyprus and the Malay States.[46]

41. Hicks Beach to Balfour, Oct. 31, 1895, Add. MS 49695. See also Hamilton memo, Oct. 28, 1895, Cab. 37/40/50.

42. Hamilton Diary, Nov. 27, 1896, Add. MS 48670; and May 26, 1897, Add. MS 48671.

43. Treasury to CO, July 6, 1897, T 7/30.

44. For the bill see *Parl. Pap.*, 1898 (H of C 302), I, 315–18. It was modelled after the Local Loans Act of 1875 under which a board, established by the Treasury, granted loans to local authorities and Parliament later perfunctorily approved. The reason for delay in presenting the bill was probably explained by a controversy which developed between the Colonial Office and the Treasury on the rate of interest to be charged.

45. This opposition, although annoying was not significant. Sidney Buxton, a former Liberal parliamentary under-secretary at the Colonial Office, withdrew his criticism when the bill was altered. There were left only Henry Labouchere, the vitriolic critic of all imperial activity, his following of a few members and the Irish MP's to adopt obstructive tactics. *Hansard*, 4th ser., LXII, 181–82, 188–93, LXVII, 417, 579; and H. Pearson, *Labby: The Life of Henry Labouchere* (London, 1936), p. 280.

46. Crown Agents to CO, April 13, 1897, CO 323/415/7841.

Table 1. *Statement of Imperial Loans Advanced to Colonies under Colonial Loans Act of 1899–1910*

Colony	Proposed Use of Loan	Amount Asked for by C.O. July, 1899 (£)	Amount Advanced (£)	Rate of Interest	Amount Outstanding March, 1910
Gold Coast	Railway Construction	578,000	nil		
	Harbor Works	98,000	nil		
Lagos	Railway Construction	792,500	792,500	3¼	nil
Niger Coast Protectorate	Harbor Works	43,500	nil		
Sierra Leone	Railway Construction	310,000	nil		
Jamaica	Public Works (Kingston)	105,000	85,000	3½	65,000
	In Aid of Revenue	150,000	20,000	2¾	nil
	Railway Equipment	110,000	110,000	2¾–3¼	110,000
	Interest on Railway Debentures	88,000	88,000	2¾	88,000
Trinidad	Railway and Road Works	110,000	nil		
Barbados	Hurricane Relief	50,000	11,649	2¾	11,649
St. Vincent	Hurricane Relief	50,000	16,077	2¾	16,077
Mauritius	Public Works	32,820	nil		
Seychelles	Roads and Surveys	20,000	20,000	2¾	20,000
Malay States	Railway Construction	500,000	nil		
Cyprus	Railways, Harbor Works, Irrigation	314,000	314,000	3	314,000
Total		3,351,820	1,459,226		624,726

Sources: *Parl. Pap.*, 1899 (H of C 98), I, 237–40; and 1911 (H of C 27), XLV, 254.

The agents, rather than raise loans in the open market, as they had done successfully in the past,[47] tided over the colonies with funds from various accounts at their disposal pending passage of the loans act. Should the bill be dropped, the agents, forced into the open market, would have difficulty raising funds on short notice.

Meantime Hicks Beach had second thoughts when he learned of the calls the Colonial Office intended to make on the proposed loan fund. Chamberlain asked for eighteen loans for thirteen colonies amounting almost to £3,500,000. Only three of the loans, totalling £160,000 for Barbados, St. Vincent and Cyprus, had received Treasury approval. The remainder, most of which were for railway construction in West Africa, Hicks Beach thought not absolutely necessary, nor advantageous to the imperial government, nor financially sound. He was not prepared to proceed with the loans bill until he was assured that the Colonial Office would relinquish complete authority to the Treasury to determine what loans would be presented to Parliament.[48] Although Chamberlain conceded that the financial viability of a loan must, of course, be determined by the Treasury, he stressed his right to appeal to the cabinet when questions other than financial were subjects of dispute between the two departments.[49] But the chancellor, who disagreed sharply with Chamberlain's optimistic estimate of the economic potential of the crown colonies, did not want the cabinet to act as arbiter.[50] He had objected unsuccessfully when, at Chamberlain's insistence, the cabinet agreed to send during 1897–1898, armed expeditions into West Africa to forestall French penetration and to peg out areas for development in the hinterlands of the Gold Coast and Lagos.[51] He also protested unsuccessfully the cabinet's decision to revoke the

47. Between 1890 and 1898 the Crown Agents raised loans at rates of 3 to 4½ per cent, very few of which were appreciably discounted and mostly for public works totalling more than £4,000,000 for several West Indian colonies, Ceylon and Hong Kong. *Stock Exchange Official Intelligence*, 1899, XVII, 192–219.

48. Treasury to Colonial Office, July 12 and 17, 1899, T 7/31; and *Parl. Pap.*, 1899 [C. 9433], [C. 9440], LVIII, 145–55.

49. CO To Treasury, July 15, 1899, CO 323/443/18121.

50. See Chamberlain to Hicks Beach, Jan. 5, 1898, Hicks Beach MSS, PCC/86, in which Chamberlain tried to overcome the chancellor's scepticism.

51. See Robinson and Gallagher, *Victorians*, pp. 402–409; and Perham, *Lugard*, I, 657–58.

Royal Niger Company's charter, though he was able to work out directly with Sir George Goldie the terms of compensation.[52] He was not prepared to give Chamberlain another opportunity to get the cabinet to override his objections. He abandoned the bill.

Hicks Beach did, however, agree to assist the Colonial Office with its immediate problem. His office drafted a new bill to obtain £3,351,820 from the local loans funds to cover the projects to which Chamberlain had already committed the colonies. The bill also included provisions for repayment and the Treasury's right to set the interest rate on each loan separately.[53] The proposed act—styled the Colonial Loans Bill—reached the House late in the session; again a few opposition members delayed its passage in committee. Chamberlain intervened. Had not the bill just dropped, he explained, been introduced by the Treasury in the first place, the loans could have been obtained in the open market. They had, he said, all been "damnified" by the delay, were absolutely necessary, as a large portion was about to be spent; and were, therefore, to meet an emergency, not an attempt to lay down the principle of a great scheme of loans.[54] The bills' opponents remained adamant but he spoke to a House in which the government had a preponderant majority. With only 170 members in attendance, it obtained majorities of more than three to one in each of seven divisions.[55]

Although Chamberlain's development program had its critics in the House, the original bill was dropped not because of their opposition but because Hicks Beach took exception to the specific purposes to which Chamberlain intended to put imperial loans and because he feared that the colonies would be unable, without government assistance, to repay the loans. Indeed, Hamilton thought opposition in Parliament negligible,[56] while Hicks Beach continued to be much disturbed by rising expenditure. Army and

---

52. J. E. Flint, *Sir George Goldie and the Making of Nigeria* (London, 1960), pp. 280–82, 307–10.
53. *Parl. Pap.*, 1899 (H of C 98), I, 237–40. In paring down the Colonial Office's requests, the chancellor refused a loan for railway construction in British Guiana and chopped £50,000 from a loan for Jamaica.
54. *Hansard*, 4th ser., LXXV, 1064, 1156.
55. *Ibid.*, cols. 1152–98.
56. Hamilton Diary, July 21, 1899, Add. MS 48675. Cf. with Robinson and Gallagher, *Victorians*, p. 401.

navy estimates, he said, were "enormous" and the financial picture for 1899 "very black." [57]

The Colonial Loans Act enabled the Crown Agents to meet their most pressing obligations, but they found its terms very unsatisfactory. The Treasury raised the interest rate from 2¾ to 3¼ per cent on calls made of the local loans fund to secure it for imperial government borrowing needs which increased sharply with the outbreak of war in South Africa.[58] In addition, the agents thought too burdensome a proviso that repayment must come from a first lien on the revenues of a borrowing colony. They might instead go to private sources of capital, but investors were not interested in these colonial investments in 1900. Surplus capital was diverted into industry and imperial war loans. Even the self-governing colonies, which heretofore found it easy to issue loans, felt the pinch. Furthermore, private investors were discouraged by the government's abandonment of the ambitious loans scheme put forward in 1897–1898, and the first lien on revenue for the repayment of the much more modest scheme finally passed.[59] The agents' actions to finance railway construction in Lagos was a case in point. They delayed as long as possible using the £792,500 provided under the act for the project. By June, 1900, however, they could obtain no further advances to cover expenditure. "The generally unsettled feeling in the money market," they explained, "renders bankers unwilling to lock up their resources and they are pressing us to name a time when we will pay off our present advances." They had no option but to go to the Treasury under the Act although the terms of repayment seriously impaired the power of the colony to raise future sums.[60] Potential investors in West African issues were also scared off at this time by a check to gold mining operations caused by the Ashanti revolts just when they were beginning to attract attention. "The luck," minuted Chamberlain, "has been against us and we are driven into the arms of the Treasury." [61]

57. Hicks Beach to his wife, Jan. 26, 1899, Lady Hicks Beach, *Hicks Beach*, II, 76.
58. Minute by Hamilton, Feb. 4, 1904, T 168/62.
59. Ommanney to CO, March 23, 1900, CO 323/452/9313.
60. Crown Agents to CO, June 21, 1900, CO 147/152/19706.
61. Minutes by Ommanney and Chamberlain, June 22, 1900, *ibid.*

The agents persisted in attempts to relieve the colony of the disadvantageous loan, particularly when, by 1902, the cost of railway construction far exceeded original estimates. But the uncertainty of conditions in which money could be borrowed for the West African colonies persisted until late 1904. Finally in February, 1905, they issued on behalf of the Lagos government a £2,000,000 loan bearing 3½ per cent interest at a discount of 97. It was to cover costs in excess of original estimates for building the line as far as Ibadan, to provide for an extension to Oshagbo, but also to pay back the Treasury the £792,500 borrowed in 1900.[62] Rather than tap the local loans fund for railway construction in the Gold Coast, the agents issued a loan at a heavy discount on the open market in 1902.[63] Thus loans made under the Colonial Loans Act were not extensive and some of them temporary. By 1910, £1,457,226 or less than half the sum provided by the act was outstanding.[64]

III

The cost of the war in South Africa prompted Hicks Beach to threaten to resign if his colleagues did not adopt retrenchment budgets. Expenditure in the period 1895–1902 increased annually an average of £7,000,000 and reached £147,500,000 in the estimates for 1901–1902.[65] Even Chamberlain found the increase startling. He pleaded the necessity of devoting large sums to reconstruction in South Africa, but he admitted "that there is serious ground for caution and for careful examination of all new estimates." [66] Furthermore, by 1902 he had to concede that his earlier hope for rapid development of the African estates was

---

62. Crown Agents to CO, Aug. 3, 1904, CO 145/172/27348; *Stock Exchange Official Intelligence*, 1906, XXIV, 56, 65.
63. It was for £1,035,000 at 3 per cent discounted at 91 to cover the cost of building a railway from Sekundi to Kumasi. Its highest quotation in 1906 was 87–5/8. *Ibid.*, 1907, XXV, 56.
64. *Parl. Pap.*, 1911 (H of C 27), XLV, 254. See also Table 1.
65. Hicks Beach to Salisbury, Sept. 13, 1901. Salisbury MSS; and cabinet memo on growth of expenditure, Sept. 12, 1901, Cab. 37/58.
66. Chamberlain to St. John Brodrick, Sept. 9, 1901, JC 11/1; and to Hicks Beach, Sept. 30, 1901, Hicks Beach MSS, PCC/86.

Table 2. *Amounts Granted by the Imperial Government in Aid to the West Indian Colonies in Each of the Eight Years Ending 1904–1905* (thousands of pounds)

	1897–1898	1898–1899	1899–1900	1900–1901	1901–1902	1902–1903	1903–1904	1904–1905
Grants in aid of deficiency of general revenue	90.	20.	20.	20.	20.3	20.	7.	—
Grants in aid of agricultural instruction and experiment	—	*3.9	*13.5	*13.3	*12.6	*12.4	*12.2	*12.2
Agricultural department, salaries and incidental expenses	—	*1.5	*2.8	*4.	*4.4	*5.	*5.2	*5.
Salaries, &c. of governors	5.2	5.2	5.1	5.1	5.	5.	5.	5.
Steamship subsidies ᵃ	—	*5.	*35.	—	*10.	*25.	*33.5	*33.5
Grant in aid of roads and land settlement	*30.	—	—	—	—	—	—	—
Grant in aid of central sugar factories ᵇ	—	10.	—	—	—	—	—	—
Grant in aid of sugar industry ᶜ	—	—	—	—	—	250.	—	—
Grant in aid of hurricane relief								
Barbados	—	40.	—	—	—	—	—	—
Leewards	—	—	17.	—	—	—	—	—
St. Vincent	—	25.	—	—	—	—	—	—
Total	125.2	110.6	93.4	42.4	52.3	317.4	62.9	55.7

* Only sums marked with asterisks can be said to have been legitimately for colonial development. Other sums were essentially designed as financial aid to meet emergencies or traditional expenses such as governors' salaries.

a. Grants under this head were for services provided under contract by three British shipping companies.

b. This grant was never used but returned to the imperial exchequer in 1905.

c. This grant was a relief rather than a developmental measure.

Source: Parl. Pap., 1910 [Cd. 5369], XI, 219, CO 884/8/132, pp. 8–10.

illusory. As he told Flora Lugard, the wife of his Northern Nigerian governor,

If I were a despot I would make a large investment in railways, but we must not go much in advance of public opinion for fear of a reaction. I am afraid the slow progress and the enormous cost of the Uganda Railway has rather influenced public opinion against too rapid progress, and until the promise of trade is more evident than can be expected at present, it would be difficult to obtain a grant for any very large undertaking which would appear to people in this country to be speculative.[67]

In West Africa the railway program proceeded more slowly and was more expensive than initial surveys had anticipated.[68] Substantial imperial grants were provided but primarily to cover deficiencies in the operating costs of colonial administrations.[69]

In the West Indies too, relief and development programs had not attracted private investors or improved economies appreciably. A substantial portion of the imperial aid was spent to alleviate distress caused by hurricanes.[70] Chamberlain had again to raise in cabinet the issue of retaliatory tariffs. This time he was more successful. Hicks Beach, although he had placed a modest tax on sugar to help pay for the war, still opposed discriminatory tariffs. Chamberlain, however, obtained a statement from the cabinet which threatened retaliation if European states did not stop subsidizing their sugar exports. On the continent, meanwhile, the discovery that sugar cartels were making enormous profits encouraged a reaction against the bounty system. These developments led an international conference to meet in Brussels and to ratify an agreement to abolish subsidies in March, 1902.[71] The agreement was to go in effect in September, 1903. Hicks Beach agreed that in the interim the West Indian sugar industry should receive an imperial grant of £250,000. This sum, like much of the money spent or lent in the West Indies, was to meet an emergency.[72] Neither this direct aid nor the end of the bounty system had much of an effect, other than as a short-term measure

67. Perham, *Lugard*, II, 170.
68. *Parl. Pap., 1905* [Cd. 2325], LVI, 378–82.
69. The Northern Nigerian estimates for 1902–03, for example, provided £67,000 out of a total planned expenditure of £355,000 for "extraordinary public work"—that is for the completion of a tramway, removal of government headquarters to a new site, telegraph construction, dwelling houses for officers in the civil administration, two government boats to replace two that had been condemned, and a railway survey. See Treasury to CO, April 12, 1902, T 7/32, in which the Treasury sanctioned a grant of £290,000 while at the same time expressing the hope that "extraordinary" expenditure would not recur on future estimates.
70. Hurricanes struck St. Vincent and Barbados in 1898, and Nevis and Montserrat in 1899; a rainstorm brought distress to St. Kitts and Nevis in 1901 and volcanic eruption devastated St. Vincent in 1902.
71. R. W. Beachey, *The British West India Sugar Industry in the Late 19th Century*, (Oxford, 1957), pp. 166–68.
72. See Table 2.

to alleviate a crisis, particularly because the beet sugar industry continued to dominate the British market, and because the grants had not been enough to solve satisfactorily the islands' deep-rooted economic problems.[73] By 1904 the Colonial Office could only hope that what the Treasury called "temporary and exceptional" imperial aid would, if continued beyond the time period (ten years) set by the Norman commission, keep West Indian administrative finance solvent until, at some future date, the sugar industry became more stable and other products were developed.[74]

In Cyprus railway and irrigation systems planned in 1896 were completed although there was considerable delay, the consequence of a strain placed on the colony's revenues by drought during 1902–1903.[75] Here as in all the crown colonies the Treasury's first consideration, maintained throughout its correspondence with the Colonial Office, was that a colony with a depressed or developing revenue system could receive temporary imperial aid to offset the costs of administration. A colony with a viable tax system, on the other hand, should pay for its own development schemes.

Self-governing colonies were, of course, by this time expected to take care of their own financial needs without imperial assistance. However, Canada had as early as 1887 urged that colonial stocks be put on the list of government approved securities in which trust funds could be invested. Payment and rates of interest on stocks put on the list of trust securities were subject to parliamentary control. Two objections had blocked previous efforts to meet the colonial request: Parliament could not impose controls on the borrowing practices of self-governing colonies, and the colonies were not legally bound to defer to judgments of British courts in litigation upon stocks.[76] Canada renewed its request at the imperial conference of 1897 and Chamberlain re-

73. S. B. Saul, "The Economic Significance of 'Constructive Imperialism'," *Journal of Economic History*, XVII (June, 1957) 173–92.
74. CO to Treasury, April 20, 1904, CO 884/8/132.
75. CO 883/6/57, pp. 197–98; and CO 883/6/58, p. 6.
76. For the history of these efforts see Treasury to CO, Nov. 2, 1897, T 7/30.

ferred it to the Treasury. By 1899 it overcame its initial financial scruples to obtain a political objective—closer imperial relations. For here was an opportunity to make a tangible concession in return for Canada's grant of tariff preferences to British manufacture and the self-governing colonies' contribution to the war effort.[77] Besides, by the turn of the century, the viability and profitability of colonial loans had been proved. Indeed, they were to many a more attractive investment than Consols which yielded less.[78] Such proven reliability made the Treasury more amenable to concession, if in addition, certain conditions under which colonial stocks would be admitted to the trustee list were acceptable to the colonies. Participating colonies agreed to accept the decision of British courts, and accept disallowance by the imperial government of any subsequent colonial legislation adverse to trustee stockholders. Also trustees were forbidden to invest in stocks yielding over one per cent more than Consols. These measures were incorporated into the Colonial Stock Act of 1900. It, rather than serving to encourage investment in colonial government stock, merely recognized what had come to pass— that British investors had a marked preference for such securities.[79]

What was perhaps more significant was the subsequent application of the Act to the securities of crown colonies. Here again, to get on the list the colonial stock must meet certain conditions drawn up by the Treasury. To qualify, each colony had to pass enabling legislation to insure payment and prevent default.[80]

77. See Hamilton to Wingfield, May 8, 1899, CO 323/442/17193; and Hamilton to Herbert, Jan. 5, 1900, *ibid.*, /35949.
78. Hamilton to Bramston, July 6, 1897, CO 323/417/14674.
79. See A. R. Hall, *The London Capital Market and Australia, 1870–1914* (Canberra, 1963), pp. 57–58.
80. By 1903 the following colonies had passed legislation meeting conditions to obtain a place on the trustee list and most of them had issued loans under the Colonial Stock Act: Barbados, British Guiana, British Honduras, Canada, Ceylon, Gold Coast, Grenada, Hong Kong, Lagos, Mauritius, Natal, New South Wales, New Zealand, Queensland, St. Lucia, St. Vincent, Sierra Leone, South Australia, Straits Settlements, Tasmania, Trinidad and Tobago, Victoria, and Western Australia. Digest of Colonial Stock Act compiled in the Treasury, Jan., 1903, CO 323/484/3591.

IV

The most revealing commentary on the Treasury's influence and its reluctance to provide funds for the spending departments was made by the prime minister. Salisbury asserted publicly that the Treasury, by exercising the power of the purse, claimed a voice in all decisions of administrative authority and policy. He claimed that "much delay and many doubtful resolutions have been the result of the peculiar position which, through many generations, the Treasury has occupied." [81] In private he further explained:

The traditions of the Office are very bad; but I think they are more actuated by the fear of the future demands which any concession may bring upon them than by the actual outlay involved in the concession. They are more likely, therefore, to be open to persuasion at the end of a liability than at the beginning of it. Their great error to my mind is that they are more afflicted at giving way to a small demand than to a larger one. [82]

Cabinet ministers might blame Treasury parsimony for inaction or mistakes rather than their own miscalculations or procrastination. After all, cabinet authority, not Treasury control, ultimately decided policy. Yet that control gave the Treasury opportunity to make many minor administrative decisions which could distort policy or even make the cabinet change its collective mind. Chamberlain tried to implement his imperial estates program. Indeed, he managed to launch part of it before the war and his own disillusionment set in, but he was discouraged initially from formulating long-term commitments in West Africa and the West Indies by the chancellor and Treasury officials. They even, inadvertently, made it difficult for the Crown Agents to obtain private finance capital for development projects underway. Others they dissuaded Chamberlain from beginning. He wanted, for example, to take over the territory of Rhodesia from the British South Africa Company. But the Treasury, he admitted, "would never give me the money that would be required to place

81. Jan. 30, 1900, *Hansard*, 4th ser., LXXVIII, 32.
82. To Lord Cromer, April 24, 1896, PRO, Cromer MSS, FO 633/7.

the administration on a proper footing and at the same time to develop the estate." [83] The imperial government had to provide the means for maintenance of viable colonial administrations and new territorial acquisitions. It need not, in the Treasury view, provide British taxpayers' money as risk capital to enable private enterprise to flourish.

If the Colonial Office under Chamberlain dropped its long-held inclination to avoid new overseas responsibilities and reduce expenses in the existing colonial empire, the tradition of non-involvement and economy was carried on by the Treasury. In the case of imperial development it made the tradition effective. [84]

83. To Sir Robert Herbert, June 10, 1897, JC 10/8.
84. The Colonial Office lapsed into its old attitudes once Chamberlain had left. Hyam, *Elgin and Churchill,* pp. 470–74.

·5·

South African Crisis: The Erosion
of Administrative Restraint

It must be remembered that that town [Johannesburg] is probably the most immoral, corrupt and generally dishonest place probably existing today in the world. . . .

Nearly all the information transmitted to England from Cape Town [is] worked by what might be justly termed a colossal syndicate for the spread of systematic misrepresentation and I am therefore very careful to insist upon the verification and examination of intelligence before transmitting it to you.

The bane of South Africa for the last twenty-four years has been the false information sent home. . . .

Sir William Butler, acting high commissioner and
governor of South Africa, to Chamberlain
December 18, 1898, Chamberlain MSS, JC 10/9.

I

Chamberlain's South African policies have been frequently studied by historians. His complicity in the Jameson plan has been well documented. His crude brinksmanship, in some measure inspired by Milner, which led to the Boer War, has been stressed. And a new assessment of his South African objectives as part of late nineteenth-century British imperial expansion has been attempted. These studies,[1] essentially concerned with policy

1. Jan van der Poel, *The Jameson Raid* (Cape Town, 1951); Ethel Drus, "The Question of Imperial Complicity in the Jameson Raid," *EHR*, LXVIII (October, 1953), 582–93. The most ingenious but still unconvincing apologist for Chamberlain is Elizabeth Pankenham, *Jameson's Raid* (London, 1960); J. S. Marais, *The Fall of Kruger's Republic* (Oxford, 1961); R. Robinson and J. Gallagher, *Africa and the Victorians* (New York, 1961), pp. 410–61.

objectives, have paid partial, and perhaps insufficient, attention to administrative problems. For example, the most exhaustive study of Chamberlain's policymaking assumes, erroneously, that the Colonial Office's organization was "excellent." [2] Another monograph states, but does not adequately explain why, Chamberlain "lost command" of the South African situation to the "militant imperialist" Milner, who deflected the course of the British policy and drove it "far beyond its traditional objectives." [3] Several facets of imperial administration were severely tested by crises in South African affairs.

II

In the 1880's the discovery of gold in the Transvaal on the Witwatersrand produced a bustling, industrial enclave in the heart of a sedentary, parochial agricultural society. Foreigners or uitlanders, mostly British by origin but including representatives of many nationalities from diverse social backgrounds had, apart from the quest for wealth, little enough in common, but they had even less in common with the original white settlers—the Afrikaners. Economic disparities between the old and new economic groups were exacerbated by language problems and political and moral disagreements between Boer and Briton.[4] The ultimate goal of the two most powerful South African leaders was to create some form of political federation which would include the British self-governing colonies of the Cape and Natal and the Afrikaner republics of the Transvaal and the Orange Free State. Paul Kruger, president of the Transvaal, envisaged a Boer South Africa under its own flag. Cecil Rhodes, the gold and diamond magnate who became premier of the Cape, dreamed of a united country closely linked by numerous ties with Britain. Moderates like Jan Hofmeyr, a leader of the Cape Afrikaners, who sought to overcome the differences between these two men,

2. R. H. Wilde, "Joseph Chamberlain and the South African Republic, 1895–1899," *Archives Year Book for South African History,* I (1956), xiv.
3. E. Stokes, "Milnerism," *Historical Journal,* V (1962), 60.
4. C. W. de Kiewiet, *A History of South Africa* (Oxford, 1941), p. 122.

wanted an independent, federated nation based on Boer-Briton equality. But hopes of political co-operation were compromised by the racial tension in the Transvaal. Furthermore, Kruger's government, enriched by income derived from the Rand gold-fields, found it could adopt a course of action increasingly independent of the British colonies.

The threat Boer separatism posed to British hegemony in South Africa was apparent to officials and politicians in both London and Cape Town; but they had been unable to devise satisfactory means to contain it. Their efforts were limited by the Pretoria and London Conventions of 1881 and 1884 which determined relations between the South African Republic and Britain and under which the republic enjoyed internal independence, it having only to submit its foreign relations to British scrutiny. Rhodes tried to make the Transvaal dependent on the Cape's railway system. He also pegged out claims for his chartered British South Africa Company along the Transvaal's western and northern borders. In London successive colonial secretaries, Lord Knutsford and Lord Ripon, assisted Rhodes in his objectives and labored to prevent the Transvaal from gaining access to the sea through expansion eastward. They too hoped ultimately to include the Boer republics in a South African federation loyal to the British connection.[5]

By 1895, it was obvious these measures were not working. The Transvaal's wealth was fast making it, rather than the Cape, the dominant political and economic entity in South Africa, a trend highlighted in 1894 by the completion of a rail link between Pretoria and the Portugese port of Lourenço Marques on Delagoa Bay. At this junction, Britain's governor of the Cape and high commissioner in South Africa, Lord Loch, suggested a plan to overthrow Kruger's government by precipitating a revolt of the uitlander community and following it with armed imperial intervention. Ripon, who was prepared to contain but not coerce the Transvaal, recalled his impetuous administrator. However, Rhodes took up Loch's plan.

Desperate measures to save Britain's hegemony in the face of

5. Robinson and Gallagher, *Victorians,* pp. 410–11.

Afrikaner nationalism were, then, under consideration when Chamberlain made his appearance in Downing Street. Rhodes's agents in London approached the colonial secretary to grant the South Africa Company the Bechuanaland protectorate for administrative as well as development purposes. Rhodes, however, particularly wanted the area to provide a jumping-off point for an armed force which was to come to the aid of a rebellion that he was fomenting on the Rand.[6]

Chamberlain, in office less than six weeks, "had been entirely unable, owing to the General Election, to master the details of [his] work," when he was caught up in these intrigues.[7] He had to rely on his staff and administrators on the spot for guidance. Meade, his permanent under-secretary, had specialized in South African affairs as had Fairfield, the first assistant under-secretary. In Cape Town, Sir Hercules Robinson, whom Ripon had chosen on Rhodes's recommendation to replace Loch, provided insights gained from previous work in South Africa. Meade and Fairfield supported Rhodes's demands and Chamberlain granted him a strip of territory along the Transvaal border in which ostensibly to build a railway. But Chamberlain soon learned "unofficially" that an armed force was being created in the territory by Dr. Leander Starr Jameson, one of Rhodes's underlings in the chartered company.[8] The conspiracy also required that the imperial government would intervene on behalf of the uitlanders once the rebellion began. Chamberlain was led to believe uitlander unrest was extensive and genuine. Unless uitlanders got substantial political concessions there would, he was told,

be an armed demonstration in the Transvaal. The majority of the visitors from or connected with South Africa seen by me were of opinion that in this manner the desired reforms would be obtained; but others expressed entire disbelief in the reality of the movement. It was impossible to arrive at any solid basis of fact on which to form a judgment as to what was likely to happen.[9]

6. Van der Poel, *Raid*, pp. 1–27.
7. Memo by Chamberlain, June 12, 1896, quoted in Ethel Drus, "A Report on the Papers of Joseph Chamberlain Relating to the Jameson Raid and the Inquiry," *Bulletin of the Institute of Historical Research*, XXV (Nov., 1952), 47.
8. Wilde, *Archives*, I, 9; Garvin, *Life*, III, 33–34; Marais, *Kruger*, p. 87.
9. Memo by Chamberlain, June 12, 1896, quoted in Drus, *BIHR*, XXV, 48.

What doubts minority reports raised in the mind of the colonial secretary must have been overcome by Robinson. The high commissioner, no doubt inspired by Rhodes, told his chief that "it seems almost certain . . . that a revolt will take place sooner or later." [10] Not only did Robinson give Chamberlain advice but offered the line of action to be pursued. On the outbreak of an uprising Robinson would go to Pretoria to mediate between the Boers and the uitlanders and request that the latter be given the vote and that the republic be made a self-governing colony under the British flag. Chamberlain approved.[11]

He had fallen in with Rhodes's schemes. But he was not one to watch from the sidelines. Assured by Rhodes and Robinson that the impending rebellion had every chance of success, he determined to set it off at a time most advantageous to imperial interests. Through Fairfield, who was in close contact with Rhodes's agents in London, he conveyed his desire to the Cape premier. The longer it was delayed, he wrote, "the more chance there is of foreign intervention. It seems to me that either it should come *at once* or be postponed for a year or two at least." [12] No sooner had Fairfield complied with his chief's instructions than the colonial secretary learned that the "Transvaal business" was going "to fizzle out" and that Rhodes had "miscalculated the feeling of the Johannesburg capitalists." [13] However, Jameson, ignoring Rhodes's instructions to enter the Transvaal only if the uitlanders revolted, crossed the border with his small force and headed for the Rand, hoping to precipitate the revolution.

Chamberlain realized that Jameson's action would be considered "a flagrant piece of filibustering for which there [was] no justification." [14] He publicly repudiated the Raid and both he and Robinson ordered Jameson, by telegraph, to turn back. But the impetuous doctor persisted, only to be captured by the Boers. His action and subsequent inquiries revealed Rhodes's South African intrigues. Chamberlain's prompt repudiation and the

10. Nov. 4, 1895, quoted in Garvin, *Life*, III, 60.
11. *Ibid.*, pp. 48, 60–62.
12. To Meade, Dec. 18, 1895, *ibid.*, p. 72.
13. Chamberlain to Salisbury, Dec. 29, 1895, Salisbury MSS.
14. Chamberlain to Salisbury, Dec. 31, 1895, quoted in Garvin, *Life*, III, 95.

calling of a parliamentary inquiry allayed but did not remove suspicion that he and the Colonial Office were guilty of connivance. But the Raid discredited Rhodes (he resigned as premier of the Cape), and weakened the imperial government's prestige throughout South Africa.

The incident also provides graphic testimony to how its guilty participants assumed erroneously that telegraphic communication would help to exploit and control South African developments. Rhodes in Cape Town received confused if not distorted reports from his cronies in London of their negotiations with Fairfield and Chamberlain.[15] His own efforts to direct the armed force on the Transvaal's border failed when Jameson ignored his telegrams. Meanwhile Robinson deliberately or inadvertently fed the office inaccurate information of affairs in Johannesburg. It, in turn, issued Robinson directives in the false hope that because they were timely they would be effective. Ultimately records of some of the telegrams which passed between Rhodes and his representatives in London came to light, discrediting him and embarrassing Chamberlain. The telegraph intensified involvement but denied Chamberlain its corollary, control.

Yet Chamberlain persisted, only to be curtailed by his own administrators. Robinson went to Pretoria as had originally been planned. A naval squadron was commissioned to be ready to sail into South African waters, and Chamberlain had the War Office order its commanding officer at the Cape to send troops to Mafeking on the Transvaal's border. This show of force coupled with "firm language" from Robinson would, Chamberlain hoped, still enable the imperial government to extract concessions from Kruger for the uitlanders.[16] Robinson objected. He now thought it prudent to avoid further interference. There was a serious risk of war, as the Boers were much incensed by Rhodes's tactics and, despite his denials, by what they believed to be Chamberlain's involvement. Robinson, therefore, objected to the suggestion to move troops to Mafeking, declined an offer by Chamberlain to

15. C. M. Woodhouse, "The Missing Telegrams and the Jameson Raid," *History Today*, XVI (June and July, 1962), 395–404, 506–14.
16. *Parl. Pap.*, 1896 [C. 7933], LIX, 493, 515, 519.

have the Cape garrison reinforced, and refused to press Kruger for reforms. "Any attempt," he told Chamberlain, "to dictate in regard to the internal affairs of [the] South African Republic at this moment would be resisted by all parties in South Africa, and would do great harm." Finally, once order had been restored in Johannesburg, he returned to Cape Town without discussing the uitlander case with Kruger. Though his actions annoyed Chamberlain, they were supported by Meade and Fairfield, and the colonial secretary reluctantly accepted the high commissioner's policy of moderation.[17] Some two months later, in April, 1896, his staff again successfully persuaded Chamberlain not to resort to intimidation in relations with the Transvaal.[18]

During late 1896 and early 1897 significant changes occurred in Colonial Office and colonial service personnel. The office lost Meade and Fairfield through accident and illness.[19] They had encouraged Chamberlain to support Rhodes's schemes but discouraged him from plunging imperial authority into the breach left by Rhodes's eclipse, for they had supported Robinson. No longer would experienced and cautious officials check Chamberlain. Meade was replaced by the malleable Wingfield. Graham, who succeeded Fairfield, had neither the time nor the inclination. In addition, new responsibilities in South African work were given to young clerks in an attempt to overcome the mounting burden of office business. Two of these, George Fiddes and Henry Lambert, pressed for strong measures. Only Hartmann Just, the senior clerk in the South African department, injected a note of thoughtful caution in the routine minuting of despatches set before Chamberlain. But he had neither the status nor the force of personality to make much impact on Chamberlain.[20] Robinson, meanwhile, gave up initiative for imperial policy. Neither his policies nor his temperament were liked by Chamberlain, who thought him a weak man.[21] In fact, Chamberlain was impatient to

17. *Ibid.*, pp. 498, 524; Garvin, *Life*, III, 99; Wilde, *Archives*, I, 23–24.
18. *Ibid.*, p. 38; Marais, *Kruger*, pp. 116–18.
19. See Chapter 2 above.
20. Wilde, *Archives*, I, 52.
21. Garvin, *Life*, III, 138.

replace him. But he was popular with Afrikaners and with the Liberal opposition in Parliament and could not easily be recalled. When age and illness incapacitated the veteran colonial administrator, Chamberlain devised an administrative expedient to bypass the high commissioner in negotiations with Kruger. Robinson's agent in Pretoria, Sir Jacobus de Wet, was replaced by a career diplomat recruited from the Foreign Office's consular staff. The new British agent, Sir Conyngham Greene, who was fluent in Dutch, was to negotiate with Kruger on the basis of instructions received directly from the colonial secretary. In addition, he was authorized to send and receive despatches unimpeded by the high commissioner. Greene was soon sending alarmist despatches to Chamberlain about the ineptness of the republic's government and the grievances of the uitlanders.[22]

The results of these administrative changes on policy implementation and control became quickly apparent when a new crisis in relations with the Transvaal developed. A law, passed by the Volksraad (Transvaal's legislature), controlling immigration had been found by Chamberlain and his staff to impinge unfavorably on the status of the uitlanders, and he pressed for its cancellation. The Pretoria government replied that it would not "tolerate any interference or meddling, however . . . well meant, in [the Transvaal's] internal affairs."[23] Protracted correspondence culminated in March, 1897, when Chamberlain told Kruger's government that he expected it would repeal or suspend the law. Greene, in fact, was instructed to impress Kruger that the despatch represented an ultimatum.[24] Freed of the restraint of senior advisers Chamberlain had gone on as well to convince the cabinet that diplomacy should be backed by a show of force and the South African garrison strengthened. Reinforcements (1,500 men) were sent to Natal and a British squadron appeared in Delagoa Bay. The Volksraad repealed the immigration law. Kruger, in the parlance of the time, had climbed down.

<hr />

22. Greene took up his post in Dec., 1896. See C. Headlam, ed., *The Milner Papers* (2 vols.; London, 1931–33), I, 36–37; and Marais, *Kruger,* pp. 136, 148.
23. *Parl. Pap.,* 1896 [C. 8063], LIX, 577.
24. *Ibid.,* 1897 [C. 8423], LXII, 193–97; Marais, *Kruger,* pp. 149–50.

III

Although he obtained an initial commitment to strengthen the South African garrison, Chamberlain encountered considerable obstruction from both the cabinet and the War Office. The latter's intelligence department reported that in the nine-month period prior to November, 1896, the Transvaal had "imported 50 field and position guns, 26 maxims, 45,000 rifles, more than 20,000 rounds of large ammunition, and 30,000,000 rounds of rifle ammunition." [25] He wanted to counter this formidable arms buildup, one largely triggered by the Raid, by doubling the 5,000-man garrison through adding to it a mobile force provided with land transport and capable of acting at a distance from rail lines. In putting his case to the cabinet he admitted that Robinson thought a troop increase might cause the Boers to take the offensive. But he claimed that every "non official Englishman," he had spoken to opposed this view. To his mind there were

very strong reasons, which I may call 'Diplomatic reasons,' for largely strengthening the Imperial forces in South Africa.
1. It would be a visible demonstration of the determination of the Imperial Government to maintain the *status quo*, and to insist on the observance of the Convention.
2. It would strengthen the loyalty of all the English in South Africa— greatly shaken by successive defeats and humiliation—and give them confidence in the Imperial factor, which there is now too much readiness to 'eliminate' at short notice.
3. It would be a warning to the Boers that we are in earnest, and that they must not proceed too far in their policy of intrigue and opposition. A display of strength has always impressed them.[26]

Hicks Beach did not look kindly on the increasing costs of the military establishments, but economy was not the only objective he had in mind when he voiced disapproval of Chamberlain's request. While he agreed with Chamberlain that British hegemony must not suffer he differed sharply with his colleague

25. Cabinet memo by Chamberlain on British military strength in South Africa, Nov. 10, 1896, Cab. 37/43/45. By mid-1899 it was estimated that the two Boer republics had more than 70 artillery pieces, 31 machine guns, 62,950 rifles, 6,000 revolvers and sufficient ammunition "for a protracted campaign." CO 417/275/ 21343.
26. Cab. 37/43/45.

on the question of how best to protect it. In his view too large a military buildup might give the Boers a valid excuse to start a war:

If Kruger's Govt. really mean to fight, the utmost patience on our part is absolutely necessary, in order to make them put themselves clearly in the wrong; for otherwise we should not get on our side such an amount of public opinion both in the Cape Colony and here, as is essential to a successful issue. If they do not really mean to fight, the natural increase of the Rand population will in time secure all that is necessary, as, but for Rhodes' folly, it would probably have done by this time. But, if the stories one hears about Boer insolence are true, they *will* put themselves in the wrong before long—and then Majuba Hill will be wiped out.[27]

Salisbury and Balfour too, wanted to avoid the impression of aggressive intent. Not only so as to not provoke the Boers but also because "any adventurous policy" against the Transvaal "would turn a vast amount of European opinion against us." [28] However, all three ministers were prepared, albeit reluctantly, to acquiesce in Chamberlain's requests. Reluctance stemmed from their knowledge of Chamberlain's aggressive tendencies, agreement from their lack of knowledge as to the situation in South Africa.[29] Maybe Chamberlain's arguments were valid. As Salisbury told Lansdowne, "I came to the conclusion that as Chamberlain based his demand principally on the effect of inaction upon colonial opinion, it was hardly possible for us, who have not had his opportunities of watching that opinion, to refuse him the reinforcements he requires." [30] Lansdowne, himself, had serious reservations. These originated in the condition of the army, the state of his own department, and an assessment of South Africa based on military rather than political considerations. The home army,

27. Headlam, *Milner*, I, 33.
28. Blanche Dugdale, *Arthur James Balfour* (2 vols.; London, 1936), I, 247–48; Lord Newton, *Lord Lansdowne* (London, 1929), p. 145.
29. A body for interdepartmental and empire-wide military planning had been established by the Salisbury government in 1895; but during its existence (1895–1902), "Salisbury was completely uninterested in it . . . and Balfour, himself the primary founder, became so engrossed in the leadership of the House of Commons that he too largely ignored it. . . ." F. A. Johnson, *Defence by Committee: The British Committee of Imperial Defence, 1885–1959* (London, 1960), pp. 34–35.
30. Newton, *Lansdowne*, p. 145.

which totalled some 530,000 men including reserves in 1896, could muster only 150,000 in sufficient health, equipped and trained for combat on short notice. India was adequately garrisoned (almost half the effective British army was quartered there), but the rest of the empire, including Britain itself, depended primarily for security on the ability of the navy to maintain its command of the seas. Besides, the ten colonial wars the British army waged between 1878 and 1896 on the borders of the Indian empire, and in South, West and North Africa, required small troop commitments.[31]

If, in terms of numbers and preparation, the British army was inadequate, its administration made it more so. Since 1856 the Duke of Cambridge had been commander in chief. As a strong advocate of tradition and the status quo he had blocked many efforts of in-service reformers and deterred politicians from imposing new controls. Finally in 1895 the Liberal government arranged that the Duke would retire and it fell to their successors to appoint a replacement. Salisbury chose Field-Marshall Garnet Wolseley. His government also partly instituted administrative reforms recommended by the Liberals designed to reduce centralization in the War Office and make it more responsible to the civil government. Wolseley, as commander in chief, was to exercise general command and be the secretary of state's principal adviser. But the various department heads in charge of training, transportation, fortifications, weapons and finance had direct access to the minister and were accountable to him. Lansdowne, who fashioned these reforms as a deliberate compromise hoped they would give the commander in chief "real though limited" responsibility.[32] Wolseley, however, by temperament and training deeply resented acting the role of adviser to a non-expert and complained bitterly of a system which failed to stress a hierarchical chain of command consistent with military practice. He clashed not only with Lansdowne but also with some of the department heads. War Office morale was further hindered by Wolseley's blatant acts of favoritism. He preferred for new senior

31. R. A. Preston, *Canada and 'Imperial Defense': A Study of the Origins of the British Commonwealth's Organization* (Durham, N.C., 1967), pp. 203–04.
32. Memo of Nov. 9, 1895, Cab. 37/40/58.

appointments in the office or in the army at home or abroad, members of his famous gang, hand-picked men who had fought with him in the colonial wars. Finally Wolseley's own once-renowned capacity for command and imaginative reform was hampered by increasing bad health: indigestion, fever and memory lapses.[33] An exchange, one of several, between one of Wolseley's gang, General Sir Charles Redvers Buller, the adjutant general charged with army discipline and training, and Lansdowne is instructive. "At the present moment," Buller complained in April, 1896, "it is not an unfair description of this Office to say that no one of the military Branches knows to whom it ought to turn to receive instructions." Lansdowne explained how the regulations should work to meet objections, but neither Buller nor Wolseley was converted.[34]

If Chamberlain headed a department overworked and under-staffed, Lansdowne headed another disturbed by dissension and confusion. Given the state of his department, the condition of the army, his own temperament, which inclined him to settle problems through compromises, and experience, which led him to anticipate real or imagined political effects of military acts, Lansdowne had little sympathy with Chamberlain's proposal. In the first instance, Chamberlain rather than he had presented the cabinet with the disturbing reports of the War Office intelligence department which was under the supervision of the commander in chief.[35] Lansdowne wondered if a troop increase might not provoke the Boers and, when Wolseley pointed out that the army in its present strength could promise only 3,500 troops instead of 5,000, he was inclined to think the smaller number sufficient. And, when the War Office financial department pointed out the cost of the contingent was so large (£500,000) that it could not be met out of existing army funds, Lansdowne sided with Hicks Beach, who complained that special provision for the contingent in the

33. J. H. Lehmann, *All Sir Garnet: A Life of Field Marshall Lord Wolseley* (London, 1964), pp. 384–86.

34. Minutes by Buller, April 23; Lansdowne, May 10; Buller, June 30; and Wolseley, July 2, 1896. Public Record Office, WO 32/155/7968/7253.

35. Wolseley sent an officer to South Africa in April, 1896, to begin an intelligence survey. His and subsequent intelligence department reports were proved later to be accurate in their assessment of Boer military strength and deployment. J. Symons, *Buller's Campaign* (London, 1963), pp. 62–63, 88.

estimates would alarm the opposition in Parliament and the Boers as well.[36] So in *ad hoc* fashion the cabinet decided to use £ 200,000—part of a budget surplus[37]—to send 1,500 troops—mostly artillery and no cavalry. This was hardly the force Chamberlain wanted. Although it might be effective as a threat to back diplomatic objectives, it had little military value. The War Office claimed the South African garrison was not strong enough to meet the forces of the Transvaal in the field "with reasonable prospect of success." Very large reinforcements would be needed—30,000 to 40,000 men in the event of war. Until such a force arrived in South Africa "it appears to be open to question whether upon purely military grounds there is much to be gained by sending out small additional bodies of troops for service on the frontier." They could not stop the Boers and could be easily cut off from bases.[38] The military and political heads of the War Office might disagree on many issues and argue conclusions from different premises, but Wolseley (because the army was unfit for war) and Lansdowne (because aggressive war was politically undesirable and financially prohibitive) agreed in 1896–1897 that the Boers should not be rushed.

During the crisis of early 1897 connected with the immigration law, Milner replaced Robinson. His commitment to empire was intense, his administrative ability immense and his political skill without flexibility.

He had a remarkable flair for finance and a prodigious capacity for work, and he was logical and lucid to a fault. Indeed, he was that somewhat rare phenomenon, an Englishman with a doctrinaire cast of mind. . . . By the time he arrived in South Africa in 1897 the rigidity was there, and in the South African milieu it became more and more pronounced.

. . . It was his basic premise that 'the British race' has a special mission to perform in the world. . . . He considered, however, that the British 'race' was in the process of disintegrating through the drift

36. Lansdowne to Chamberlain, Nov. 6, 1896, with enclosure from Wolseley; Hicks Beach to Chamberlain, April 4, 1897, and its enclosure; Lansdowne to Hicks Beach, same date, JC 5/4; and *Lansdowne*, pp. 144–45.
37. Of the surplus (£ 1,500,000), Goschen obtained £ 500,000 to accelerate shipbuilding and £ 350,000 went to the GPO to increase postal and telegraphic facilities. Hamilton Diary, Add. MS 48671, f. 42.
38. War Office to Colonial Office, April 29, 1897, WO 32/269/40270/21.

towards autonomy of the great colonies of settlement . . . [and he] regarded it as his mission to transform South Africa from 'the weakest link in the imperial chain' into a strong and effective link.[39]

Within a year of his arrival in Cape Town he came to the conclusion that Chamberlain's policy—diplomatic intervention backed by the threat of force—would not retain South Africa for the empire. "There is no way out of the political trouble in S. Africa," he remarked, "except reform in the Transvaal or war." [40] That is, unless Kruger granted uitlanders political influence through which they in turn would at best support the imperial factor or at least take economic and political power out of the hands of Afrikaner nationalists, then that factor must be brought to Pretoria by British troops. He soon rejected the first alternative for the second.

But neither the British public, the cabinet, nor even Chamberlain were in 1898 prepared to fight a war. Indeed, for the time being at least, Chamberlain was even reluctant to threaten the Transvaal. He had discovered that there was little support in Britain for taking a harsh line with Kruger's government, and that not only would war be unpopular but "it would involve the despatch of a very large force and the expenditure of many millions." In addition, imperial rivalries with European powers elsewhere, particularly with France in the Sudan and West Africa, looked as if they might involve armed hostilities. Even though "the temper of the Transvaal has not improved [he said], and . . . their insolence and neglect of friendly representations is most irritating . . . we must refrain from pressing [cause for offence] in any public or peremptory fashion." [41]

While Milner contemplated drastic measures and attempted to get them accepted in Whitehall, he was also occupied with laying an elaborate network of communication and influence which made use of both public and private channels and which left him in a unique position of power. Not only did he manipulate and control in South Africa, but he was able to do so in London as well. One of his first acts was to insure that Greene in

39. L. M. Thompson, *The Unification of South Africa, 1902–1910* (Oxford, 1960), pp. 5–6.
40. Milner to Chamberlain, Feb. 23, 1898, Headlam, *Milner,* I, 221.
41. Chamberlain to Milner, Feb. 23, 1898, *ibid.,* pp. 227–28.

Pretoria would not communicate directly with the Colonial Office.[42] He also took a leading role in drawing up administrative reforms to insure that Rhodes and his cronies connected with the British South Africa Company would not be able to take the initiative away from the imperial government again, but rather be used in the creation of his own design for South Africa. All police forces in Rhodesia would be in imperial hands and administrators were to be "the 'eyes and ears' of the H[igh] Commissioner and of H[er] M[ajesty's] Govt." and "not the Co.'s tool[s]." In addition, he rejected Chamberlain's suggestion to improve administration by relieving him of Rhodesian work by giving it to a separate high commissioner. He viewed "with alarm the injury to his position and prestige, if Rhodesia were taken out of the sphere of his authority. . . . To weaken the [high commissioner] in any way is to weaken the most powerful factor, in fact the *only* factor worth mentioning, on the imperial side."[43] The governor of Natal, Sir Walter Hely-Hutchinson, proved willing to take his cues from Milner. And Fiddes, the Colonial Office expert on Transvaal affairs who was sent out to serve as Milner's imperial secretary, was as much if not more inclined to rush the Transvaal than the high commissioner himself.

So Milner was able to sift and funnel and comment upon the information which Chamberlain and his staff used as the basis for decisions. He did so with alacrity. As he confided to Fiddes:

. . . Joe may be led but he can't be driven. I go on pegging mail after mail, month after month, and I think it tells, but if I were *once* to make him think that I am trying to rush him, he would see me to the devil and we might as well shut up. I put everything in the way most likely to get him to take our view of *himself*. Whether he takes it, or rather when he takes it, depends on the amount of external pressure and excitement corresponding to our prodding of him from within. If only the Uitlanders stand firm on the formula 'no rest without reform' and can stand on it not 6 days but 6 weeks, or six months, we shall do the trick yet my boy. And by the soul of St Jingo they get a fair bucking up from us all one way and another.[44]

"Prodding from within" was promoted through the office's parlia-

42. *Ibid.*, pp. 36–37.   43. *Ibid.*, pp. 119, 122.
44. Jan. 3, 1899, quoted in Stokes, *Historical Journal*, V, 62.

mentary under-secretary, Lord Selborne, a personal friend to whom Milner often wrote and who frequently put Milner's case not only to Chamberlain but to his father-in-law, Lord Salisbury, as well. "External pressure" was brought to bear through several contacts in high places. They ranged from cabinet ministers such as Goschen, his former patron; to civil servants like Hamilton, a former admiring colleague at the Treasury; to newspaper editors like George Buckle of *The Times*, a Balliol contemporary.[45] In letters to these acquaintances and on the occasion of a visit to England in late 1898 and early 1899 he forcefully put his solution to the South African problem.

In the self-governing Cape Colony, Milner ignored established precedents. He refused to allow for colonial sensibilities as did his colonial service colleagues in Canada and Australasia. Perhaps his most blatant infringement of role and precedent occurred in March, 1898, when, during a heated election campaign invoking Afrikaner and English racial antagonism, he chose, without Chamberlain's sanction, to admonish Cape Afrikaners in public for not sufficiently encouraging the Transvaal to submit to his advice. He further cast aspersions on their loyalty and alienated moderates like Hofmeyr.[46] The speech made it that much more difficult for the Colonial Office to find a way for imperialism and nationalism to co-exist in South Africa.

Milner's network of influence and power enabled him to manipulate and consolidate to a considerable degree uitlander unrest on the Rand, to magnify and distort the extent and nature of that unrest to his superiors in Whitehall, and to suppress and minimize evidence of efforts by Transvaal officials to redress uitlander grievances. Milner and Greene encouraged the uitlanders to present the British government with a petition of grievances and pressed the Colonial Office to take up the case in the early spring of 1899. In Milner's own words:

The game has been admirably played so far, but it cannot be won by one or two moves. It requires, above all things, steady persistence. British Govt. is slow to move. Public opinion has been quite averted

45. See Headlam, *Milner*, I, 76–78, 472–73; and Add. MS 48672, ff. 98–100.
46. E. A. Walker, *Lord de Villiers and His Times* (London, 1925), p. 323.

from S. Africa and is only gradually regaining interest in that subject. Considerable progress has been made in this direction lately, but after all it is only a beginning, though a very good beginning, and what the Uitlanders have to do is to keep on pegging away. A certain number of the weaker members will no doubt fall away, but if any considerable section have the capacity to stick to their guns I believe they will win almost universal support in Great Britain.[47]

Milner was able to get the Colonial Office to accept the petition and prepare to remonstrate with Kruger over the grievances alleged in it, a step that could not easily be reconciled with powers enjoyed under the Conventions and therefore a serious departure which required cabinet approval. As was by now his habit, Milner sent the Colonial Office a series of despatches and telegrams elaborating distorted arguments for intervention. One was his well-known "helot" despatch, so strong in its condemnation of the Transvaal government that Chamberlain remarked on receiving it "if it is published it will make either an ultimatum *or* Sir A. Milner's recall necessary." [48] It was by no means the most vitriolic. The others Chamberlain suppressed, but the "helot" despatch was used by him in putting the case for intervention before the cabinet and (in edited form) subsequently to justify intervention to the public. Chamberlain obtained cabinet sanction for a stiff despatch but it was not sent pending the outcome of the Bloemfontein conference of early June between Kruger and Milner called largely at the insistence of South African moderates.

Chamberlain and his staff (particularly Just and Graham) reviewed the possibilities of a negotiated settlement's emerging from the conference. They were not optimistic but cabled Milner advice designed, from their point of view at least, not to preclude a settlement. Chamberlain particularly wanted W. P. Schreiner, the moderate prime minister of the Cape, to attend.

Suppose [he wrote], that Milner and Kruger are at first far apart. It is inconceivable that Schreiner should support Kruger in his extreme views. If he supports Milner we have gained enormously. . . .

47. Milner to Greene, April 3, 1899, Headlam, *Milner*, I, 345–46. For the not inconsiderable efforts of the able state secretary, Jan Christian Smuts, to eliminate corruption and inefficiency in the Transvaal's government which some uitlanders complained about see W. K. Hancock, *Smuts, The Sanguine Years, 1870–1919* (Cambridge, England, 1962), pp. 67–106. Also see Chap. 6 below.
48. Quoted in Wilde, *Archives*, I, 102.

The only danger is that Kruger should accept his [Schreiner's] proposals and that Milner should decline. No doubt this will throw him into Kruger's arms but how are we worse off than if the Conference breaks down in his absence and he is able to say that the fault lies with our unreasonable attitude.

In my opinion there is therefore nothing to lose in taking Schreiner and a probability of something to gain. But having expressed my own views I am ready to leave decision to Milner who is on the spot.[49]

Though he left Milner "as free a hand as possible," he thought the high commissioner "should lay all the stress on the question of franchise." Finally, he instructed Milner to be patient and not break off discussion hastily. None of the cables had an effect. Milner ignored Chamberlain's suggestion to include Schreiner; he argued rather than negotiated with Kruger on the franchise; his day-to-day reports of conference proceedings were brief and incomplete but revealed his impatience with Kruger. He, in fact, terminated the meeting before Chamberlain's last cautionary telegram reached him.[50] Clearly the telegraph did not extend the office's opportunities for learning of or controlling events in South Africa. In fact, its operation reinforced the office's passive characteristics, and the activist propensities of the man on the spot.

IV

Milner thought it imperative to strengthen Britain's military posture in South Africa. But his efforts received a sharp rebuff from an unexpected quarter. It came from the commanding officer of the South African garrison. Illness resulted in the necessity of finding a replacement for General W. H. Goodenough, who, had he been fit, would have acted in Milner's place while the latter was absent in England attempting to secure support for his policy. Milner urged Chamberlain to press the War Office for an able replacement.

. . . I need not tell you [he wrote his chief], that it is of vital importance to get a really good man . . . of energy and resource and of some political sense. It would be really disastrous if, because things

49. *Ibid.,* p. 105. 50. *Ibid.,* pp. 105–11.

are quiet for the moment, the War Office thought they could use the opportunity to provide for some worn-out Lt.-General for whom they were anxious to find a billet. No doubt, even that is not the worst that might befall us. . . . My object is . . . to call your attention to the fact that a new appointment . . . may be near at hand, and in case you think fit to use your influence to get the appointment filled by special selection and not the ordinary departmental routine.[51]

Before this letter reached Chamberlain, Goodenough died. When the colonial secretary intervened, he discovered a replacement had been found and his name submitted to the Queen. Lansdowne was reluctant to withdraw it.[52] As a consequence, Lt. Gen. Sir William Butler, whom Chamberlain had little opportunity to brief, went to South Africa on a ship which passed another bringing Milner to England.[53] Butler had been one of Wolseley's men in the colonial wars. But, as an ardent Irish Catholic, he was sensitive to the national aspirations of other peoples, including the Boers. He had previously served on Wolseley's staff when the latter had been temporary governor of Natal in 1875 and again during the Zulu war. Largely self-taught, the author of several volumes of imaginative reminiscences, anti-Semitic like many of his fellow officers, convinced capitalism was unethical and exploitive, Butler was uniquely qualified to dispute Milner's assessment of South African politics. In Milner's absence he attacked uitlander political agitation on the Rand, refused to accept a petition on their grievances, and urged Chamberlain to adopt a policy of conciliation.[54]

Milner, a frequent visitor to the Colonial Office while he was in England, discounted Butler's political views to the satisfaction of most of its staff (only Wingfield had lingering doubts), and he was, on his return to South Africa, to resume his agitation. Meanwhile Butler sent reports to the War Office warning that conflict would be in the nature of a civil war and the "greatest

51. Oct. 19, 1898, Headlam, *Milner*, I, 228.
52. Lansdowne to Chamberlain, Oct. 28, 1898, JC 5/4.
53. Chamberlain saw Butler for a half-hour on November 7 and the interview was "barren" of discussion of difficulties Butler could expect to encounter. W. F. Butler, *Sir William Butler: An Autobiography* (London, 1911), p. 386, and E. McCourt, *Remember Butler* (London, 1967), pp. 218–19.
54. See for example Butler to Chamberlain, Jan. 25, 1899, CO 879/56/572. Butler arrived in Cape Town on Nov. 30, 1898, served as acting governor until mid-Feb., and was recalled Aug. 9, 1899.

calamity" South Africa ever witnessed. At the same time he made little effort to calculate the resources needed or the strategy to be adopted if war came. He did estimate, as the young Jan Smuts carefully noted, that England would need at least 150,000 men to deal with the Boer army. Yet he did so in a book published in 1899, not in his despatches to the War Office.[55] By late June Milner found what Butler was doing or not doing was intolerable, as one of his diary entries complained: "Found letter from Butler enclosing his telegram to War Office about reinforcements. Sent strong telegram to S[ecretary] of S[tate], objecting to this. . . . Things have become critical now. Butler or I will have to go." [56] Chamberlain became concerned about Butler's obstruction as reported by Milner but accepted Lansdowne's argument that the general's recall "would strengthen the hands of the opposition immensely" and "make a martyr of him and give all the friends of the Boers the enormous advantage of quoting him in that character." Anyway Milner, he felt, was "overstrained" and rather "trying." [57]

Butler remained for more than another month in command of a force of some 8,000 men, one which in his own estimate could not and should not bring pressure to bear on the Transvaal government. He thereby served to support Lansdowne who was reluctant to increase the garrison despite strong pressure from officials in his department to do so. It was not readily apparent at first to the War Office staff that the politicians were contemplating war, particularly in light of their concern with expenditure, but by April, 1899, Wolseley realized that it would only be a matter of time before hostilities began. He urged Lansdowne, with Chamberlain's support "to largely augment the force at the Cape." On June 8 he wanted to "prepare for war" by quietly

55. See Smuts to Hofmeyr, Aug. 22, 1899. W. K. Hancock and Jean van der Poel, eds., *Selections from the Smuts Papers* (4 vols.; London, 1966), I, 301–02; and Butler's *The Life of Sir George Pomeroy-Colley* (London, 1899). Butler engaged the War Office in heated correspondence during 1901–02 claiming he had anticipated the prolonged resistance of the Boers when Chamberlain publicly asserted that no one in authority had done so. His despatches spoke out strongly against war but did not calculate what would be needed if it came. See PRO 30/60/36 and CO 417/366/5214A (secret).

56. June 24, 1899, Headlam, *Milner*, I, 510.
57. Chamberlain to Lansdowne, June 26, 1899, JC 10/4.

mobilizing an army corps (50,000 men), in England and collecting large quantities of food and stores in Cape Colony and Natal. On June 7 he requested that 10,000 men be sent immediately to South Africa and that transport mules be collected there for them. These requests Lansdowne refused to sanction. Instead he permitted as a suitable demonstration the despatch of a few hundred troops to Natal on August 2.[58]

In the meantime Butler received a private letter from someone in the War Office suggesting he resign. Thinking a conspiracy was afoot against him, he confronted Milner, who admitted he had not found the general co-operative. Butler thereupon sent a letter of resignation to Lansdowne. It was accepted on August 8 and Butler left South Africa two weeks later,[59] but not before he had seriously interfered with Milner's schemes. As the high commissioner told Chamberlain in mid-August:

If we had had a man who wanted our fighting strength on the spot to be as great as possible, instead of one who was only too glad of any excuse for keeping it down, he would have forced the W.O. to do the right thing. . . . The advice of a civilian is necessarily of less weight. The result is that we have had the maximum of fuss out here about increase of armaments, with the minimum of result. The fuss did no harm—good rather at first—but by this time mere bluff is of no more value. I do not see why pressure could not have been applied in a manner which would at the same time, as it alarmed the enemy, have actually increased to a more substantial extent our defensive strength.[60]

By this time Milner's agitation, War Office protestation and Chamberlain's willingness to back both had swung reluctant cabinet ministers (Salisbury, Hicks Beach, Balfour and Lansdowne) into accepting the high commissioner's policy of reform or war.[61] The cabinet began contemplating an ultimatum and

---

58. Index compiled by Wolseley of efforts to prepare for war, Dec. 3, 1902, WO 32/269/40270/20. Two of Milner's contacts, George Wyndham, parliamentary under-secretary at the War Office, and Fleetwood Wilson, the assistant under-secretary, who were in sympathy with Milner's objectives and methods informed him of departmental and cabinet deliberations and likely confided in Wolseley. See Stokes, *Historical Journal*, V, 54–56.
59. He was replaced by Lieut.-General F. Forestier-Walker.
60. Aug. 16, 1899, Headlam, *Milner*, I, 516–17.
61. See Salisbury to Lansdowne, Aug. 30, 1899, quoted in Newton, *Lansdowne*, pp. 156–58.

decided on September 8 to send a substantial force to South Africa—6,000 troops from India to arrive in Natal in five weeks and another 4,000 from Britain and stations in the Mediterranean a week later—thereby raising the South African garrison to some 20,000 men. The decision to send troops was publicly announced as was a hint that an army corps might be mobilized. Kruger's government, interpreting these announcements to mean Britain intended war, contemplated striking first. Milner learned of this reaction and urged Chamberlain to delay the despatch of an ultimatum until more troops reached South Africa. Delay was also urged by Wolseley. Indeed, he wanted the cabinet to prolong negotiations to postpone war until the preparations he had earlier pressed for and which he had been refused could be taken. He particularly wanted to have an army corps deployed in South Africa before hostilities broke out. The ultimatum was held up so it would reach South Africa along with the corps. Meanwhile Kruger's government had composed an ultimatum of its own and when British troops from India disembarked at Durban on their way to the Transvaal frontier the document, which in effect was a declaration of war, was delivered to Greene in Pretoria on October 9.

Two days before, Chamberlain wrote a remarkable letter to the chancellor of the exchequer. He had previously expected the Boers would always climb down in the face of threats. He now claimed they would be easily defeated.

My own opinion is [he said], as it has always been, that both Milner and the military authorities greatly exaggerated the risks and dangers of this campaign. . . . When all the reinforcements [the 10,000 men recently sent] are landed my own feeling is that we shall be quite a match for the Boers even without army corps.[62]

Wolseley on the other hand complained bitterly to Lansdowne that diplomacy had outrun military preparations, permitting one of the greatest blunders possible in war—it gave the enemy the initiative.

---

62. To Hicks Beach, Oct. 7, 1899, quoted in Marais, *Kruger,* pp. 320–21. The corps disembarked on October 20, the day on which the first action of the war took place.

V

If Chamberlain had been unable to take a decisive role in determining Britain's military posture in South Africa and had been at the same time unrealistic in his assessment of it, he failed also in an attempt to curtail the Transvaal's arms buildup. This effort centered on the status of the Portuguese port of Lourenço Marques at Delagoa Bay. Through this port and the railway linking it with Pretoria, the Transvaal obtained most of the armaments, the amounts of which were disturbing the Colonial Office. Both Rhodes and the Colonial Office had considered British control of the port necessary to continued hegemony in South Africa and Chamberlain shared the view. "Delagoa Bay," he told the prime minister, "is the key of the situation in S. Africa —and it is to us of supreme importance." [63] In 1897 Salisbury let Chamberlain negotiate directly with the Portuguese ambassador. The colonial secretary intended to have the British government alleviate Portugal's acute financial difficulties by getting the Rothschilds to provide a loan. In return Britain would get practical control of Delagoa Bay. These efforts proved futile. Salisbury, aware of the difficulties, skeptical of Chamberlain's intrusions into foreign policy, and in declining health, gave little leadership or support in the negotiations. The bankers wanted a government guarantee but the chancellor thought the financial risk too great.[64] The delay caused by the financial impasse permitted Germany to learn of the proposal and block it. Indeed, her diplomats tried to use the opportunity to obtain colonial concessions in return for any advantages Britain obtained from Portugal.[65] Not until mid-July, 1899, when war appeared inevitable, did Salisbury apply strong diplomatic pressure to stop the arms shipment. Contrary to a previous trade agreement with the Boers, Portugal reluctantly consented to detain "the first large consignment of cartridges for the republic's new Mauser

63. Dec. 16, 1896, Salisbury MSS. Milner agreed. See Headlam, *Milner*, I, 267.
64. Note by Francis Bertie, March 1, 1897, with comments by Salisbury, n.d., FO 63/1359.
65. For the subsequent Anglo-German convention, largely Balfour's creation, which satisfied neither government see J. A. S. Grenville, *Lord Salisbury and Foreign Policy* (London, 1964), pp. 190–98.

rifles." [66] But French and German diplomats in Lisbon applied pressure of their own and the shipment was released on August 29. Further shipments were not stopped until after the war had been declared under the secret Anglo-Portuguese agreement of October 14, 1899.[67]

VI

British administrative procedures and institutions were particularly susceptible to individual wills and idiosyncratic behavior. During crucial events and negotiations in South Africa, three new men on the spot ignored or abused their functional roles. Greene at Pretoria provided misleading rather than informative despatches. Milner imposed his own policy in the local situation and through extraordinary methods got London to accept it. Butler also was out of step with London. He failed to make his political views acceptable but largely ignored his military responsibility. In London the hierarchy of the Colonial Office, disrupted and distracted by the loss of Meade and Fairfield and overwork, lost the opportunity to apply restraint, leaving Chamberlain's impulsiveness and impatience to be exploited by Milner.[68]

The cabinet reluctantly and with great misgivings accepted Milner's formula of reform or war. Its drift into the war was largely the result of a passive acceptance, through lack of knowledge, of Chamberlain's forceful presentation of Milner's views. From an administrative point of view the Foreign Office, the

66. Wilde, *Archives*, I, 128.
67. For its terms see Grenville, *Salisbury*, pp. 260–62.
68. Although written in 1900 the following excerpt from a letter by Graham to Milner is illuminating: "Work here is overwhelming. . . . It is all that Just and Lambert can do to keep pace with the routine work and take a share in the more important, and the less experienced members of the South African Dept., clever as they are, cannot write an elaborate draft on general instructions. So I have myself to take my share in drafts. . . . I find that my digestion is suffering and sometimes think life is not worth living. But I am kept up by the hope that one is now working for some purpose, and feel cheerful when I compare the present with the awful days of /98 and /99 when every week one had some fresh case to get up against Kruger or some long winded argument to meet— knowing all the time that no good would ever come of it. . . ." Aug. 14, 1900, Milner, MSS, XXV.

Admiralty and the India Office traditionally presented the cabinet with the great questions of imperial strategy and security. Now it was the Colonial Office and the War Office which were most directly involved. And the latter department like the Colonial Office, but for different reasons, could not question effectively or provide the means needed to carry out Milner's policy. Graham at the Colonial Office revealed by implication the contradiction in imperial administration when he wrote:

We are trusting and rightly trusting largely to a High Commissioner of singular ability; but I begin to think that there is something excitable in the South African air which prevents man taking a cool and dispassionate view and that possibly Sir A. Milner is being as rapidly carried away in one direction as Sir Wm. Butler in the other. . . .[69]

He might have added that Milner had carried the imperial factor with him. Where individuals with extraordinary ability and fanatical commitment to causes are granted power and authority, trust is a poor substitute for effective restraint.

69. Quoted in Grenville, *Salisbury*, p. 252. Of course, throughout the nineteenth century activist administrators on the spot, particularly in South Africa and India, eluded restraint from the center. Milner, however, was the extreme example. Cf. with J. S. Galbraith, "The 'Turbulent Frontier' As a Factor in British Expansion," *Comparative Studies in Society and History*, II (January, 1960), 150–68.

· 6 ·

The Response of Business
to Imperial Design

The latter [the Johannesburg capitalists] are a lot of cowardly selfish blatant speculators who would sell their souls to have the power of rigging the market.

Joseph Chamberlain, April 5, 1896, quoted in Ethel Drus, "Select Documents from the Chamberlain Papers Concerning Anglo-Transvaal Relations, 1896–1899," *Bulletin of the Institute of Historical Research,* XXVII (November, 1954), 161.

I

Special interests and different needs of business enterprises which shaped and composed the imperial economic impulse were exceedingly diverse. Shipping magnates, manufacturers and financiers did not easily co-operate in economic activities. Their pressures and demands on government were different as well. Government in turn found that these representatives of the British and colonial economies were as difficult to persuade as colonial legislatures when it came to obtaining support for its imperial designs. Indeed, antagonism and suspicion more than co-operation and trust featured prominently in the relations between that part of government, on the one hand, and that sector of the business community, on the other, involved in overseas undertakings.[1] Significant changes in the organization and scale of business units in the late nineteenth century exacerbated these

1. Cf. with W. K. Hancock, *Survey of British Commonwealth Affairs,* II, *Problems of Economic Policy* (London, 1940), p. 31.

relations. Larger more fully integrated operations were formed from the combination or collaboration of units engaged in the same or related aspects of production and transportation to cut costs and fix prices. These larger units could be developed through greater use of increasingly complex machinery and more elaborate productive processes, encouraged by refinements in the division of labor and clearer divisions between management and capital, and secured by better communications and different methods of distribution. This trend received further impetus from foreign competition, while in some instances even international rivalry gave way to co-operation.[2]

Shipping was particularly susceptible to combination. A rebate system, first tried in 1875–1877 in trade to Calcutta, was applied to practically all the chief outward trades from Britain demanding liner services. Under the arrangement a conference of shipping lines offered firms rebates of 5 to 10 per cent, withheld these for six months, refused payment if any freight was shipped by independent means, and even penalized through higher rates shippers who would not co-operate. The system could ruin competitors, lead to rate fixing, and result in discrimination in favor of foreign shippers. By the 1890's all the major ocean trade routes were dominated by shipping monopolies offering liner service which, in contrast to tramp ships, required careful organization and large capital outlay. Furthermore, these monopolies were mostly international in character and included German, French and American as well as British lines. The rebate system and the growth of shipping combinations alarmed the government for two reasons: they appeared to raise inordinately the shipping costs which British exporters and colonial importers paid and complained about, and they permitted foreign companies to obtain a share of the all important carrying trade. Important strategic and economic objectives were threatened and the government tried to cope with the challenge.

In February, 1902, the American capitalist, J. P. Morgan,

2. Even the Birmingham screw firm in which Chamberlain had been active came to an agreement in 1905 with a German combine with which it had long been in competition. Allen, *Birmingham*, p. 367. See also H. W. Macrosty, *The Trust Movement in British Industry* (London, 1907), Chaps. i and xii.

reached an agreement with several British and German shipping firms in which they agreed to merge all their business properties through the transfer of shares to an American holding company— International Navigation. The British firms included one of the major Atlantic carriers, the White Star Line of the Oceanic Steam Navigation Company (capital £750,000), and the Leyland Line of Frederick Leyland and Company (capital £3,114,350). Because the takeover was made at an inflated price the shareholders of White Star benefited considerably. White Star, under a contract for subsidies from the British government, had agreed to sell to the Admiralty on request eight fast vessels which could be converted into merchant cruisers. Not only had American owners obtained control of important British lines but also, it seemed, could deny the navy access to valuable ships.[3] Lord Selborne, now first lord of the Admiralty, learned belatedly of the merger, complained bitterly of the loss of ships, but felt powerless to change the agreement.[4] Much alarm was expressed in the press when it was revealed; only then did the government make an effort at least to reserve the fast liners for naval duties. Selborne, along with Chamberlain and Gerald Balfour, the president of the Board of Trade, whose departments were most concerned with the repercussions of the merger, saw Morgan. Even when Morgan indicated the merger need not invalidate White Star's arrangement with the Admiralty, Chamberlain objected strongly, partly because the government had not been taken into the shipowners' confidence, partly because the merger menaced British trade interests.[5]

To counter the effects of the merger, Chamberlain and Balfour proposed to obtain the merchant cruisers from White Star and resell them to a rival combine headed by Cunard. Negotiations with Sir Christopher Furness, Lord Inverclyde, Sir Ernest Cassel, Sir Alfred Jones, and other shipping magnates produced a plan for a combine of Cunard, the eight ships from White Star, the

3. Board of Trade Memo, April 7, 1902, PRO 30/60/45. Since 1887–88 the Admiralty had subsidized many ships for use as auxiliary cruisers in wartime. Fifty were being subsidized at the end of 1900. A. J. Marder, *The Anatomy of British Sea Power* (New York, 1940), p. 102.
4. Selborne to Salisbury, March 12, 1902, Salisbury MSS.
5. Dawkins to Milner, May 9 and 23, 1902, Milner MSS.

Beaver, and the Elder, Dempster lines. The combine would build three new fast prestige ships and receive a £1,000,000 annual government subsidy. The proposal, suggested by the shipowners, appeared attractive to the government negotiators but in 1902 so large a financial commitment was not possible. Cassel, for his part, pointed to the substantial aid French, American and German governments gave their privately owned commercial fleets and claimed that Cunard could not compete with the American combination without state aid.[6]

Finally an agreement was reached. For a low interest government loan of £2,600,000 and a twenty-year annual subsidy of £150,000, Cunard would build two ships for the Atlantic run which could be converted for use in war. Their officers and one-half their crews were to belong to the naval reserve. They, along with the whole Cunard fleet, were at the disposal of the Admiralty to charter or purchase; they, along with other company vessels over seventeen knots, could not be sold without Admiralty consent. In addition the company agreed not to sell shares to foreigners or employ them as directors and not to raise rates unfairly or give a preference against British subjects. Direct government intervention in company affairs was limited; disputes between it and Cunard were to be settled by an independent arbitrator; the cabinet refused an offer for the government to be represented on the company's board.[7] These measures bolstered the naval fleet and improved Cunard's image in passenger competition on the Atlantic run. Yet Chamberlain claimed that if he were a dictator he would have taken stronger measures to help the company engage in "a great commercial war" with the Morgan combination.[8] The nation's security more than its commerce benefited from this neo-mercantilistic arrangement.[9]

While the last bits of the agreement with Cunard were falling

6. Balfour to Chamberlain, May 9; Furness to Chamberlain, May 29; and Cassel to Chamberlain, Aug. 1, 1902, PRO 30/60/45.

7. Cabinet Memo by Gerald Balfour, Chamberlain and Selborne, Aug. 15, 1902, Cab. 37/62/128.

8. Chamberlain to Devonshire, Sept. 22, 1902, JC 11/2.

9. Surprisingly enough the agreement was reached without Treasury consultation, the new chancellor complaining from abroad that neither he nor his department had been informed but later accepting the *fait accompli* furnished by his colleagues. Ritchie to Balfour, Sept. 10 and Oct. 4, 1902, PRO 30/60/45.

into place the government continued its negotiations with the Morgan trust. Morgan and his agent, Clinton Dawkins, assured Gerald Balfour that in their view the takeover had not impugned the nationality of British ships and that, therefore, the White Star vessels were still on call to the Admiralty. They traded on this assurance in the hope of obtaining the opportunity to build subsidized prestige ships that could be converted for naval work, and to extract a promise from the government that it would not discriminate against the trust's lines. Balfour saw the advantages in coming to an amicable arrangement which would not commit the government. Chamberlain did too, but he was adamant that such an agreement would specifically state the government would not be bound to promise giving equal opportunity in tendering for construction of additional fast ships. It did provide that the trust's ships would be treated on the same footing as British lines for mail service contracts. The trust in turn promised that British companies in the combination would continue as such, a majority of directors would be British subjects, no British ships would be transferred to foreign registry without the consent of the president of the Board of Trade, that they be officered and manned by British subjects and be available to let or sell to the Admiralty. The agreement was to run for twenty years but could be terminated at any time. Chamberlain thought it vague, of little advantage, and a "sop to Cerberus," for ultimate control of the trust lay in American hands.[10] "Private speculation," wrote the informed Dawkins, "has been mixed up with patriotic suggestion by certain advisers of the Govt all through this shipping business to a very unpleasant and discreditable extent." [11] Government, nonetheless, temporized in tackling the shipowners. It, and particularly Chamberlain, showed an inclination to get directly involved but ended up adopting a position through which it could secure naval assistance in the event of military war but from which it could do little to direct or aid in a "trade war."

Government concern with the character and composition of

10. Chamberlain to Devonshire, Sept. 22, 1902, JC 11/2. For the agreement between the government and the Morgan trust see *Parl. Pap., 1903* [Cd. 1704], LXIII, 101–08.
11. Dawkins to Gerald Balfour, Sept. 9, 1902, PRO 30/60/45.

the carrying trade was not confined to new inroads by foreign combines but was also prompted by the activities of existing shipping conferences including some dominated by British lines. That concern was activated by memorials and deputations sent to the Board of Trade in 1899 by the Association of Chambers of Commerce of the United Kingdom and the British Iron Trade Association. The chambers even alleged that profits made through rates charged on shipments from Britain were used to pay for losses incurred in granting special rates to foreign shippers.[12] Persistent complaints were also made against the conferences by colonial politicians and governors as well as Chamberlain's staff. The office in fact despatched a circular to several colonies in August, 1899, to inquire into the effects of the conferences on imperial trade.[13] One of these was the Eastern Shipping Conference which included thirteen lines, of which six were subsidized and foreign, one (Peninsular and Orient) subsidized and British. It, claimed the governor of the Straits Settlements, had reduced sharply tramp traffic in the area, which as a rule was British owned, and had increased the opportunity for foreign goods to be sold in the area.[14] Also the government-subsidized Royal Mail Steam Packet Company had exerted an effective monopoly in the West Indian trade. Its position was thought by the Colonial Office to be detrimental to West Indian progress because of its indifference to development. Ommanney and Chamberlain welcomed the opportunity to aid a competitive undertaking. Elder, Dempster and Company, controlled by Sir Alfred Jones, was granted an annual subsidy of £40,000 to establish a service between Bristol and Kingston which would ship bananas to Britain.[15] Both Chamberlain and Ommanney, however, were critical of Jones's successful efforts to impose a shipping combination on the coast of West Africa because that conference included

12. *Parl. Pap.*, 1909 [Cd. 4669], XLVII, 140.
13. See *ibid.*; and CO 845/35 for copy of the circular, Aug. 23, 1899; and CO 885/17/197.
14. Sir Alexander Swettenham to Chamberlain, Feb. 20, 1900, CO 273/256/8759.
15. Minutes by Ommanney and Chamberlain, Feb. 17, 1900, CO 318/300/5054. Jones's venture was commercially unsuccessful and the subsidy terminated in 1911. Saul, "Constructive Imperialism," *Journal of Economic History*, XVII, 180.

a German carrier (the Woermann Line) and because, under its rebate system, the Crown Agents could lose discounts on freight shipped to *all* West African colonies if they used another carrier to any *one* colony.[16] Jones's rebate system was also anathema to a major private exporter to West Africa, his fellow Liverpudlian, John Holt.[17]

Among the combinations the most noted for its "autocratic spirit" and "arbitrary action" was the South African conference or ring formed in 1882, composed of several lines, and dominated by the Union-Castle Mail Steamship Company which was managed by Donald Currie and Company. South Africa's agriculture and mining were practically wholly dependent on this shipping group. Farmers complained of the high rates the ring imposed on their exports, mine owners of the exorbitant cost of importing machinery. The latter even asserted that the ring charged more than French and German lines to ship gold.[18]

The Colonial Office became particularly concerned with the conference's operations when it learned from the Crown Agents of the high rates charged for shipment of material required for Milner's reconstruction programs. The Crown Agents, for example, found it cheaper to order and ship cement (much needed for mining and railway building) from Germany even though English firms charged the same price. Ommanney and Chamberlain agreed that the agents should offer the ring a chance to meet the German rates, but if it did not the orders for cement would go abroad.[19] An opportunity to gain concessions from the ring occurred when a rival line attempted to break into the South African trade by starting a rate war. The agents put freight contracts be-

16. Minutes by Ommanney and Chamberlain, May 21, 1903, CO 147/168/ 13049.
17. He, as well, found the German carrier more efficient and better equipped than Jones's firm—British and African Steam Navigation Company. *Parl. Pap., 1909* [Cd. 4670], XLVII, 533–60.
18. See Milner to Chamberlain, March 22, and minute by Just, April 21, 1899, CO 417/259/8691.
19. Minutes by Ommanney, Oct. 14, and Chamberlain, Oct. 15 and 20, 1902, CO 323/474/39637. This cement case prompted the office to send out a circular to colonial governors and the agents stating that when a distinct advantage was gained by the colony a foreign tender should be accepted but when the benefit was marginal or doubtful the home market should be used. See minute by Lucas, July 8, 1904, CO 273/304/23875. The circular was dated Aug. 25, 1903.

fore the ring, which ran daily sailings, and the interloper, the firm of R. P. Houston, which sent four ships a month. Chamberlain and Milner inclined to let Houston have the contract even though his service and rates were not as good as those offered by the ring because it would strengthen his hand in offering competition. However, as Ommanney rightly guessed, Houston wanted to join the ring, not compete with it. He also had slashed rates more drastically on freight sent from the United States to South Africa, thereby handicapping British exporters. Ommanney also thought that once the tariff war ended the public would have to reimburse the victor through increased rates.[20] By his recommendations and negotiations with Currie and Houston, the agents obtained a rate one-half the published tariff for shipment of 50,000 tons of materials and an option to ship up to 200,000 tons during the following year.[21] Once it appeared that Houston would be accepted into the ring its members lost interest in offering the agents special rates in future and refused to bid on a contract which would give the agents an option to ship outside the conference without loss of rebate.[22]

The government, Ommanney thought, was powerless, apart from exploiting a temporary rate war, to defend the public interest against the monopoly. Firstly, the agents might charter ships when sufficient freight was on hand as they had done in supplying the Uganda railway project.[23] But this expedient was ruled out because much of the material required in South Africa was needed on short notice. Secondly, it could demand reasonable rates for its shipping requirements, but it was impossible to determine what represented a just tariff.

The difference [wrote Ommanney] in the cost of running steamers of dissimilar types, the facilities for obtaining return cargoes, the risks of detention at the ports of discharge, the varying prices of coal, the fluctuations in the rates of wages, and many other considerations enter

20. Memo by Ommanney, March 18, 1903, CO 879/80/720.
21. Chamberlain to Milner, June 16, 1903, CO 879/90/716.
22. Minute by Ommanney, Dec. 18, 1903, CO 417/378/45346. Houston's line joined the conference in January, 1904.
23. They chartered fifty-seven ships over a period of six years to send the bulk of the supplies needed for constructing the East African line. *Parl. Pap.*, 1909 [Cd. 4670], XLVII, 738.

into a problem, the solution of which is not an easy one, even for those whose interests and whose daily business are directly connected with questions of this kind.[24]

Thirdly, the government could, as in the case of railways, declare steamships common carriers and subject them to uniform rates. But the difficulties of applying such controls to ocean traffic seemed too difficult.[25] When it became public knowledge that the government had temporarily gained special rates from the ring, yet another complaint was added to the growing list of dissatisfactions which led to inquiries in South Africa and Britain but to no new imperial government intervention.[26]

II

The "official mind" has been isolated and studied as an important dynamic of imperial expansion, that is, the collective mind of Whitehall official, colonial governor and Westminster cabinet minister.[27] No comparable work has probed the collective mind of financiers and investors. Hobson evoked an image of financiers, monolithic and conspiratorial, manipulating "the patriotic forces which politicians, soldiers, philanthropists, and traders generate." [28] A more convincing analysis claims they were "a mere aggregate of specialists, each with a horizon no broader than current bargains." [29] The City's financial aristocracy, investment bankers such as the Rothschilds and Baring, facilitated access of governments to the London money market. Their decisions were derived more from assessments of politics than from economic trends, and their dominance in the market was challenged by investment financiers, such as Rhodes and Cassel, with

24. Memo by Ommanney, CO 879/90/720, p. 8.
25. *Ibid.*, p. 11.
26. See recommendations of majority report in *Parl. Pap.*, *1909* [Cd. 4668], XLVII, 91–96, that associations of shippers should obtain fair agreements from the shipowners and where disputes arose the Board of Trade might be called in by the parties as arbitrator.
27. See Robinson and Gallagher, *Africa and the Victorians*, especially pp. 19–21.
28. J. A. Hobson, *Imperialism: A Study* (2nd ed.; London, 1938), p. 59.
29. S. G. Checkland, "The Mind of the City, 1870–1914," *Oxford Economic Papers*, n.s., IX (October, 1957), 261.

wealth recently acquired in mineral exploitation or shipping. The "new men," in contrast to the establishment, were more inclined to take the initiative in relations with government. Financiers generally had difficulty comprehending the contemporary experience, particularly changes fostered by technological innovation. Midland industrialists found the City unresponsive to their long-term financial needs. Government officials also found financiers difficult, partly because of their self-interest but also because of their lack of unity and expertise.

Indeed, though the world might think of the City in a general way as the brain of the world's commerce, the City itself had few illusions. It could judge a particular proposition, or advise governments on the short-term effects of particular policies. But to understanding the laws governing the general working of the economy it made no claim.[30]

Chamberlain and his staff not only tried to prod the Treasury to finance colonial development, they also sought commitments from the private sector through negotiations with individual capitalists. When Thomas Lipton, the self-made millionaire merchant, showed an interest in marketing West Indian sugar the way he had promoted Ceylonese tea in his shops, the Colonial Office made a concerted effort to get him to sink capital in the venture. To obtain a supply of marketable sugar Lipton initially proposed to invest £500,000 to £600,000 in sugar factories in Barbados, Antigua and St. Kitts and tested Chamberlain to see what concessions he could get. Chamberlain consulted Lucas and Ommanney, met and corresponded with Lipton and his advisers. He offered to have the colonial governments take up debentures up to two-fifths of the amount of capital invested in their respective islands, to abolish export duties on sugar products, and to introduce coolie labor.[31]

Two difficulties proved insurmountable. In Barbados, the island best suited for such operations, no workable agreement for obtaining cane for the factories from the planters could be reached. They feared "placing their whole industrial fate in the

30. *Ibid.*, p. 278.
31. Lipton to Chamberlain, July 1 and Aug. 10, 1899; and memo of negotiations with Lipton, Aug. 23 or 24, 1899, CO 318/298/21749.

hands of an absentee capitalist or company taking all the profits."[32] Efforts to get Lipton at least to build factory and transportation facilities in Antigua failed to overcome his scepticism
which grew the more he examined the venture. He concluded
that cane sugar would not likely compete with subsidized beet
sugar. Unless the imperial government would guarantee possible
financial losses he would not attempt it. Chamberlain was prepared to provide modest subsidies to offset any increased bounties on European beet sugar, to aid in building transportation
facilities, even to have the colonial government provide these
services. But he would not cover losses incurred in the building
of the factory or the manufacture and sale of sugar: "I am afraid
that any guarantee of the original capital would not only be
entirely unprecedented, therefore unlikely to be accepted by
Parliament, but that it would be found in practice quite un-
workable." The government would have to exercise close supervision over the business and there would be constant dispute
over what part of the capital had been lost, assessment of assets
and depreciation allowances, and profits.[33]

Lipton was a wealthy capitalist who could not be persuaded to
invest in empire or to conduct his activities along lines seen by
government to be in the imperial interest. Another type of en-
trepreneur were promoters whose financial resources were sus-
pect. They dealt in highly speculative undertakings and sought
assistance from government to entice investors or stave off bankruptcy. They were active in colonial areas of marginal economic
potential and proved somewhat of a dilemma to Colonial Office
officials who wanted to follow their chief's dictum to support
private ventures but not encourage badly conceived or financed
schemes.

Railway construction and mineral development in British
Guiana were in the hands of such speculators.[34] The Demerara
Railway Company had for many years operated a short line out
of Georgetown. In 1896, under a contract with the Crown Agents
acting on behalf of the colonial government, it began two exten-

32. Memo by Olivier, Oct. 23, 1899, *ibid.*
33. Chamberlain to Lipton, Aug. 14, 1899, *ibid.*
34. For what follows see CO 884/6/102, *passim.*

sions. The government promised that on completion it would grant an annual subsidy of 4 per cent for fifty years (or less if net earnings were sufficient to pay dividends) on the capital of £312,500 raised in the money market to build the lines. It also had the right of pre-emption. By 1900 the company claimed it was without funds to continue to operate one section just completed or to finish the second. It had paid appreciable dividends to shareholders (7 per cent on preference shares and from 4 to 2 per cent on ordinary shares), and spent money unwisely in construction. Faced with bankruptcy, it asked the colonial government to exercise its option, but the agents advised against a takeover of the extensions. Ommanney had no sympathy for the company in its self-inflicted predicament. He also thought the colony would have great difficulty obtaining a loan to buy it out. The company's credit was nil, the money market tight, and the colony's standing weakened by its exclusion from the Colonial Loans Act. Let the company attempt to solve its difficulties. If it failed, the government might, at a future date, acquire the entire railway operation on very favorable terms.[35] The law officers, despite company protest to the contrary, interpreted the contract to mean that pre-emption was not obligatory if construction and operations ceased. Under instructions from London the colonial government promised to continue the subsidy if the company got on with the job. It reluctantly issued £70,000 of debentures in 1901. These had not been taken up in 1903 and the company had not declared a dividend for two years.[36]

Several speculators wanted Chamberlain to grant them advantageous arrangements to prospect for gold and diamonds in the interior of British Guiana. He delegated to Everard Im Thurn, an office staff member with knowledge of the region, the task of drawing up guide lines with which to handle concession seekers.[37] Im Thurn had spent several years in the colonial service of

35. Ommanney to Chamberlain, Feb. 5, 1900, *ibid.*
36. *Stock Exchange Official Intelligence*, XXII (1904), 290–91. With the aid of the subsidy and a curtailment of dividends the company continued as a private undertaking.
37. Minute by Chamberlain, Jan. 29, 1900, CO 111/525/2309.

the colony before joining the Colonial Office's first division in 1899 and had published works on its anthropology, geography and history. He interviewed speculators, long on plans and short on capital, such as one Julius Conrad, a director of the British Guiana Diamond Syndicate which, with £10,000 nominal capital, wanted rights to search for precious stones on a 2,000 acre tract in the central district of the colony.[38] He also consulted Sir Walter Sendall, the colony's governor. Both stressed that concessionaires should be discouraged if they did not have sufficient capital. They should, Im Thurn set out in his guide lines, post a bond on obtaining exploration rights and forfeit it if they abandoned their workings; if they obtained leases these must be forfeited if work did not begin within or stopped for a year. Under lease arrangements they could farm and cut timber as well as mine or build railways, but only after an interval of years could they obtain freehold rights and these for only part of the leased area used for permanent buildings and works. Tax concessions would be considered only for leases over 5,000 acres. No concessionaire could expect a rebate on export duties. No agreement could be inconsistent with existing legal rights including those granted to aboriginal Indians. Needed police for selected areas would be government controlled although their cost might be charged to the concessionaires.[39]

The value of British Guiana's gold production was falling in this period. It was considered in the London investment market to be part of the unprofitable West Indies. Railway operations were in difficulty. The Treasury would not consider financial aid. Nor would the Colonial Office concede that British speculators might trigger an economic boom if given broad concessions or indirect aid.

III

His intense commitment to empire and the capital at his disposal made Cecil Rhodes unique among financiers with whom

38. CO to Conrad, Feb. 10, 1900, *ibid.*
39. For Im Thurn's recommendations see CO 884/6/107.

the Colonial Office dealt. Although the Raid had reduced his influence in South African politics he was still a powerful factor in Central African affairs. For more than a year beginning in April, 1898, Rhodes sought imperial government assistance to extend the rail link recently completed from the Cape through Bechuanaland to Bulawayo northwards to Tanganyika. The line from Mafeking to Bulawayo was owned and operated by the Bechuanaland Railway Company, assisted by an annual £20,000 government subsidy, and controlled by the chartered British South Africa Company. Both companies were under Rhodes's personal aegis. As an additional step in furthering his "Cape to Cairo" dream, he placed various proposals before Chamberlain to obtain assistance in financing construction at least as far as the Zambezi. He wanted the government, along with the chartered company, to guarantee interest on loans issued by the railway firm. He particularly wanted the railway company to issue debentures for £3,000,000 to convert its existing capital of £2,000,000 at 5 per cent and provide an additional £1,000,000 to construct the first 250 miles of the extension. The new loan would be at 2½ per cent.[40]

Chamberlain was sympathetic. He agreed with Frederick Graham that there were good reasons for supporting the extension: it would encourage mineral and commercial development, shore up public confidence in the chartered company, cut costs of administration if the government had to take over the task from the company, and reinforce the imperial factor's position in Central Africa.[41] Chamberlain, however, had to proceed with caution. Rhodes's integrity was questionable and, despite his reputed wealth, the finances of both companies were weak. Cape Colony should be made to contribute. The Treasury had to be called in. Then the incompatible personalities and imperial priorities of Hicks Beach and Rhodes clashed. "Rhodes," commented Chamberlain, "is very unreasonable in the way he expects his demands to be taken on trust and Beach—well Beach is Beach." [42]

40. Rhodes to Chamberlain, April 28, 1898, and Jan. 17, 1899, Cab. 37/49/26.
41. Chamberlain to Rhodes, July 29, 1898, *ibid.;* undated memo by Graham on Beach to Chamberlain, April 18, 1899, and Chamberlain to Beach, April 19, 1899, JC 10/8.
42. Chamberlain to Arthur Balfour, Feb. 2, 1899, JC 5/5/81.

The chancellor conveyed to the cabinet his profound distrust of Rhodes and his dislike of aiding private investors.

. . . Other persons have greater interests in this extension than we have. The shareholders in the Bechuanaland Railway; those who have invested, or desire to invest, money in Rhodesia; the Cape Government, on account of the increased traffic that would be brought into its railways. None of these are to help at all; we are, directly or indirectly, to provide for the whole construction of the extension by our guarantee. There is, of course, the invariable suggestion, in such cases, that we shall never be called upon to pay. But that is not business. I do not believe in Mr. Rhodes' estimates of the net profits of the Bechuanaland Railway. . . . No one can judge of [the chartered company's] solvency from the published accounts. . . . But it is notoriously living on its capital; and the supply of fresh capital depends on Mr. Rhodes' life, on the public confidence in him, and on the, as yet, very doubtful success of gold mining in Rhodesia. . . . It does not appear that from a commercial point of view Mr. Rhodes has any real need of our help to secure the construction of this extension. . . . He says he can do it; large sums are reputed to have been already subscribed; the prospects of the Bechuanaland Railway and of Rhodesia are both [he claims] at the present 'booming'. Why does he, in such circumstances, persistently press for our help, and why does the Press, which his friends control, clamour so loudly for it? . . .

In my opinion, it is most probable that Mr. Rhodes himself does not believe in [the Bulawayo-Tanganyika, and 'Cape to Cairo' schemes] and that he and his supporters are really pressing this request with quite another object: namely, as the first step in obtaining the financial support of the Imperial Government for the South African Company; and that if their request were granted, we should very soon see that the Stock Exchange so interpret it. I think you would share my strong objection to anything of the kind. I have seen enough of the men who control the Company, and their methods, from Mr. Rhodes downwards, to distrust them utterly; and I would sooner ride any expenditure that might be imposed on us by the failure of the Company, than I would embark on a policy of 'backing thin bills'. . . .

I am, therefore, clearly of opinion that Mr. Rhodes' requests should be declined. . . .[43]

Although he was more sanguine about the financial strength of the two companies and the economic potential of regions beyond

43. Beach to Chamberlain, April 18, 1899, Cab. 37/49/26.

the Limpopo, Chamberlain agreed Rhodes's proposals were unacceptable because of the risks involved. But "the most influential representative of British influence and opinion in South Africa," should not be handed a "curt and uncompromising negative." So Chamberlain contrived to have the negotiations terminated by Rhodes.[44] With cabinet approval he offered to lend the railway company funds at 2¾ per cent to pay off its debenture holders and to ask the Cape government to contribute to repayment of the imperial loan if operating profits were insufficient. In return the imperial government and the Cape or a future South African federation would have the right of pre-emption. Direct aid for extensions beyond Bulawayo would not be made. Indeed the company must post a bond to show its intention to build the extension in order to receive the loan.[45] Rhodes sharply criticized and refused to accept these terms.[46] Thus, as Hamilton put it, "an awkward and perhaps dangerous precedent [was] avoided." [47] Without tangible government support the railway company issued debentures, principal and interest to be guaranteed by the chartered company, for £3,125,000 at 4 per cent in May, 1899.[48]

More significant than his efforts to push a rail line into central Africa were Rhodes's schemes to secure the Transvaal for the empire by using his economic interests in the republic for political ends. In addition to his financial interests in the Kimberley diamond fields (De Beers) and lands and mines in Rhodesia (the chartered company), he had a large stake in the Rand gold mines. Consolidated Gold Fields of South Africa, of which he was a managing director and through which he had fomented rebellion in Johannesburg, was one of the Rand's ten major mining groups.[49] Apart from Rhodes these groups were dominated

44. Chamberlain to Beach, April 19, 1899, *ibid.*
45. Graham to Rhodes, May 1, 1899, JC 10/8.
46. Rhodes to Graham, May 9, 1899, *ibid.*
47. Hamilton Diary, April 21, 1899, Add. MS 48674.
48. For the company's prospectus see CO 417/275/12193. For relations between government and another chartered company, the Royal Niger, see Flint, *Goldie.* In this instance a conflict between the needs of the company's shareholders and imperial interests led to loss of the charter but "extraordinarily generous" compensation for the company. *Ibid.,* pp. 307–08.
49. These holding companies, in addition to Rhodes's group, were Wernher, Beit & Co. whose Transvaal agents were Hermann Eckstein & Co.; Johannesburg Consolidated Investment Co. formed by Barney Barnato; the Joseph B. Robinson

by such self-made financiers as Alfred Beit, Julius Wernher, Hermann Eckstein, Joseph Robinson, Barney Barnato and George Farrar. Their personal power and wealth had been acquired in South Africa. Most had made fortunes in the diamond fields. With financial resources derived from their diamond operations, share issues, the financial houses of Rodolphe Kann and the Rothschilds, and private banking houses in Germany and France, they had spent the better part of a decade developing the Rand's gold-bearing reefs.

Consolidated Gold Fields and Rand Mines (a creation of Wernher, Beit and Company), were involved in a particularly precarious venture. They bought up properties and floated mining companies to extract gold from the reefs at considerable depth, while all the productive, dividend-paying mines were working at or very near the reefs' outcrops. Consolidated Gold Fields, which had staked everything on the success of the deep-levels, soon discovered that the new mines were far more costly and difficult to bring into production than its expert advisers originally thought. Moreover, in 1895 the collapse of a "Kaffir boom" had seriously reduced the company's main source of income—capital got by shares issued at very high premiums—for financing the mines. Because of its particularly vulnerable position, Gold Fields, and Rand Mines as well, had a powerful economic reason for toppling Kruger's government, whose taxes, regulations and administrative inefficiency made deep-level operations that much more hazardous.[50]

---

group; S. Neumann & Co.; George Albu's General Mining; Adolf Goerz & Co.; Anglo-French-Farrar holdings; the Lewis and Marks group; and Abe Bailey's enterprises. In 1899 the market value of their shares, about 80 per cent of which were believed to be in British hands, was probably more that £ 200,000,000. Actual capital invested on the Rand was considerably less, about £70,000,000 in 1899. In 1894 the Rand produced 2,024,164 ozs. of gold valued at £6,960,000 which represented about 1/5 the world's production. In 1898 it produced 4,295,602 ozs. valued at £15,250,000 which made the Transvaal the world's most important gold-producing country. In 1899, the Rand in nine months of operation (the mines closed when the war broke out) produced 4,101,447 ozs. See P. H. Emden, *Randlords* (London, 1935), p. 207; Milner to Chamberlain, April 18, 1900, CO 879/63/611; S. H. Frankel, *Investment and the Return to Equity Capital in the South African Gold Mining Industry, 1887–1965* (Oxford, 1967), pp. 23, 116; *The Mining Manual*, 1900, pp. xx, 720.

50. See G. Blainey, "Lost Causes of the Jameson Raid," *Economic History Review*, XVIII (1965), 350–66, who argues that Randlords working the outcrops

Whatever the company's motives, and whatever there is to be said about the Randlords' ethnic background and business ethics (several were Jews [51] and some, like Rhodes, unscrupulous in financial dealings), they did not present a united front in relations with either the republic's government or the imperial factor; nor were most of them much concerned with political reform. Rhodes had Beit's support and the aid of other deep-level operators in planning and subsidizing the revolt. But Charles D. Rudd, a managing director of Gold Fields, was primarily concerned with its financial operations and opposed using its assets for political agitation. Other Randlords, including Adolf Goerz, George Albu, Robinson, Samuel Marks and Barnato, refused to participate in the conspiracy.[52] They complained about labor regulations, monopolies and railway rates which complicated mining operations. But these difficulties were not so crippling that they felt the need to overthrow the republican regime and replace it with one more efficient and closely attached to the empire. Some had obtained concessions from Kruger or influenced Volksraad members with gifts. In 1895 these magnates were more concerned with the sharp decline in the market value of gold shares—a fall set off by their own manipulations, which had driven up gold shares to ridiculously inflated prices. By 1898, however, the share market had recovered from its worst excesses while mining regulations and labor shortages, though chronically restricting, were not fatal to either the deep-level or outcrop mines. By then the deep-level mines had been proved, they were producing at a profit and paying dividends; their parent companies were confident of future prospects.[53] In other words, on the eve of the

---

and making profits stood aloof from Rhodes's conspiracy while through it he drew on the support of deep-level interests and risked "political power in order to preserve economic power."

51. Johannesburg Jews were not a homogenous group. A distinction, for example, could be made between South African born and Anglicized Jews on the one hand, many of whom were financiers and identified with the English, and eastern or Russian Jews many of whom were traders and laborers and who were sympathetic to the Boers. See G. Saron and L. Hotz, eds., *The Jews in South Africa, A History* (London, 1955), pp. 193–96.

52. Emden, *Randlords*, pp. 119–20, 141–45, 209–10; Marais, *Kruger*, pp. 62–63.

53. The Consolidated Gold Fields of South Africa, *The Gold Fields, 1887–1937* (London, 1937), pp. 48–51, 62–63; and *The Mining Manual*, 1899, pp. xii–xiii, 717–29.

outbreak of war the doubts which had beset the industry had disappeared, and despite complaints about Kruger's regime, the all important cost per ton of ore refined had decreased with improved methods of management, mining and extraction. Meanwhile Rhodes's eclipse prevented him from taking the lead in getting the mining magnates to act in concert in the interests of British hegemony. This task had to be taken up by the imperial factor itself, which found the mining groups, satiated with profits and prospects, difficult to interest in political change.

Dynamite, essential for blasting operations in the mines, was produced under concessions obtained from Kruger by a company in which two explosive manufacturing combinations, one Anglo-German and the other French, had recently obtained major interests. Mine owners complained, with some justification, that its prices were too high and that it used bribery to entrench itself with the administration. The government received a modest tax on sales but stuck with the unpopular monopoly as a potential source of direct aid in the event of financial need and as part of its effort to make the republic self-sufficient. In December, 1898, Kruger proposed an extension in the period of time for which the monopoly was to run. Milner took this opportunity to urge Chamberlain to lodge a protest against the monopoly and encourage the Randlords to agitate against it. Some of the mining financiers were glad to oblige. These included Percy Fitzpatrick, a partner in the firm of Eckstein and Company, who had been a leader of the reform committee instrumental in planning the rising of 1895.[54] His business colleague, Georges Rouliot, president of the chamber of mines, was approached by Edmund Fraser, the acting British agent in Pretoria. Fraser, following instructions from Chamberlain, who had accepted Milner's advice, urged Rouliot to speak out against the monopoly. He did and on behalf of the chamber offered to loan Kruger £600,000 to compensate the concessionaires if their monopoly was cancelled. Fraser also delivered Chamberlain's official protest to Kruger. The Transvaal

---

54. Wernher often thought Fitzpatrick's political activity detrimental to the firm's business interests and image and was noticeably relieved when he finally left it in 1907. A. P. Cartwright, *The Corner House* (Cape Town, 1965), pp. 253–54. Also see Marais, *Kruger*, pp. 243–47.

government challenged Chamberlain's right to intervene in the republic's internal affairs, turned down the chamber's offer, and obtained the Volksraad's consent to prolong the monopoly in return for a substantial decrease in the price of dynamite.

The imperial factor deliberately espoused a mining magnate's grievance to obtain their support in undermining Kruger's position. But as late as March, 1899, Milner was not certain they were either united or dependable in their identification with imperial objectives.

The danger [he wrote Selborne] is that the big financial houses will think only of themselves, and, if they can get the questions, which specially affect their pockets, settled satisfactorily, will give away the bulk of the Uitlander population, and the Imperial Govt. to boot. They would be making a fatal mistake if they did, but money-bags are apt to be short-sighted. There are certainly some of them—Fitzpatrick, for instance, and I believe both Beit and Wernher—who are capable of taking the broader and more statesmanlike view. I think they will follow our advice if only we give it. And we ought to give it. No use trying to escape responsibility in the matter.[55]

Milner's particular concern was prompted by an effort of Kruger and his advisers to meet the mining magnates' outstanding economic complaints and grant some franchise reform for support of a government loan and a boycott of the South African League —the imperially oriented political pressure group on the Rand. Selborne, on Chamberlain's instructions, pressed Wernher to block any settlement which omitted provision for the uitlanders to have a substantial say at the municipal level. Chamberlain took the same tack with Lord Harris, a director of Consolidated Goldfields, who was inclined to accept Kruger's proposals.[56] Milner preferred the magnates should stress franchise reform. At a meeting in London on March 16, attended by Harris, Beit, Robinson, Neumann and Farrar, the financiers considered sympathetically the points on which Kruger wanted to base a set-

55. Milner to Selborne, March 8, 1899, Headlam, *Milner*, I, 324–25.
56. "I may say," wrote Harris to Chamberlain, "that we are by no means ill disposed towards Kruger. We wish he could establish an honest executive, & thereby secure the observance of the provisions of the drink Laws: but we don't think the principle of taxing declared net profits of Mining Cos. unfair, or that we are working under a crushing tyranny." Nov. 20, 1898, JC 10/4. Harris became the company's chairman the following year.

tlement. These included adjustments in the franchise, the appointment of an impartial state financial adviser, and regulations controlling mining operations and labor recruitment. Significantly they did not press for a prompt end to the dynamite monopoly.[57] Chamberlain and Milner were relieved when Fitzpatrick ruptured negotiations by publishing prematurely correspondence between Kruger's government and the Randlords. The mineowners were not so united, so reliable, so vitally concerned to be trusted to refuse a settlement along the lines Kruger desired. As Britain's agent in Pretoria described their position:

> The truth is that the Uitlanders of Johannesburg are lacking, as before, in cohesion, and it is impossible to hold them, for an indefinite interval, together. This was the case at the Raid time, and again you will recollect the long time that elapsed before even the Mining Groups agreed to come together and amalgamate. The same influence is at work to-day. The Groups have with difficulty been got to make common cause with the Uitlander Community . . . but if this opportunity is passed by the Home Govt., and *no result* ensues, it will be a long day, if indeed it ever comes, when we need expect any combined movement again.[58]

Although the Randlords could not be expected to sustain an identification with the imperial cause, they had been sufficiently influenced not to obstruct its pursuit. For example, in 1898, Chamberlain persuaded both Lord Rothschild (who had capital invested on the Rand and who had issued a £2,500,000 loan for the republic in 1892), and Lord Harris from assisting Kruger obtain a new loan.[59] If one mining magnate, Rhodes, had triggered the South African crisis, it was the imperial government, unencumbered by either encouragement or restraint from the Randlords, who thereafter perpetuated it.

The characteristics of informal negotiations and conflicts of interest between the imperial government and the financial community were also apparent in the efforts made by Chamberlain to extract contributions from the Transvaal to finance reconstruc-

57. Report of the meeting enclosed in Milner to Chamberlain, April 5, 1899, CO 879/56/572.
58. Greene to Milner, April 7, 1899, Headlam, *Milner*, I, 346.
59. Chamberlain to Rothschild, Nov. 30, 1898, JC 10/4; and Chamberlain to Salisbury, same date, Salisbury MSS.

tion and reimburse Britain for part of the cost of the war. Once the republic had become a British colony and the plight of its Boers became evident, it was obvious that only the mining community could make such contributions. But, as Milner pointed out, the mines must not be crippled by a heavy war levy if his recovery programs were to succeed. The mine owners, suffering from the dislocations of war and driven by the profit motive, looked on any contributions as anathema. Still Chamberlain felt that the British public demanded some relief from gold production for debts and taxes caused by the war.[60]

Both Ommanney and Hamilton consulted financial leaders in the City to determine what form loans to meet these contributions might take. These included Lord Revelstoke (E. C. Baring), a director of the Bank of England, Lord Rothschild and Cassel. Instead of the imperial government's issuing securities on behalf of the Transvaal, they advised it guarantee a colonial loan. Such loans were invariably issued at a higher interest rate than Consols. "The difficulty," commented Hamilton, "of getting any advice from City people is that they always regard things from one point of view—their pockets, leaving out of account all Parliamentary and political considerations." [61]

Meanwhile in meetings with mining representatives during his South African tour, Chamberlain found he had to scale down the terms and amounts of the contributions he wanted. He had to be satisfied with small sums payable over a short period from available tax surpluses. For purposes of reconstruction, debt redemption and development the imperial government would guarantee a £30,000,000 loan. A further £30,000,000 would be raised as a second mortgage on revenues to contribute to war costs. This loan would not be guaranteed by the imperial government but rather backed by the mining interests, who promised to take up a third of it at once and the remainder within three years.[62] At least the war contribution scheme seemed to have the

60. Memo by Chamberlain, Nov. 17, 1902, CO 879/79/711.
61. Hamilton Diary, March 24, 1902, Add. MS 48679.
62. To cover part of the first £10,000,000 the following pledged a million each: Wernher, Beit & Co.; S. Neumann & Co.; Barnato Bros.; Consolidated Goldfields; L. Albu; and Goerz & Co. Messrs. Eckstein and Co. to Milner, Jan. 21, 1903, CO 879/79/714.

advantage of giving the British taxpayer some immediate relief before the colony could raise its own political voice and repudiate the liability or before subsequent events proved a large contribution unwarranted. These proposals were accepted in principle by the London representatives of the mining firms and Chamberlain's colleagues. However, the interest rate to be set on the development loan was contested. The Treasury wanted it issued at 2¾ per cent; Rothschild and Cassel wanted 3 per cent. A loan at the lower rate might not, they said, be fully subscribed and this would put the colony at a real disadvantage if, as seemed likely, it would have to float additional loans in the near future. Their arguments and influence prevailed.[63] In addition, the slow recovery of the Rand gold field permitted the mine owners, with Milner's support, to default on the war contribution.

IV

Under Chamberlain's inspiration the imperial government did not hesitate to attempt to ally itself with capital and industry on the high seas, in the impoverished West Indies, in strife-torn South Africa. However, the alliance was not easily forged. Political necessity and the felt needs of national interest on the one hand clashed with the profit motive and self-interest on the other. In particular situations the economic units were either powerful enough to resist government persuasion or so weak as to be of little use to a government unwilling to provide substantial direct aid. It continued to use the well established precedent of granting subsidies to help provide improved communications and strengthen naval power. It relied largely on the private sector's assessment of itself, though by accident more than design it did possess experts such as Ommanney and Im Thurn whose advice on particular economic matters was invaluable. But such permanent officials as Ommanney and Hamilton had an instinctive dislike of government intervention in economic activity. Even Hicks Beach and Chamberlain differed in degree and not in kind

63. For the final arrangement see Hamilton to Ommanney, May 7, 1903, T 7/33.

on the role of the state. Business operations became more complex in organization and larger in scale as technological innovation opened new vistas for profit seekers. The administrative arm of government, aware of these changes, and driven by its own set of objectives, felt the need of guiding business to act in the imperial interest, but did not have and did not want legislative or bureaucratic devices to achieve its desire. Nonetheless, the personal intervention of a Chamberlain or a Milner did on occasion get business to act, if not in concert with the imperial factor, at least not against it.

Science and Empire: The Office
Attacks the Mosquito

Chamberlain had done some good (and won much political capital) by suggesting the schools of tropical medicine; but in my opinion, his refusal of a proper sanitary organisation for the colonies largely cancelled, then and since, the benefits which might have accrued. . . . Probably the fault lay with the permanent officials; but in either case my dreams of general British action against malaria vanished. . . .

Ronald Ross, *Memoirs*
(London, 1923), pp. 436–37.

For many years tropical disease specialists conjectured that malaria might be transmitted by insects rather than by "bad air." Surgeon-Major Ronald Ross of the Indian Medical Service proved they were right. His discovery that the malaria parasite was conveyed in birds by the bite of infected mosquitoes was announced to the medical world by his friend and mentor, Dr. Patrick Manson, in July, 1898. Manson, in turn, conducted experiments which confirmed that certain mosquitoes transmitted the disease in man.[1] Other scientists corroborated these findings, showing that the malaria parasite in the blood of the infected was sucked into the *anopheline* mosquito, developed in it, and later injected into the healthy. By 1900 medical and entomological research had pro-

---

1. Manson had discovered the connection between mosquitoes and elephantiasis. He had speculated the same link might exist between the insect and malaria. For the antecedents to discovery and the co-operation between Manson and Ross see P. H. Manson-Bahr and A. Alcock, *The Life and Work of Sir Patrick Manson* (London, 1927), Chaps. ix and x. See also R. E. Dummett, "The Campaign Against Malaria and the Expansion of Scientific, Medical and Sanitary Services in British West Africa, 1898–1910," *African Historical Studies,* I (1968), 153–60.

vided crucial knowledge with which to fight a disease that had played havoc with man's activity in the tropics.[2]

Often that part of the lay public which might derive most from scientific breakthroughs learns only belatedly to accept and use (or abuse) them. The response of administrative establishments is notoriously slow. Yet in this case a positive reaction in the Colonial Office was instantaneous. Manson had recently become its medical adviser and Chamberlain his enthusiastic supporter. In 1897 Manson heard from a friend in Whitehall that the post had fallen vacant. Before he could make application he learned, on a visit to the office, that the list was closed. However, Herbert Read, Chamberlain's private secretary, recognized him in a corridor, knew his reputation, and intervened on his behalf. This chance encounter coupled with a testimonial from Lord Lister, president of the Royal Society, got Manson the job. Read also insured that Chamberlain's desire to innovate was well fed and the office's procedural inertia circumvented. He drafted concise memos for action, arranged committee work, interceded with Chamberlain and the senior permanent officials, and acquired much specialized knowledge. As Herbert, supported by Antrobus, minuted, "I should like to confirm all that is said . . . of the value of Mr. Read's work and his able memorandum speaks for itself. From the beginning he has made the subject [of tropical medicine] his own."[3]

Read's assistance and Chamberlain's support gave Manson the opportunity to get government help for a project to which he was devoted. He wanted to create a special center to develop research and education in tropical medicine, one which would also

2. Although the death rate among Europeans in such notorious regions as West Africa was high (between 1881 and 1897 the annual average among the small group of officials was 76 on the Gold Coast and 53 in Lagos), it was probably half what it was before 1840. Better hygiene, quinine prophylaxis and the abolition of such harmful antidotes as bloodletting and harsh laxatives accounted for the improvement. P. D. Curtin, *The Image of Africa: British Ideas and Actions, 1780–1850* (Madison, 1964), p. 362. Of 175 European officials on the Gold Coast in 1895, 17 died and 24 were invalided; of 176 in 1896, 15 died and 26 were invalided. These were called two "exceptionally unhealthy seasons." CO 885/7/119, p. 27.

3. Minutes by Herbert (as a member of the committee of management of the Seamen's Hospital), Nov. 11, 1902, and Antrobus, n.d., CO 323/480/45838. See also above Chap. 2, and P. H. Manson-Bahr, *History of the School of Tropical Medicine in London* (London, 1956), p. 28.

train medical officers for work in the colonies. He selected the Seamen's Hospital at the Albert Dock, which admitted patients suffering with tropical diseases from all over the world, as the site for the school. Two immediate problems had to be overcome: where to find funds for facilities and salaries, how to overcome the opposition of sceptics and special interest groups. Manson's own published findings challenged practices and theories of some of his colleagues who responded with criticism impugning his ability. The staff of the Royal Victoria Hospital for Soldiers at Netley, who trained Indian Medical Service personnel, complained because their institution was ignored and their curriculum by implication judged deficient. Chamberlain countered opposition by backing Manson in public, speaking from informative briefs prepared by Read, and obtaining co-operation from the other great departments. The Treasury even agreed to a modest grant of £1,775 if, as was done, the colonies would match it.[4] Chamberlain presided at a fund-raising dinner in 1899 which brought in £12,000.[5] Read's statistics emphasized the need for a colonial medical officer program. There were 74 permanent medical posts in Britain's eight African possessions in which 12 new appointments to fill vacancies were made in 1897. With temporary postings attached to military expeditions and railway construction sites, openings were numerous. Doctors completing a three-month course at Seamen's Hospital would be guaranteed employment and their tuition fees paid by the colony to which they were sent.[6]

The school opened October 2, 1899. By late 1902 its professional status was recognized, when it became part of the University of London, and its need proven, as 234 students had used its facilities.[7] As the school expanded it received additional funds

---

4. The sum was to cover one-half the cost of a school building and was to defray the shares of all exchequer-aided tropical colonies and protectorates. The hospital's board of management had already decided to add a new wing costing £10,000 to increase bed space from 18 to 45. *Parl. Pap., 1903* [Cd. 1598], XLIV, 4–5.

5. He also raised £11,000 in 1905. Manson-Bahr, *Tropical School*, p. 47.

6. Memo by Read, Dec. 2, 1897, CO 885/7/119; and CO 323/448/25134.

7. A breakdown of enrollment to 1902 and 1905 (in parentheses) was from the Colonial Office, 87 (220); Foreign Office, 10 (22); Indian Medical Service, 8 (32); Army Medical Corps, 1 (5); Royal Navy, 3 (12); others including a large

from the imperial government, the colonies and private sources. Of £25,000 raised up to the end of 1902 less than 20 per cent came from government and most of that, including £1,000 donated by India, from the colonies.[8] To collect and allocate funds the office established an advisory committee of experts. With Chamberlain absent on his South African tour, the office, on initiatives begun by Read and taken up by Lucas, asked the colonies for more money to further the study of tropical diseases and their prevention. Lucas anticipated that a co-ordinating committee would be needed to advise Chamberlain on how these funds should be spent.[9] By November, 1904, about £1,600 a year for five years had been pledged by the crown colonies, £500 a year for a similar period by the Treasury on behalf of state-aided protectorates, and a further £500 under the same arrangement by the government of India. Later Australia agreed to contribute £200 annually, but New Zealand and Canada, not affected by tropical illnesses, refused assistance. The advisory board of the tropical disease research fund was established in 1904 to administer these funds. It was composed of Manson, Sir Michael Foster, secretary of the Royal Society, Sir Thomas Barlow, a London physician, Sir Joseph West Ridgeway and Sir Ralph Moor, former governors representing the crown colonies, Lucas and Read from the Colonial Office, and two officials representing India. The board allocated most of the money raised to schools of tropical medicine (particularly Manson's institution) for salaries of teachers and researchers.[10]

Another committee struck on Manson's initiative drew up a set of practical suggestions for use in the colonies to combat malaria. Chaired by Lord Onslow, the parliamentary under-secretary, it included Read and canvassed the Crown Agents and

---

number from missionary societies, 125 (291). Memo by Read, Nov. 16, 1902, CO 885/8/143; and Manson-Bahr, *Tropical School*, p. 271.

8. By 1911 the school had received more than £75,000 of which almost one-half was made up of private contributions.

9. Minute by Lucas, Nov. 12, 1902, CO 323/480/45838. His idea was incorporated in a circular despatch to the colonies asking for aid of May 28, 1903 [Cd. 1598], XLIV, 15–25.

10. CO. 885/9/170, pp. 36, 48, 70, 85; and CO 885/9/173, pp. 5–11.

the consulting firm of Messrs. Shelford and Son to determine the best wire netting and cloth gauze for buildings and beds.

These findings, other suggestions for prevention, along with a poster by Manson illustrating how mosquitoes transmitted malaria were sent under circular despatch to all the colonies in April, 1901. The office knew the information would have limited effect. "If these recommendations," observed Ommanney, "so far as they affect the action of individuals, are to be given the force of regulations . . . penalties for their contravention will have to be specified—which seems to be quite impracticable." [11] Response depended upon how open colonial officials were to innovation, their initiative and the nature of the local problem. Tasmania reported no malaria but Fiji wanted 100 additional copies of Manson's poster and a sample of the recommended gauze. [12] Lugard had already written Chamberlain from northern Nigeria asking for wire netting to try on two newly erected houses to see if it would at least cut down the mosquito count but he doubted its efficacy:

I confess that it does not appear to me that any very great step towards the extermination of malaria would be gained, even if it were demonstrated that complete immunity could be effected by the exclusion of anopheles from a room by night. The mosquito bites all day and not only at night; and it is absolutely impossible in the climate of West Africa to exclude the free passage of air by means of gauze, through which little or no breeze can come. The warm night would be unbearable in such circumstances, and still more the day; during which, moreover, the conditions of work necessitate exposure to mosquito bites. [13]

Onslow's committee also examined the merits of an ingenious lamp designed to destroy mosquitoes found inside rooms and netting. The lamp was sent from Penang but was also obtainable in Bond Street. A dozen were forwarded for testing in West Africa. Unfortunately the committee failed to provide instructions for its use and the Gold Coast governor reported the lamp exploded when filled with petroleum. Feeling the incident dis-

11. Minute of Jan. 28, 1901, CO 323/469/3377.
12. CO 862/12, ff. 119–20.   13. June 23, 1900, CO 885/7/129.

credited the office's reputation, Antrobus quickly had drafted a despatch stating the lamps should be used with vegetable oil and pointing out their reputed success in China.[14]

More serious setbacks to good intentions befell a research team sent to Central Africa to investigate malaria and blackwater fever. The inquiry was sponsored jointly by the office and the Royal Society and responsible to a committee drawn from the two institutions on which Lucas and Read represented the former. It was financed out of colonial contributions and a small grant from the society but depended on the African Lakes Company and a telegraph firm to cover part of the travel costs. Two of its members nominated by the society, John Stephens and Samuel Christophers, quit the expedition, complaining that the region near Blantyre where studies were conducted had few malarial cases and inadequate hospital facilities. The leader of the expedition, Charles Daniels, seconded from the colonial medical service by the office, stayed on, managed to acquire valuable information at Blantyre and on the coast, but almost died from the very diseases he was investigating.[15]

Meanwhile a research team was sent out to West Africa under the auspices of private initiative. Sir Alfred Jones, who sought an alliance between commerce and government, was also instrumental in forging a link between business and science. He founded the Liverpool School of Tropical Medicine which opened April 2, 1899, six months before Manson's institution. He provided funds from his own pocket (£350 annually for three years as a beginning) and helped the school collect £120,000 by 1910. Donations came from Leopold II, Lord Rothschild and telegraph companies, but mostly from Liverpool business firms whose members, in the words of John Holt, were most anxious "to be rid of the dread effects of malaria, which in the past had been the bugbear of our trade, and the vital enemy to European existence in West Africa."[16] The first of many expeditions the

14. CO to Nathan, June 20, 1902, CO 323/473/22622.
15. CO 885/7/119, pp. 82, 90, 126, 137, 143–44; and CO 885/7/129, p. 18. Daniels, Stephens and Christophers became major contributors to research and teaching in tropical medicine.
16. Holt to T. H. Barker, Dec. 6, 1902, Liverpool Chamber of Commerce MSS, Liverpool Public Library, 380 COM, 3/1/1; *Sixth Annual Report of the Incor-*

school sent to West Africa and elsewhere was headed by Ross and went to Sierra Leone in mid-1899. The Liverpool School asked for government aid and, when Ross found malaria mosquitoes, Jones requested the Colonial Office send out medical men to combat them. Although it instructed local authorities to give every assistance to the expedition, it declined to provide a grant. Funds, it said, collected for its own malarial investigation "will barely suffice." [17] However, Stephens and Christophers, financed largely by local funds, were sent to West Africa in late 1899. [18]

By early 1900 the malaria committee of the Colonial Office and Royal Society had received preliminary reports from Ross as well as its own research team. He advised that still pools near human habitation which served as breeding grounds for *anopheles* be either filled in or coated with kerosene and that European dwellings be built on high ground. On the basis of the evidence presented by their team the committee advised against large expenditure on these measures. Breeding of *anopheles* was not limited to pools; they also laid eggs in running streams during the wet season. Filling pools would lessen, not eradicate malaria. Kerosene too would only have a temporary effect, and it was not definitely proven that high elevations prevented attacks of the disease. [19] Stephens and Christophers stressed constant use of mosquito netting. They also discovered that while native adults had built up an immunity to malaria it was very common among children, so much so that they were prime agents in the infection of Europeans. It followed that Europeans should avoid contact with Africans. Here was a prophylatic measure which the secretary of the Royal Society, Sir Michael Foster, thought to be of the "first order." [20] As the two researchers later asserted,

since we first put forward segregation as a principle to be followed whenever opportunity offered it has been recognised by some authori-

porated *Liverpool School of Tropical Medicine* (Liverpool, 1904), pp. 16–19; and A. H. Milne, *Sir Alfred Lewis Jones* (London, 1914), p. 85.
  17. Liverpool School to CO, June 14, and CO to school, July 1, 1899, CO 885/7/119.
  18. They visited Accra and Lagos as well as Freetown. Daniels also visited West Africa in 1901 under arrangements made by the Liverpool School to observe its activity in Freetown.
  19. Sir M. Foster to CO, Feb. 24, 1900, CO 267/456/6196.
  20. Foster to CO, April 24, 1903, *Parl. Pap.*, 1903 [Cd. 1598], XLIV, 27.

ties [including Manson] as the first law of hygiene in the tropics; on the other hand it has met with criticism. . . . Segregation as an anti-malarial measure does not . . . mean the avoidance of intercourse with the native. Nor does it mean a lessening of the power of control of the native. . . . In India segregation is almost universal . . . yet . . . there can be no question of loss of touch with the natives—rather on the contrary, an increased respect on their part. . . .

Before malaria is made to decrease among Europeans in Africa . . . men will refuse to allow in their compound squalid grass and palm leaf huts; they will cease to build their bungalows among or on the outskirts of villages; they will be extremely careful where they sleep when travelling, and it will be the duty of the medical officers of mining camps, railways, and military expeditions to absolutely forbid the forming of any camps near native huts, or to allow these to spring up in the more permanent camps.[21]

Ross, with less emphasis, also advocated segregation and admitted his methods would not exterminate the *anopheles*. But he argued that his control measures would seriously disrupt the life cycle of the mosquito and significantly reduce its numbers in areas of European habitation. To prove the point he implemented his recommendations at Freetown in 1901 with the support of local authorities and the aid of interested businessmen who provided money, shovels and kerosene. Ross claimed the campaign was very successful but not followed up by local or imperial authorities.[22]

Indeed he was alienated by what he felt to be imperial lethargy and obstruction. In March, 1901, a deputation visited Chamberlain from the Liverpool School and the chambers of commerce of London, Manchester and Liverpool with specific recommendations which had emerged from Ross's work in Sierra Leone. To reduce European illness and mortality in the major West African towns, it wanted the local governments to launch systematic sanitation measures to remove garbage, drain ponds, clear under-

21. J. W. W. Stephens and S. R. Christophers, *Summary of Researchers on Native Malaria and Malarial Prophylaxis; on Blackwater Fever, Its Nature and Prophylaxis* (London, HMSO, 1903), pp. 7–9. Copies of such reports and publications of the Liverpool School were distributed throughout the empire by the Colonial Office.

22. J. P. Coates, a Glasgow businessman contributed £2,000. Jones, Holt and F. Swanzy also helped. R. Ross, *Memories of Sir Patrick Manson* (London, 1930), p. 23; and by the same author, *Mosquito Brigades and How to Organise Them* (London, 1902), pp. 87–92.

growth and move African huts away from European residences. To see these undertakings were begun and continued it wanted the Colonial Office to appoint "sanitary commissioners" who would repeatedly visit the colonies and report to it on the performance of local authorities. Chamberlain, presumably guided by his experts' views, refused to adopt the suggestions, which were, he said, impracticable. Furthermore, local authorities, not scientific experts, best knew what was possible granted the immensity of the task of sanitation and mosquito control. He feared that visiting inspectors who did not understand the financial problems of the colonies might force local administrators to adopt projects which revenues could not meet.[23] Ross, who attended the interview, denied his proposals were prohibitively expensive compared to the cost and suffering caused by malaria. He soon also could point to the startling results achieved by the American army in Havana. As part of a rigorous sanitation program it began in 1901 to attack the breeding spots of the *culex* mosquito which transmitted yellow fever. Within months of the start of the campaign, the city was practically freed of the dread disease. A campaign against the malaria-transmitting *anopheles,* whose breeding places were different from the *culex*'s, was also very effective.[24] He blamed jealousy of the Liverpool School, hostility towards scientists and unjustified parsimony, particularly among the permanent officials, for Britain's administrative inertia.[25]

Ross's temperament, the obstructions put in his way by officialdom in India, and the controversy which flared over who first discovered the malaria parasite in mosquitoes, made him exceedingly sensitive to authority and the possibility of conspiracy. And his indictment of the Colonial Office is largely without foundation. In Read the office had an influential official, knowledgeable

23. *The Times,* March 16, 1901.
24. "From an average of 1,047 a year in 1898–1900, malaria deaths dropped precipitately [in Havana] to only 151 in 1901, 77 in 1902, and an average of only 44 a year for the decade following the turn of the century. By 1912 they had dropped to only four a year." J. M. Gibson, *Physician to the World, The Life of General William C. Gorgas* (Durham, N.C., 1950), p. 90. This biography, by its examination of American administrative attitudes and practices, provides illuminating contrasts with British experience. See especially Chaps. iii–viii.
25. R. Ross, *Memoirs* (London, 1923), pp. 434–37.

about and receptive to science. Read, naturally enough, followed Manson's suggestions and the latter inclined to emphasize research more than its application. At the same time the scientists themselves were by no means in agreement on what were the best methods of attack. Read's summation of the situation is instructive:

An almost illimitable field of investigation has been opened up by the discovery of the part played by the mosquito in conveying disease. It is difficult to say what diseases these insects diffuse and how they diffuse them. Quite recently yellow fever has been brought into the category of mosquito-produced disease. Already some 500 species of mosquito are known each of which has to be studied in its bearings on human pathology. As regards the important question of malaria, our investigations are only in their infancy. We know that certain mosquitoes convey malaria, but we do not know all the mosquitoes which convey it, nor under what conditions they act.[26]

Initially the office offered little encouragement to the rapidly developing Liverpool School. But in 1900 it recognized the institution's graduates on a par with London's for appointments in the tropics. And the advisory board of the tropical disease research fund granted Liverpool an annual £500 for five years beginning in 1904.[27] Given the contemporary attitude towards and problems of colonial finance, the aid accumulated for the study and control of tropical disease was substantial. Indeed, the concerted effort made to raise funds was a self-inflicted task hardly in keeping with the public image of the permanent official's function.

The usual difficulties London encountered in making its instructions effective on the local level were also partly overcome. Dependence on governors' assessments and initiatives, sensitivity of other departments, varying abilities and shortages of medical officers, and the diversity in local health problems limited the center's opportunities for action. Nonetheless, the office diligently followed up with reminders, unanswered circular despatches asking for funds or information. Following Manson's suggestion the office issued new forms on which more complete and uniform

26. Memo by Read, Nov. 16, 1902, CO 885/8/143.
27. CO 885/7/129, p. 28; and CO 885/9/173, pp. 11–12.

medical reports could be returned, but the response of local medical officers was not encouraging.[28] The office also had sent to the natural history section of the British Museum specimens of winged insects including mosquitoes for identification and study.[29] These and other related efforts were suggested and supervised by the office's advisory committees. Manson, for example, advocated the establishment of central laboratories in several regions of the empire—in West Africa, the West Indies, East Africa and the Far East. Diseases indigenous to each group of colonies could thus be systematically and continuously studied, exchanges made between directors of these laboratories and experts at home, and a body of beneficial information and experience accumulated. To this purpose a laboratory, financed out of local funds, was established at Kuala Lumpur in 1900. However, in 1904 the governor of the Federated Malay States, Sir John Anderson, questioned its need. Could the states at that stage of development afford to support an institution devoted primarily to research when the practical problems of public health were so obviously in need of further attention? The office consulted Manson and on the basis of his brief, pointed out benefits to be derived from research, how the institute might be maintained at less cost, and aid more directly the local health department. Although still inclined to stress its practical side, Anderson agreed to continue the center.[30]

While Lugard might question the use of mosquito netting and think training African women as nurses as part of hygiene improvement programs for native towns "a hopeless project" (none, he claimed, was fit for or interested in the work), he, nonetheless, welcomed other recommendations of the experts. He was, he said, a strong advocate of practical segregation. When he took over from the Royal Niger Company he abandoned the European

---

28. No reliable and uniform statistics on malarial deaths and cases were compiled. See *Parl. Pap., 1903* [Cd. 1598], XLIV, 17. Ross was consulted in 1910 but the forms he devised to record mosquito-born diseases were also unevenly answered. See *Parl. Pap., 1914* [Cd. 7261], XLVIII, 625 ff., and *ibid.*, 1914–16 [Cd. 7796], XXXVII, 1–254.

29. *Parl. Pap., 1903* [Cd. 1598], XLIV, 16.

30. Anderson to Lyttelton, Aug. 18, Manson to CO, Sept. 28, Lyttelton to Anderson, Nov. 11, 1904, CO 885/9/170; and CO 885/9/178.

section of Lokoja, which was surrounded by African dwellings, for a site one mile away, where he began building cantonments on the Indian system. He also provided for the reduction of mosquito breeding areas, and a local sanitary inspector for the new town to work with the director of public works and the medical officer, and empowered to control native access to the cantonments.[31] Another administrator responded differently to expert advice. Sir William MacGregor, the governor of Lagos, and a former medical officer, whom Ross thought particularly receptive to his malaria control measures, opposed segregation.

The policy [wrote MacGregor] followed in Lagos in this as in other matters is to take the natives along with the Europeans on the way leading to improvement. Here they cannot live apart nor work apart, and they should not try to do so. Separation would mean that little, or at least less, would be done for the native, and the admitted source of infection would remain perennial.[32]

In Ceylon Manson's posters were translated into the vernacular and quinine was distributed free to villagers.[33] In Mauritius netting and screening helped keep government house mosquito free, quinine depots were established and sanitary works launched. But initiative lagged after an initial burst of activity and sanitary measures were not maintained. More than 4,400 fever deaths in a population of 370,000 were reported in 1912.[34] Various anti-malaria programs in southern Nigeria seemed to have more positive results, at least for the health of Europeans. Although their numbers at Lagos almost doubled between 1897 and 1906 deaths from malaria declined.[35] Whether measures adopted by governors, public works officials and medical officers to cut the death

31. Lugard to CO, June 16, 1904, CO 885/9/170. See also W. Fosbery, acting high commissioner of southern Nigeria, to CO, March 1, 1904, *ibid.*, for efforts at segregation, drainage and fill programs at Akassa and Spaele, and establishment of a research laboratory and a native nurse training program at Old Calabar.

32. Quoted in Ross, *Mosquito Brigades*, p. 75. For a detailed account of MacGregor's work and the efforts of several other governors in Britain's West African possessions to introduce measures against malaria see Dummett, *African Historical Studies*, I (1968), 179–88.

33. See enclosure in Henry McCallum, governor, to CO, Sept. 10, 1907, *Parl. Pap.*, 1908 [Cd. 3992], LXXXVIII, 642–45.

34. See Cavendish Boyle to CO, Nov. 29, 1906, *ibid.*, pp. 645–46, and *Parl. Pap.*, 1914 [Cd. 7261], XLVIII, 632–701.

35. See enclosure in J. J. Thorburn, deputy governor, to CO, Dec. 9, 1907, *Parl. Pap.*, 1908 [Cd. 3992], LXXXVIII, 652–59.

rate had immediate effects, they did reflect a significant degree of local response to the suggestions of science passed on by London.

Committees, including non-governmental personnel, were an accepted feature of nineteenth-century imperial administration. But their main function had been to gather information and make recommendations. They had not become intimately involved in the formulation and execution of policy. In this context the committees struck to further the study and prevention of tropical diseases, especially malaria, were a new departure. They were for the most part composed of men noted not for their social position, vested interest, or political allegiance, but rather for their expertise. They were either medical specialists, experienced colonial administrators, or particularly qualified office staff. As such, encouraged by Chamberlain, they actively advised. More than this, however, they made crucial decisions on how funds might be gathered and spent, what priorities were to be given to research and its application, what preventative measures available should be stressed, and how government was to further study and research at the center rather than to initiate health projects at the local level. Given the complexity of local situations and the particular state of man's knowledge this was understandable. They were, as well, Euro-centric in disposition and imperialistic by necessity. The colonies must pay for the research which ultimately would provide the means to make them safer for Europeans to live in.[36]

36. Malaria did not stop being a serious disease for Europeans until the late 1940's. By then insecticides, new knowledge about the life history of the malaria parasite in humans, and man-made drugs more effective in the cure and prevention of malaria and with less detrimental side effects than quinine made the disease "less to be feared than . . . influenza." P. Manson-Bahr, *Patrick Manson* (London, 1962), p. 157. It still of course takes a heavy toll in sickness and death among impoverished indigenous peoples of the tropics.

· 8 ·

Administration and Trade: The
Problem of Imperial Preference

Under a different system, he really might federate the Empire effectively and live in history with the Richelieus. . . .
[But] even Joe can make nothing great with this *system*
[with its] . . . inadequate regard for trained knowledge and
complete information . . . old divisions of [political] parties
no longer corresponding to any real differences . . . [and]
a huge unwieldy Cabinet [which] . . . cannot give *continuous thought and study* to the *vital,* being eternally distracted by the local and *temporary.*

Lord Milner to Lady Edward Cecil,
May 16, 1903, C. Headlam (ed.),
The Milner Papers, II, 447–48.

I

The elections of 1900 returned the Unionist alliance to office.
Though its margin of the total popular vote was slim, it retained
an impressive majority in the House of Commons where it again
faced a deeply divided Liberal opposition. Within three years
the crisis over imperial preference had ruptured the alliance,
united the Liberals, and forced Chamberlain to resign. The
essential question in the fiscal dispute was clear—would free
trade arrangements continue to best serve Britain's economy or
were tariff adjustments needed?—but the political maneuvers of
the cabinet ministers involved were very intricate and confused.
These complications were made worse because the government's
administrative arm could not provide a conclusive answer to the
question and because some of its officials interfered decisively in
the ministers' deliberations and calculations.

II

Trade problems had been Chamberlain's primary concern from the outset. Immediately on entering office he began "seriously contemplating the possibility and expediency of giving Colonial produce a preference over foreign produce."[1] In late July, 1895, before the South African crisis developed and before he confronted the Treasury with crown colony development, Chamberlain initiated a project to determine the extent to which foreign imports were displacing British goods in the markets of the empire. Why did colonies import certain lines of foreign manufacture when they might have British? He wanted "to get facts" which he could "send to . . . English manufactur[ers] & which will put them on the scent of this trade & enable them to take the trade from their foreign competitors."[2] An elaborate circular despatch of inquiry was drawn up by the office and sent to the colonies on November 28. Local officials were asked to provide returns for the years 1884, 1889 and 1894 which itemized foreign trade articles. An appendix to the despatch, which listed the articles to be enumerated under some 70 heads and 130 subheads, was based on Board of Trade categories amended by British chambers of commerce. The exhaustive list included bottles, boots, buttons, bed steads, clocks, chemicals, carpets, curtains, paint, pickles, plate, paper, sail cloth, steam engines, shovels, shirts, screws. Even the major "free ports" of the empire (Gibraltar, Singapore and Hong Kong), which benefited as much from foreign trade as British, were asked to participate. These ports either did not record or kept "inflated and fallacious" trade statistics, but "they could tell [the office] a good deal about the fate of British trade as it passes under their eyes." Chamberlain agreed with Selborne's remark that since the colonists might "think that we are not caring for their interests but only for those of the British producer," the inquiry should also make token provision for them to express views on how their exports to Britain might be increased. In addition, the colonial representatives in

1. Hamilton Diary, July 5, 1895, Add. MS 48667. The Treasury official had obtained his information from his good friend and colleague, Meade.
2. Minute of Aug. 19, 1895, CO 323/403/13432.

London, the agents general from Australasia and the Canadian high commissioner, were assured that the project was not an attempt to challenge the protectionist policies of their respective governments. To insure that the needs of British industry would be met, the office submitted first drafts of the circular to eighteen chambers of commerce for comment, and the colonies were asked to forward samples of imported foreign manufacture to London. Finally, to mollify resentment of the Board of Trade at this encroachment into its preserve, it was asked for comment.[3] The inquiry, then, was to be thorough and comprehensive and designed to assuage the sensibilities of special interest groups.

Senior office officials, less sensitive to the interests of British industry than their chief and more sceptical about obtaining accurate information, saw little advantage in pursuing the inquiry. They pointed out that colonial trade statistics were unreliable because customs officials were more concerned with levying duties and less with the origin, function or description of imported articles. For example, goods from Europe sent by way of London in British ships were often not distinguished from English products. "My experience," Round later wrote, "of Colonial Customs houses & colonial statistics would lead me to distrust the accuracy of a good deal of the 'particular' as opposed to general information received in reply to the Circular."[4] Most of the work connected with the inquiry was given to a single junior clerk, Charles Alexander Harris. He soon bypassed the office hierarchy (including Round to whom the work properly belonged and the under-secretaries), and communicated directly with Selborne or Chamberlain himself. He also established a close liaison with the secretary of the London Chamber of Commerce. These arrangements avoided office bottlenecks, but they meant Chamberlain had to become familiar with much detail to make minor decisions which Harris was not inclined to do on

3. Minutes by Fairfield, Aug. 10; Charles Alexander Harris, Oct. 3, and Selborne, July 29, 1895, *ibid.*
4. Minute of Jan. 11, 1897, CO 323/407/13882. Inaccurate information and the indifferent attitude of consular representatives to business activity also made commercial intelligence gathered by the Foreign Office of questionable validity. See D. C. M. Platt, *Finance, Trade and Politics in British Foreign Policy, 1815–1914* (London, 1968), pp. 102–40.

his own. For almost two years the junior clerk kept busy prodding tardy colonies to provide returns, gathering statistics as they came in, and obtaining commentary by British industry on the foreign trade samples. In August, 1897, the Colonial Office issued a six-hundred page blue book based on the inquiry. Because the stastistics gathered were neither exhaustive nor particularly accurate, they did not, as the report admitted, "afford a perfectly secure basis for generalisation." Nonetheless, Harris calculated that in the decade 1884–1894 foreign exporters had increased their share of the colonial import trade by 6 per cent (from 25.8 to 31.5). Despite the inconclusiveness of the statistics the report did show how foreign competitors obtained access to colonial markets—by underselling their British counterparts and by adapting selling techniques and products to the colonial situation.[5]

British industry showed a keen interest in the report and the foreign samples and expressed a strong desire for the government to expand this service. The Association of Chambers of Commerce of the United Kingdom, representing eighty-seven local organizations, urged the Colonial Office to appoint special trade officers in the colonies to report on agricultural, commercial, mineral and industrial trends. Also the India and Foreign Offices and the Board of Trade, as well as the Colonial Office, were pressed by the association for additional information to meet the needs of specific industries to be gathered through a trade intelligence center established in London.[6]

III

While the inquiry to provide information for British exporters was proceeding, Chamberlain engaged in speculation about a more ambitious venture—the creation of an imperial *zollverein*. Under such a plan, he told a meeting of the Congress of Chambers of Commerce of the Empire, Britain would "consent to place

5. *Parl. Pap., 1897* [C. 8449], LX, 3–12.
6. H. Stafford Northcote, M.P., president of the association, to the Colonial Office, Oct. 16, 1896, and Jan. 1, 1897, CO 323/412/21759; and May 21, 1897, CO 323/425/10950.

moderate duties upon certain articles which are of large production in the colonies." They, in turn, "while maintaining their duties upon foreign commodities, would agree to a free interchange of commodities with the rest of the Empire, and would cease to place protective duties on any products of British labour."

The details of such a scheme [he continued], would require the most careful examination. [And it would not] be either wise or practical that a proposal of this kind should come in the first instance from the United Kingdom. We know how strenuously the colonies cling to their own independence, and their own initiative. If they desire, as we believe they do, this closer union, if they are willing to make some sacrifice of their present arrangements and convictions in order to secure it, let them say so. Let the offer come voluntarily from them, and I believe it will be considered in this country not in any huckstering spirit, but will be entertained as part of a greater policy that is intended to unite in the closest bonds of affection and of interest all the communities which are under the British flag, and all the subjects of Her Majesty throughout the Empire.[7]

Even such a staunch free trader as Hamilton of the Treasury could admit that "the *idea* has its attractions." But he was not convinced by Chamberlain's rhetoric that Britain would have anything to gain economically through a customs union. "The Colonies," he added, "would have a good deal to lose."[8] So far as the self-governing colonies were concerned he was right. Protection against British as well as foreign articles, which competed unfavorably with the products of their fledgling industries, was already an integral part of their economic nationalism; so too was the desire to arrange favorable tariff agreements with foreign countries. During the Colonial Conference of 1897 the visiting premiers made it clear that they were not interested in an imperial common market in which protection against British manufacture must disappear. Some were, however, willing to grant Britain a tariff preference if its government would reciprocate. Indeed, in that year Canada gave a modest preference to a number of articles imported from Britain. Then the British govern-

7. Speech of June 9, 1896, quoted in C. W. Boyd, ed., *Mr. Chamberlain's Speeches* (2 vols.; New York, 1914), I, 370–72.
8. June 9, 1896, Add. MS 48669.

ment followed by denouncing trade treaties with Belgium and Germany which contained most-favored-nation clauses lest these countries benefit from the preference, which was raised to 25 per cent in 1898 and again to 33⅓ per cent in 1900.

The onus was now on the British government to do something further for imperial unity by placing a tariff on foreign imports which competed in the home market with such colonial exports as grain and sugar. But from the British point of view the risk of incurring foreign retaliation by departing from free trade practices in return for minor colonial concessions was not worth taking. Hamilton thought it necessary to put the Treasury view on record when the agents general urged unsuccessfully that colonial wines be exempted from a proposed addition to duties to increase revenues. With certain exceptions, such as tea from India and Ceylon, rum from the East and West Indies and a limited amount of dried fruits, tobacco and wine, colonial imports, which consisted primarily of food-stuffs and raw materials, entered Britain duty-free. If, he argued, existing tariffs were preferentially adjusted or new ones added to foreign imports in these categories, production costs of manufacturers who used these materials would increase. These manufacturers would be under a further disadvantage in the competitive export trade and the home consumer would have to pay more. To insure that foreign goods taxed at higher rates than colonial produce did not reach Britain by way of the colonies to obtain preferential treatment, costly administrative checks would have to be devised, and Britain's entrepôt and transit trade (which constituted 25 per cent of the entire export business of the nation), might be disrupted. Furthermore, foreign countries which took twice as much of British exports as the colonies might retaliate. He concluded that even minor preferential adjustments could thus cause very serious commercial loss to Britain and weaken instead of strengthen the cause of imperial unity.[9] Such arguments were not lost on Chamberlain at this stage. He said he believed that no such proposal as preferential trade "would justify any change in the fiscal system of this country, & that to induce considera-

9. Hamilton to Colonial Office, June 9, 1899, T 7/31.

tion of any such change on our part it would be necessary that
the Colonies should adopt the principle of Free Trade so far as
British commerce is concerned." [10]

With a *zollverein* repugnant to the colonies, imperial preference anathema to the Treasury, and South Africa his dominant
concern, Chamberlain let the Colonial Office ignore trade problems. It responded tardily to the business community's desire for
more trade information. As Selborne explained to Chamberlain
in March, 1897,

In Nov. or Dec. [1896], you minuted to me to discuss with you a
proposal for the establishment of commercial representatives in the
self-governing colonies.

Increasing pressure of other work has afforded no apparent opportunity in which you were free to take up any fresh movement.

I presume that you are, to say the least of it, sufficiently occupied
and that subject must stand over till the S[outh] A[frican] Committee
[i.e., the inquiry into the Jameson Raid], is a thing of the past.[11]

Not until 1901 did the office take up the question of appointing
commercial officials, and then only as a consequence of the
prompting of the Board of Trade.

In fact that department, stirred by Chamberlain's excursions
into trade matters, had appointed a committee in July, 1897, to
study the suggestions of the chambers of commerce. Like the
Colonial Office, the Board of Trade in the late nineteenth century
assumed various new administrative duties. Unlike the Colonial
Office, however, its staff increased significantly to meet new
business.[12] Of its six branches, the commercial and statistical department was most active compiling abstracts and returns on
domestic, colonial and foreign economic activity and advising the
other government departments on commercial matters. Its
political head, Charles Ritchie, thought the Colonial Office had
exaggerated the effects of foreign competition but agreed government should make every effort to inform British industry how
foreign competitors operated in world markets.[13] When the

10. Chamberlain to Alexander MacNeill, Canadian M.P. and ardent imperial
federationist, Aug. 19, 1899, JC 9/2.
11. Minute of March 11, 1897, CO 323/412/21759.
12. Board of Trade Confidential Print, May, 1903, PRO 30/60/45.
13. Ritchie to Northcote, June 29, 1897, BT 13/29/E12804.

Colonial Office volunteered to let a proposed information office be "under the undivided control of one head appointed by and responsible to the Board," Ritchie instructed his department to appoint a committee to prepare estimates of its staff and cost. These the Treasury approved.[14] As a part of the commercial and statistical department, the new commercial intelligence branch opened in October, 1899, with premises in the City. It acted as a central agency for the systematic collection and dissemination of commercial information furnished by traders, commercial attachés and colonial governments. In addition, the commercial department produced its own study of the impact of foreign exports on British trade from which it concluded that while "competition has undoubtedly become increasingly keen within recent years, its effect had probably been exaggerated. . . . [The study] has shown that there is little ground for the dread which has been expressed, with some authority, of serious undermining of our commercial pre-eminence."[15] Not only did the Board of Trade challenge the Colonial Office's claims about trade patterns, but it became the authoritative government department on commerce in the empire. Significantly enough Harris, once the Colonial Office trade inquiry of 1895–1897 had been completed, turned to other duties.[16] Meanwhile other imperial as well as domestic problems more than occupied Chamberlain. Well might he remark to Walter Long, a cabinet colleague in December, 1901: "Look at all these [despatch] boxes (there were a pile of a dozen); think of all the work—I don't know what you feel but I am sick of it."[17]

IV

Neither Chamberlain nor the Treasury was prepared for the

14. Colonial Office to Board of Trade, Aug. 20, 1898, BT 13/28/E16522, and Treasury to Board of Trade, March 8, 1899, BT 13/29/E13678.
15. Board of Trade to Treasury, April 29, enclosed in Board of Trade to Colonial Office, June 28, 1897, CO 323/416/14024; see also *Parl. Pap., 1897* [C. 8322], LXXXIII, 705–59. For a critical assessment of the commercial intelligence branch's effectiveness, see Platt, *Trade and Politics,* pp. 123–26.
16. Harris was involved in colonial civil service reforms in 1901. See Chapter 3. He ended up heading a new department concerned with West African colonies.
17. Recorded by Parker Smith, a private secretary, JC 12/2.

repercussions which followed on Hicks Beach's decision in early 1902 to impose a duty of 3d. per cwt. on imported grain and 5d. per cwt. on imported meal and flour to raise revenue to meet rising expenditures, the war making further unexpected demands on the exchequer. Hamilton, who had unsuspectingly advised the imposition of the tax, soon became aware of

the risk lest the corn duty is to be made a peg on which is hung the preferential treatment of Colonies. If I thought that Chamberlain was going to give way on that point to the Colonial Premiers, I should say it would be worth Beach sacrificing his reputation [i.e. by withdrawing the tax], to put a spoke in the wheel of his colleague.[18]

Chamberlain, indeed, had to face a Canadian delegation which strongly urged at the Colonial Conference that began in late June that Britain grant Canada a preference by not imposing the new duty on its grain. Also the premier of New Zealand introduced the idea that the conference study the subject of reciprocity of preferences in which Britain and the colonies would all grant each other exemptions on existing tariffs.

It would appear that if Chamberlain was not well prepared to meet these pressures, the Board of Trade was. Its statistical analysis showed that in 1901, if commodities from India and Ceylon were excluded, only 13 per cent of Britain's food-stuff imports were derived from colonial sources. (This figure was also the average for the period 1897–1901.) Furthermore, 87 per cent of grain and flour imports came from foreign countries. At the same time Britain exported manufactured goods to the Cape, Natal, Australia, New Zealand and Canada worth £44 million, to India £33½ million, and to foreign countries £136 million.[19] As Gerald Balfour, who had replaced Ritchie as president of the Board of Trade in 1900, pointed out in a memo for the cabinet, the self-governing colonies took less than one-fifth of British exports while they marketed three-fifths of their exports in Britain. And despite Canada's preference on British manufacture, Board of Trade statistics indicated little had been done to arrest the fall of British as compared to foreign imports. Canada's tariffs, de-

18. May 25, 1902, Add. MS 48679.
19. Record of proceedings of the Colonial Conference, 1902, Appendix X, CO 885/8/144.

signed to shield its industry, still decidedly discriminated against British manufacture. New South Wales and New Zealand, for example, took several times more British goods per head of population than Canada. He concluded that the field for practical tariff adjustments was so small that any adjustments, though they might give a fillip to the idea of imperial unity, had no commercial advantage for the empire.[20]

Chamberlain's opening remarks to the conference on trade matters drew heavily upon the Board of Trade briefs. He pointed out that the rate of increase of British exports to Canada "under the preferential tariff was actually less than under the general tariff."

Foreign produce [he continued], at the present time in Canada has still a lower average tariff than British produce, no doubt due to the fact that the foreign produce is . . . of a character upon which lower duties are ordinarily levied: but the result is that while foreign imports have largely increased the British imports have largely decreased. . . . The net result which I desire to impress upon you is that in spite of the preference which Canada has given us, their tariff has pressed, and still presses, with the greatest severity, upon its best customer [i.e. Great Britain], and has favoured the foreigner who is constantly doing his best to shut out her goods.[21]

Before the question could be further pursued, Chamberlain's health, which during the past seven years had deteriorated under the constant stress of work, was seriously impaired. In a cab accident on July 7 he "was more seriously hurt than was known. Very nearly killed, in fact. The skull bruised at a very thin place, and he has not been able to read or think since." [22] Chamberlain, though he had not recovered from the accident, insisted on taking part in the conference when it resumed on July 18. Despite Gerald Balfour's scepticism, the colonial secretary tried to move the conference from a general discussion of preference to detailed proposals for colonial tariff adjustments. Perhaps a substantial commitment from the colonies would yet enable him to press in future for British concessions—a rebate on present duties

20. Cabinet Memo of June, 1902, Cab. 37/62/120.
21. June 30, 1902, CO 885/8/144.
22. Lord Esher to his wife, July 15, 1902, Brett, *Journals,* I, 340.

or new ones imposed for revenue. Balfour was dubious. Only the Canadian delegation had experts with it. Though detailed negotiations might start and continue after the prime ministers left England, the matter, he said, was too complicated to sort out during the conference. Most of the prime ministers favored Balfour's argument that only a general resolution was in order. The Canadians, however, were interested in probing specifics and did so with Board of Trade representatives, especially in an effort to prove their preference was beneficial to Britain.[23]

The Board was not to be moved and Chamberlain could only try to gloss over the difficulties in the concluding sessions of the conference. He took the middle ground between Balfour and Sir Wilfrid Laurier, the Canadian prime minister. "We admit," he told the Canadians, "that the preference is valuable although we think we have shown you, and we think you yourselves are inclined to admit that it has not had all the results that we both expected from it." [24] He also agreed to a general resolution in which the premiers urged Britain to extend preferential treatment to colonial products though it in no way committed Chamberlain to extend concessions. They promised only to discuss tariffs in cabinet back home. No tangible measure emerged from the conference in its discussions of preference (nothing concrete had emerged from discussion on an imperial council or colonial contributions to imperial defense either), a conference which, significantly enough, featured the Board of Trade handling specific tariff questions and sceptical of any fiscal change.

V

While Chamberlain was recovering from his accident, the makeup of the Unionist government underwent a major change. Salisbury and Hicks Beach retired. Arthur Balfour became prime minister on July 12, but a replacement for Hicks Beach was more

23. For the statistical analyses upon which the board experts and the Canadian delegation based their different conclusions on the benefit of the Canadian preference see CO 885/8/144, Appendices XIII, XIV, and XVII.
24. *Ibid.*, p. 132.

difficult to find. Hamilton keenly felt the loss of his strong-willed mentor, particularly because there was "not a soul to succeed him":

I would sooner have Austen Chamberlain [financial secretary to the Treasury] than anyone else; but I am afraid it is impossible: it would look too much as if his appointment were a part of the terms exacted by his father for serving under Arthur Balfour. I have said I shall resign if [R. W.] Hanbury [president of the Board of Agriculture] is appointed and I have lodged a protest against Ritchie [home secretary since 1900].

But Ritchie, whom Hamilton classed as third-rate, "lazy," and inclined "to leave everything to be done by others," succeeded Hicks Beach.[25]

The retirement of Salisbury and Hicks Beach weakened the government but permitted cabinet members to pursue policies they had opposed. Balfour, for example, was able to proceed with educational reforms which the chancellor thought too costly. One section of the prime minister's Education Bill of 1902 provided for the payment of voluntary church schools out of municipal taxes. This provision greatly embarrassed the colonial secretary, who drew much of his political support from nonconformists whose agitation for free, non-sectarian and compulsory education he had vigorously supported in the 1870's. While Chamberlain was incapacitated by his cab accident, the House of Commons deleted a clause which he had inserted in the bill to make it less repugnant to nonconformists and making contributions to church schools a matter of local option. Nonconformists were scandalized and many gave up their allegiance to the Unionist party. Chamberlain pessimistically reported to Balfour:

My unfortunate accident, among many other inconveniences, has prevented me from following closely the debates on the Education Bill. . . . [But] to my mind it is clear that the Bill has brought all the fighting Nonconformists into the field and made them active instead

25. Hamilton Diary, July 14, 1902, Add. MS 48679; Add. MS 48667, f. 52; and Add. MS 48680, ff. 127–28. Austen Chamberlain did, however, come into the cabinet as postmaster-general and on the resignation of Ritchie and his father in Sept., 1903, became chancellor.

of merely passive opponents. Their representatives and appeals to
the old war cries have impressed large numbers of the middle and
upper working classes who have hitherto supported the Unionist
Party without joining the Conservative organisation. The transfer of
their votes will undoubtedly have immense importance at a general
election. . . .

I recognise that it may be too late for any compromise at all and
that there is nothing for us but to go to what I believe is certain political destruction. . . .

I cannot be hopeful of any solution, and I am perfectly ready to
accept your decision. . . .[26]

A section of the electorate supporting the Unionist government
generally and Chamberlain specifically had been alienated. Convinced of the necessity of raising other issues to rally dwindling
support, Chamberlain turned again to the empire. He set out to
put the stamp of success on the costly post-war settlement in
South Africa and to obtain tariff reforms in the name of imperial
unity which would find approval both in the colonies and at
home. He decided to make a personal tour of South Africa and to
raise in cabinet the question of imperial preference. Canada had
offered to give British manufacture further preference for a
rebate on Hicks Beach's grain tax. Equipped with this promise
Chamberlain got an initial encouraging response in cabinet to his
suggestion for a reciprocal arrangement. Balfour was not an
orthodox free trader and was in Chamberlain's debt because the
latter, although he had found it politically disadvantageous, had
supported the prime minister's education bill. Selborne, Brodrick
and Lansdowne raised no objections either.[27] However, the new
chancellor, whose background at the Board of Trade made him
well versed in fiscal orthodoxy, and the officials of his department were thoroughly alarmed. Ritchie, Hamilton noted, was

quite alive to the seriousness of the Chamberlain proposal; & of his
own accord took a very sensible & orthodox line . . . but he said he
was sure that a considerable majority [of the cabinet] was against
him, and he doubted his ability to fight Chamberlain single-handed.

26. August 4, 1902, Amery, *Life*, IV, 494–95. See also Chamberlain to Gerald
Balfour, Aug. 26, 1902, PRO 30/60/45.
27. In 1900 Selborne had succeeded Goschen at the Admiralty, Lansdowne
went to the Foreign Office and Brodrick to the War Office.

I undertook to prepare a brief for him and I recommend his circulating a strong paper on the subject.[28]

On November 19, the chancellor, briefed by Hamilton,[29] persuaded the cabinet to put off a decision on the corn duty until it came time to consider the budget early in the following year. The cabinet did, however, appear to give tacit approval to the principle of imperial preference, for just what occurred at this meeting has been the subject of considerable controversy.[30] Hamilton's account of it, which tells something of the intrigues of his own department to thwart the colonial secretary, is particularly revealing:

All that the Chan. of the Exchequer could get done in yesterday's Cabinet on the preferential question was noncommitted to Canada. She was to be written to and told with our regret that no decision could be taken about her Corn, until the Cabinet knew better how they should stand financially next year. But the outlook on the general question looks very bad. The only man from whom Ritchie got any support, & very unexpectedly, was [Lord] Londonderry [president of the Board of Education], & he had been preached at by Mowatt & Murray as well as by me. Balfour of Burleigh [secretary for Scotland] though he did not like it gave in. Even Ritchie himself said he felt that at the back of his mind there was some grain of truth & sense in the heterodox view. I gather that Chamberlain had argued the case from a Colonial point of view with great skill.[31]

Before Chamberlain could deal further with the corn duty, he embarked on a new departure in imperial administration. On November 25 he left England for South Africa. His hectic tour, crammed with speeches and interviews, has been regarded by his biographer as a personal triumph in racial reconciliation for the colonial secretary. Yet his efforts insulted more than mollified the Boer leaders. He could do little to eradicate the "arrogant superiority" which British colonists "assumed towards the Dutch,"

28. Hamilton Diary, Oct. 27, 1902, Add. MS 48680.
29. The brief is quoted extensively in Amery, *Life*, IV, 520–23, where Mowatt rather than Hamilton is said to be its author. For memos by Hamilton and Ritchie on preference see Cab. 37/63/148 and /155.
30. See Amery, *Life*, IV, 523; Dugdale, *Balfour*, I, 340; B. Holland, *The Life of Spencer Compton, Eighth Duke of Devonshire* (2 vols.; London, 1911), II, 298–99; A. Gollin, *Balfour's Burden* (London, 1965), pp. 27–32; and Fraser, *Chamberlain*, pp. 233–35.
31. Nov. 20, 1902, Add. MS 48680.

and Boer "disloyalty" in the Cape was more extensive than he had anticipated.[32] He left South Africa, if not a disillusioned at least a very tired man, on February 25, and arrived back in England on March 14, 1903.

In his absence Treasury officials continued their intrigues. Ritchie, although "anxious to avoid taking a step which might put his colleagues in a difficulty, and which might lead to disruption," following a talk with Hamilton "summoned up his courage." He "told Arthur Balfour that if preferential treatment is to be pressed, he must find another Chan. of the Exchequer."[33] On March 31 Ritchie put Hamilton's budget proposals, which included a remission of the corn duty, before the cabinet, and he won his point. Three weeks later the chancellor brought down his budget in a speech, largely prepared by Hamilton,[34] in which he announced the repeal of the corn tax. The decision brought forth vigorous protests from supporters of imperial preference, representatives of agriculture, and from manufacturers who suffered from foreign competition and who had seen the duty as a first step toward the adoption of protection. This agitation, much of it coming from the ranks of the Unionist party, prompted Ritchie to express the wish that "he had left the duty alone." Even Hamilton noted the movement was "gaining ground" but doubted whether it was going to be "really serious."[35] He was wrong.

Beginning on May 15 Chamberlain gave a series of three speeches which placed him in the vanguard of the preference movement. He thereby precipitated a cabinet crisis setting a cabal of free-trade ministers led by Ritchie against him. They, in turn, were urged on by Treasury officials, whose irregular activities so much annoyed the prime minister that he had to be persuaded not to write Mowatt a letter urging him, as a civil servant, to stay out of the controversy.[36] At the same time Chamberlain's

32. Lord Monk Bretton, n.d., impressions of the South African tour, Monk Bretton MSS, Bodleian Library. See Hancock, *Smuts,* I, 192–93, for an account of Smuts's antipathy toward Chamberlain.

33. Hamilton Diary, Feb. 23 and 26, 1903, Add. MS 48680.

34. *Ibid.,* f. 107; Dugdale, *Balfour,* I, 346; and T 168/60 and /61.

35. Hamilton Diary, May 7 and 12, 1903, Add. MS 48680.

36. Balfour regarded Mowatt's activities as "subversive of all the loyalty which has characterized the Civil Servant of the Crown," but on the advice of Hamilton and his private secretary, who feared the letter would prompt Mowatt to re-

action drove fissures into the unity of the Unionist party and gave the Liberals—long at odds among themselves—an opportunity to close ranks as staunch supporters of free trade.

Balfour, in a letter to Devonshire, thought that Chamberlain, because he had been thwarted by his colleagues, was acting with a reckless impulsiveness if not inconsistent with a preconceived commitment, at least devoid of previous preparation.

What actually happened was this. Chamberlain came back from South Africa, conscious of having done a great public work, and of having done it in a way which few could have attempted to rival. He was rather ill, rather irritable, and very tired. On his arrival he found the Bye-elections going against us, a Land Bill about to be introduced into the House of Commons on which he had never been consulted, and of which, for some reason or other (I really have never quite made out what) he chose to disapprove. He found Brodrick & Brodricks' Army Schemes the topic of universal criticism, and running counter in some important respects to his own South African projects. He found our Education Bill in its most unpopular phase, and daily alienating valuable supporters belonging to the left wing of the Unionist Party in Birmingham and elsewhere—a subject on which he is, and always has been, pardonably sensitive. Above all, he found that his scheme for employing the shilling duty on corn as a means of obtaining preferential treatment for Canada was rendered impossible by the Chancellor of the Exchequer's unexpected refusal to embody it in his Budget, and this after he had just reason to suppose that in November the Cabinet as a whole were in its favour.

It must be acknowledged that all these causes taken together made him by no means an agreeable colleague during the first months after his return to England. Sensitive, indeed over sensitive, as he is to temporary movement of public opinion, he hated the political situation & wanted a new cry. And, quite unconsciously to himself, he was perhaps influenced by the notion that his counsels had not all the weight, which his public position justified, in determining the legislative policy of his colleagues.

Though Balfour was prepared to admit Chamberlain had been sorely tried by his colleagues, he found "no justification or excuse" for the public utterances made by the colonial secretary in

---

sign and thereby embarrass the government, the letter was withheld. Hamilton Diary, July 14, 1903, Add. MS 48681. The unsent note is in the Balfour Papers, Add. MS 49855, ff. 161–63. Also see Gollin, *Balfour*, pp. 49–50. Mowatt retired at the end of September.

late May and early June urging the adoption of imperial preference and in "distinct violation of an arrangement" with himself.
Concerned with preserving party unity, Balfour was bent on pursuing a scheme designed to ditch the extremists. His proposals,
which would empower the government to force down foreign
tariff barriers through the imposition of retaliatory duties, would
be repugnant to orthodox free traders but not satisfy supporters
of imperial preference. He explained his general position to
Devonshire, hoping of course the Duke would fall in with it.
"The path of safety [he added], is not to be found in the ad-
herence to discredited dogmas, but in the cultivation of a sober
public opinion, and in the steadfast cooperation of men who are,
neither blind to new necessities, nor too easily carried away by
new enthusiasms." [37]

By the middle of September the dogmatists (Ritchie, Lord
George Hamilton, secretary of state for India, and Balfour of
Burleigh), and the enthusiast (Chamberlain), had resigned.
Devonshire, rather scandalized by the methods the prime minis-
ter had used to dismiss the extremists, and finding that he was
himself a free trader after all, left the cabinet shortly thereafter.
Just before he resigned the Duke received an exceedingly bitter
letter from the ex-colonial secretary.

For my own part [Chamberlain wrote], I care only for the great
question of Imperial Unity. Everything else is secondary or conse-
quential. . . .
    If the Cabinet and the Party had been united we might have faced
the General Election with confidence that even if we were defeated—
as I believe we should have been on Education and War Office Reforms—we should have had a policy for the future which time and
discussion would have made victorious. . . .
    I, who for the sake of the party swallowed these camels, now find
that you and others strain at my gnat!
    What did I ask of you before I went to South Africa? That you
should retain the shilling corn duty and give a drawback to Canada.
I thought you had all, except Ritchie, accepted this policy. While I

37. Aug. 27, 1903, Add. MS 49770. Balfour's references to Chamberlain's tru-
culence and illness are corroborated by a letter from Lansdowne to Balfour,
April 12, 1903, Add. MS 49728, and a diary entry by Hamilton, April 12, 1903,
Add. MS 48680. For a recent interpretation of Balfour's role in the cabinet crisis
see D. Judd, *Balfour and the British Empire* (London, 1968), pp. 108–24.

was slaving my life out you threw it over as of no importance, and it is to this indifference to a great policy, which you had yourself accepted, that you owe the present situation.[38]

Chamberlain had occasion to be bitter, but his explanation of events was both illogical and distorted. How could a concession to Canada which foreshadowed a "great policy," that of overthrowing free trade for imperial preference, be compared to the swallowing of a "gnat"? Furthermore, Devonshire had not accepted Canadian preference before Chamberlain left on his tour, though the colonial secretary and Balfour might well have thought he did. Indeed, the Duke was hard of hearing and as a consequence often not certain of what occurred at cabinet meetings. Even Balfour could not always be sure what was decided at cabinet since minutes were not kept. As he commented on another occasion to Lord Salisbury when a misunderstanding arose:

I agree with you that a brief record of cabinet decisions would be a convenience: my own memory in such matters is very untrustworthy, & I sometimes find it difficult, after our confused discussion, to recollect even the instructions which I have received on matters which I have myself brought before it.[39]

Cabinet dissension caused by such administrative inefficiency was further exacerbated by the decisive intervention of permanent officials. Hamilton and Mowatt had "preached" not only to Ritchie, but also to Devonshire. They also conspired with free traders such as Goschen and Hicks Beach, former cabinet ministers who still carried considerable weight in deliberations in Parliament and within the Unionist party.[40]

Chamberlain also did not, naturally enough, take into account the effects of his own reputation or of the precipitous course which he had taken upon those whose support he needed. Balfour thought that although several cabinet members were not dog-

38. Sept. 21, 1903, Holland, *Devonshire,* II, 355–56.
39. April 22, 1900, Add. MS 49691.
40. Devonshire likely did not understand the economic arguments presented to him (see Balfour's comment to this effect in Dugdale, *Balfour,* I, 360), but the fact the Treasury officials, from their positions of expertise, were opposed to fiscal change must have carried influence with him. For their activities see Hamilton Diaries, Add. MSS 48680, ff. 133–34; and 48681, ff. 5, 15, 24, 28. For Hicks Beach's efforts to thwart Chamberlain see Hicks Beach, *Life,* II, 187–200.

matic free traders they were "disturbed by the reflection that they might be dragged along the new path much further than they desired to go. Joe's impulsiveness, combined with his extraordinary vigour and controversial skill, thoroughly alarmed them." [41] "Joe" even alienated men who supported his program. For one of Milner's well-placed informants, who shared in Chamberlain's schemes for empire, could report:

> It is impossible to doubt that Chamberlain 'took the floor' on his return from South Africa in a spirit of somewhat self-willed infallibility. Had I been in Parliament, I should have sided with him, but I should have declared my own reservations, and should have protested against the gratuitous defiance, the uncompromising ram-rod style of his crude programme. There is no doubt that J. C. has managed to excite resentments in the Cabinet and outside, which have weakened his position more than he, I think, realizes.
>
> Looking back, I feel that the key note of his character has been pugnacity, antagonism, self-will. By good Providence those qualities have in the main been directed (since that epoch-making time in [1886]) against the enemies of his country, wh[ich] has enabled us to follow him & support him thru' thick and thin. The weak point is that these qualities are not *only* directed against the enemies of his Country, but against any personality or influence which baffles or foils him, and it would appear that his weakness increases upon him. In the long run he steadily makes new enemies but seldom makes new friends.[42]

It was not only this informed observer who was concerned about Chamberlain's "crude programme." Hamilton too, blamed him because he had "not had a scheme worked out before he made a public pronouncement." [43] He had no firm reciprocal commitment from Australasia and had yet to prove the economic advantages of Canadian preference. He admitted to Hamilton that he had "no plan whatever of a cut & dried sort. If Colonies did not fall into line—if for instance the Australian Commonwealth did not offer good enough terms, he should pass them by & pass on to another—N. Zealand." [44] W. A. S. Hewins of the

41. Aug. 27, 1903, Add. MS 49770.
42. Philip Lyttelton Gell, city financier, acquaintance of Chamberlain and confident of Brodrick, to Milner, Sept. 19, 1903, Milner MSS, XXXIX.
43. Hamilton Diary, May 19, 1903, Add. MS 48680.
44. *Ibid.*, June 30, 1903, Add. MS 48681.

London School of Economics, who later helped in Chamberlain's tariff propaganda campaign, learned that the colonial secretary did not "pretend to be an economic expert. I once [said Chamberlain] read Mill and tried to read Marshall. You must supply the economic arguments." [45] Presumably his own office had not helped or informed him. To launch a controversial campaign without previous preparation was poor tactics. To launch it in the face of entrenched opposition was courting defeat.

The adoption of imperial preference at the turn of the century would have been for Britain an economically unsound proposition.[46] Even Chamberlain himself, despite his public utterances to the contrary, adopted it less out of conviction than because of political expediency. Yet factors other than the merits of his fiscal program served to thwart Chamberlain's bid to get the cabinet to accept it. Inefficient cabinet procedure and the anomalous activity of Treasury officials conspired to render his task exceedingly difficult. His unfortunate accident, his untimely South African tour, and his political embarrassment caused by the education controversy prevented him from pursuing effectively the art of personal persuasion—an art at which he excelled. His own department was neither by inclination nor function able to provide him with a program to counter the fiscal missives of the Treasury and the Board of Trade. These departments' experts marshalled evidence which Chamberlain's office did not try to rebut even though the unreliability of statistics left ample room for challenge. He had been baffled by the weaknesses of the Colonial Office and the obstructions of other departments. He was annoyed by the intransigence or vacillation of his cabinet colleagues and probably rendered exceedingly impatient by ill health and setbacks to his other imperial schemes. Unable to make the governmental system do his bidding, Chamberlain defied it. His actions led not only to a cabinet schism that weakened irreparably the Unionist coalition, but to the removal from political power of the empire's most dynamic individual, himself.

45. W. A. S. Hewins, *The Apologia of an Imperialist* (2 vols.; London, 1929), I, 68.
46. S. B. Saul, *Studies in British Overseas Trade, 1870–1914* (Liverpool, 1960), p. 228.

Conclusion

Chamberlain began his public career in Birmingham as a municipal reformer, one who encouraged increased activity on the part of local government in the affairs of the community. He went on to demand more state activity on a national scale. He ended his career in attempting to strengthen the empire through more government control and expenditure. In seeking to make the central state a more active factor in the empire at large Chamberlain, as colonial secretary, possessed unique advantages denied his predecessors. His term of office, which coincided with a heightened public concern with the empire, was unprecedented in length. Politically he was one of the most influential cabinet ministers in a government which enjoyed the largest majority of the century, a majority pitted against an opposition weakened by factionalism and poor leadership. Despite these advantages Chamberlain's accomplishments were far less extensive than has often been suggested in the literature about this dynamic imperialist. Indeed, as in the 1880's with domestic reform and the Irish question, so too at the turn of the century with imperial reform, he was largely thwarted in the pursuit of his ambitions. In both instances the obvious symptom of that frustration was his resignation from office.

While the symptom of his difficulties as colonial secretary was obvious, the causes were not. To begin with Chamberlain came into an administrative system ill-equipped to assume more imperial burdens. Neither his office nor the colonial service possessed sufficient experienced manpower. The cabinet had not the machinery to co-ordinate the activities of the several departments when their co-operation was needed to deal with such major imperial problems as the South African situation.

Through reforms and new expenditure these inadequacies might have been remedied. But the men who operated the instruments of imperial administration were not disposed to innovate or lead. With but few exceptions, such as the efforts of a few officials to control malaria, static attitudes and functions pervaded the Colonial Office; but even more importantly featured in Treasury obstruction. Reinforced by the belief that government should pursue a passive role in the community and possessed of immense power, that department seemed at almost every turn to curtail Chamberlain's imperial initiatives. But opposition on the part of Hicks Beach and Hamilton did not simply stem from a preoccupation with the status quo. Chamberlain's methods, derived from his Birmingham business and political background, were anathemas to men conditioned in a different school of life. The colonial secretary, in Hamilton's words, "was not born, bred or educated in the way which alone secures the necessary tact and behaviour of a real gentleman." Distrust stemming from differences in background was further accentuated by Chamberlain's impulsive temperament and abrasive political style. Chamberlain did not succeed in obtaining the confidence of Treasury officials. Indeed, he drew their hostility.

If the Treasury's attitude was a decisive factor in contributing to Chamberlain's frustration, so too was the general lack of support given him by his cabinet colleagues. The cabinet was agreed that Britain must remain the paramount power in South Africa. Although his colleagues, Hicks Beach included, shared in Chamberlain's broader imperial objectives, they had serious reservations about the suitability of his specific programs and the methods with which he pursued them. Certainly there is no evidence to suggest that Chamberlain received cabinet support in his confrontations with the Treasury. There is, on the other hand, much evidence to suggest that his colleagues were disturbed by his impulsiveness and were reluctant to engage in new departures. Balfour's attitude in connection with the imperial preference dispute is a case in point. Chamberlain possessed the influence and energy but not the circumspection and patience needed to make a static administrative system adjust to the challenges of imperial expansion. His brusque methods and many schemes alienated some and overburdened other key members of that system. Without administrative support and initiatives his programs and policies were more illusory than real or even, as in the case of South Africa, destructive to the cause he had set out to foster.

Selected Bibliography:
A Note on Sources

Three guides recently published by the Public Record Office were invaluable in finding and using departmental correspondence. These are *The Records of the Colonial and Dominions Office* (1964), *List of Cabinet Papers, 1880–1914* (1964), and *List of Colonial Office Confidential Prints to 1916* (1965). The correspondence of the general department of the Colonial Office (CO series 323, consisting of some one hundred volumes for the period 1895–1903) was indispensable. It contains papers concerned with the office establishment, trade and defense. Yet minutes and despatches on these topics were often found in the records of the geographical departments. No systematic effort was made to keep dossiers on the office staff or members of the colonial service, although the *Colonial Office Lists,* unofficial publications sanctioned by the secretary of state and compiled by staff clerks, help fill the gap. Between 1884 and 1914 no parliamentary inquiry was conducted into the civil service. But newspapers, periodicals, memoirs, biographies, civil service reports and confidential prints contain important information about office problems and personalities. Treasury out-letters to the Colonial Office (T 7) and the financial papers of Sir Edward Hamilton (T 168) are essential to an understanding of the relations between the two departments. Selective searches in the records of the Board of Trade, the War Office and the Foreign Office helped to clarify the effect other departments had on Colonial Office decisions. R. B. Pugh's article and bibliography (*CHBE*, III, 711–768, 905–907) as well as his introductory notes in *The Records of the Colonial and Dominions Office* are essential sources for students of imperial administration. Recent publications which shed light on the antecedents and subsequent evolution of the office are J. W. Cell's "The Colonial Office in the 1850's" (*Historical Studies: Australia and New Zealand*, XII, 43–56) and K. E. Robinson's *The Dilemmas of Trusteeship*.

With the exception of the Monk Bretton manuscripts, the private papers cited are familiar to historians of the period. However, as in the case of the Milner papers, I have found materials not mentioned elsewhere which are valuable for administrative studies. The Hamilton diaries are crammed with political and social as well as financial and administrative information. The Chamberlain papers are disappointing. J. Amery still retained those relevant to the period 1903–1914 and some documents, quoted in part by J. L. Garvin, are missing, suggesting that papers which might have contained more administrative detail have been destroyed.

Recent studies of nineteenth-century British public administration have concentrated upon agencies of social change (i.e., emigrant traffic, poor laws, public health) and the civil service reforms of the mid-Victorian period. Although not specifically concerned with the institutions or time period studied in this work, they proved very illuminating, particularly the scholars' debate in which O. MacDonagh (*Historical Journal*, I, 52–67) and Valerie Cromwell (*Victorian Studies*, IX, 245–255) have participated. Max Weber, who wrote his work on bureaucracy before 1914 (see *From Max Weber* edited by H. H. Gerth and C. Wright Mills) must have found ample evidence in the British example to support his theories. Hypotheses which adapt and significantly modify his assertions may be found in recent numbers of the *Public Administration Review*, for example, in articles by W. S. Sayre (XVIII, 102–105) and D. Waldo (XXI, 210–225). Zara Steiner's analysis of the Foreign Office (*Historical Journal*, VI, 59–90) and Ann Burton's on the Treasury (*Public Administration*, XLIV, 169–192) are among the very few new studies of government departments in the late nineteenth century. So it was difficult, without examining vast archival materials, to make many detailed comparisons between the Colonial Office and other administrative agencies.

One of the best new bibliographical aids to the immense literature on British imperialism is *The Historiography of the British Empire-Commonwealth* edited by R. W. Winks. D. K. Fieldhouse's *The Theory of Capitalist Imperialism* is an excellent introduction to practically all the major writers who have dealt with that important if vague concept. Any study of the motives and priorities of British expansion in the Chamberlain era might well begin with the work of R. Robinson and J. Gallagher (*Africa and the Victorians*) and follow the growing body of scholarly argument their book has generated.

Archives

British Museum. London.
  Balfour Papers.
  Hamilton Papers.
  Ripon Papers.
Liverpool Public Library. Liverpool.
  Liverpool Chamber of Commerce Minute Books.
Oxford University. Oxford.
  Milner Papers, New College.
  Monk Bretton Papers, Bodleian.
  Salisbury Papers, Christ Church.
Public Record Office. London.
  Balfour Papers:
    PRO 30/60: Cabinet and departmental memos
               and private correspondence,
               1897–1903.
  Board of Trade:
    BT 13: Establishment division, correspondence
           and papers, 1898–1901.
  Cabinet Papers:
    Cab. 37: 1895–1903.

Colonial Office:

CO 67: Cyprus, correspondence original, 1897.

CO 147: Lagos, correspondence original, 1900, 1904.

CO 273: Straits Settlements, correspondence original, 1900–1903.

CO 323: Correspondence general, 1894–1904.

CO 417: South Africa, correspondence original, 1899–1903.

CO 429: Patronage, correspondence original, 1895–1903.

CO 431: Accounts Branch, correspondence original, 1896–1903.

CO 537: West Africa, correspondence original, supplementary, 1897–1898.

CO 854: Circular despatches, 1894–1903.

CO 878: Colonial Office, office minutes, 1895–1902.

CO 879: Africa, confidential prints, 1895–1903.

CO 883: Mediterranean, confidential prints, 1895–1903.

CO 884: West Indies, confidential prints, 1895–1905.

CO 885: Miscellaneous, confidential prints, 1895–1903.

Foreign Office:

FO 633: Cromer Papers.

Hamilton Papers:

T 168: Financial papers, 1895–1903.

Treasury:

T 7: Out-letters, colonial affairs, 1891–1904.

War Office:

WO 32/268: Office establishment, 1895–1899.

WO 32/269: Wolseley correspondence on the Boer War.

University of Birmingham Library, Birmingham.

Chamberlain Papers.

Williamstrip Park, Circencester, Glos.
    Hicks Beach Papers.

Government Publications

Colonial Office Lists. London.
Great Britain. *Hansard's Parliamentary Debates.*
————. *Parliamentary Papers.*

Newspapers and Periodicals

Stock Exchange Official Intelligence. London.
The Times. London.

Published Private Papers, Speeches and Memoirs

Balfour, Lady Frances. *Ne Obliviscaris.* 2 vols. London, 1930.
Boyd, C. W., ed. *Mr. Chamberlain's Speeches.* 2 vols. New York, 1914.
Brett, M. V., ed. *Journals and Letters of Reginald Viscount Esher.* 3 vols. London, 1934.
Bruce, Sir Charles. *The Broad Stone of Empire.* 2 vols. London, 1910.
Butler, W. F. *Sir William Butler, An Autobiography.* London, 1911.
Furse, R. *Aucuparius.* London, 1962.
Hancock, W. K. and Jean van der Poel, eds. *Selections from the Smuts Papers.* 4 vols. London, 1966.
Headlam, C., ed. *The Milner Papers.* 2 vols. London, 1931–33.
Hewins, W. A. S. *The Apologia of An Imperialist.* 2 vols. London, 1929.
Howard, C. H. D., ed. *A Political Memoir, 1880–92, by Joseph Chamberlain.* London, 1953.
Marsh, Edward. *A Number of People, A Book of Reminiscences.* London, 1939.

Maycock, W. *With Mr. Chamberlain in the United States and Canada, 1887–88.* Toronto, 1914.

Olivier, Margaret. *Sydney Olivier, Letters and Selected Writings.* New York, 1948.

Parkinson, Sir Cosmo. *The Colonial Office from Within, 1909–1945.* London, 1947.

Perham, Margery and Mary Bull, eds. *The Diaries of Lord Lugard.* 4 vols. London, 1959–63.

Ross, Sir Ronald. *Memories of Sir Patrick Manson.* London, 1930.

————. *Memoirs.* London, 1923.

West, Sir Algernon. *Contemporary Portraits.* New York, 1920.

Contemporary Books

Bright, Sir Charles. *Submarine Telegraphs: Their History, Construction and Working.* London, 1898.

Butler, Sir William. *The Life of Sir George Pomeroy-Colley.* London, 1899.

Hatch, F. H. and J. A. Chalmer. *The Gold Mines of the Rand.* London, 1895.

Hobson, J. A. *Imperialism: A Study.* London, 1902; 2nd ed., 1938.

Liverpool School of Tropical Medicine. *Sixth Annual Report.* Liverpool, 1904.

Macrosty, H. W. *The Trust Movement in British Industry.* London, 1907.

Contemporary Articles

Hamilton, Sir William Baillie. "Forty-Four Years at the Colonial Office," *The Nineteenth Century and After,* LXV (April, 1909), 599–613.

Morris, Sir Daniel. "The Imperial Department of Agriculture in the West Indies," *United Empire,* n.s., II (February, 1911), 73–85.

Wilson, Sir Harry. "Joseph Chamberlain As I Knew Him," *United Empire*, n.s., VI (February, 1917), 102–111.

Secondary Sources

Books

Abbott, A. W. *A Short History of the Crown Agents and Their Office*. London, 1959.

Allen, G. C. *The Industrial Development of Birmingham and the Black Country, 1860–1927*. London, 1929; reprinted with corrections, 1966.

Ashworth, W. *An Economic History of England, 1870–1939*. London, 1960.

Beachey, R. W. *The British West Indies Sugar Industry in the Late 19th Century*. Oxford, 1957.

Brown, B. H. *The Tariff Reform Movement in Great Britain, 1881–1895*. New York, 1943.

Cartwright, A. P. *The Corner House*. Cape Town, 1965.

Cowan, C. D. *Nineteenth-Century Malaya: The Origins of British Political Control*. London, 1961.

Curtin, P. D. *The Image of Africa*. Madison, Wisc., 1964.

Dugdale, Blanche. *Arthur James Balfour*. 2 vols. London, 1936.

Emden, P. H. *Randlords*. London, 1935.

Farr, D. M. L. *The Colonial Office and Canada, 1867–1887*. Toronto, 1955.

Feiling, K. *The Life of Neville Chamberlain*. London, 1947.

Flint, J. E. *Sir George Goldie*. London, 1960.

Frankel, S. H. *Investment and the Return to Equity Capital in the South African Gold Mining Industry, 1887–1965*. Oxford, 1967.

Fraser, P. *Joseph Chamberlain*. London, 1966.

Fyfe, C. A. *A History of Sierra Leone*. London, 1962.

Galbraith, J. S. *Reluctant Empire*. Los Angeles, 1963.

Garvin, J. L. and J. Amery. *The Life of Joseph Chamberlain*. 4 vols. London, 1932–51.

Gerth, H. H. and C. Wright Mills, eds. *From Max Weber.* New York, 1958 (reprint).

Gibson, J. M. *Physician to the World, The Life of General William C. Gorgas.* Durham, N.C., 1950.

Gill, C. and A. Briggs. *History of Birmingham.* 2 vols. London, 1952.

Gollin, A. *Balfour's Burden.* London, 1965.

Grenville, J. A. S. *Lord Salisbury and Foreign Policy.* London, 1964.

Hall, A. R. *The London Capital Market and Australia, 1870–1914.* Canberra, 1963.

Hancock, W. K. *Smuts, The Sanguine Years, 1870–1919.* Cambridge, 1962.

————. *Survey of British Commonwealth Affairs,* II, *Problems of Economic Policy.* London, 1940.

Heussler, R. *Yesterday's Rulers, The Making of the British Colonial Service.* Syracuse, 1963.

Hicks Beach, Lady Victoria. *Life of Sir Michael Hicks Beach.* 2 vols. London, 1932.

Hill, G. *A History of Cyprus.* 4 vols. Cambridge, 1952.

Holland, B. *The Life of Spencer Compton, Eighth Duke of Devonshire.* 2 vols. London, 1911.

Hyam, R. *Elgin and Churchill at the Colonial Office, 1905–1908. The Watershed of the Empire-Commonwealth.* London, 1968.

Jeffries, C. *The Colonial Empire and Its Civil Service.* London, 1938.

Johnson, F. A. *Defence by Committee: The British Committee of Imperial Defence, 1885–1959,* London, 1960.

Judd, D. *Balfour and the British Empire.* London, 1968.

Kelsall, R. K. *Higher Civil Servants in Britain from 1870 to the Present Day.* London, 1955.

Kendle, J. E. *The Colonial and Imperial Conferences, 1887–1911.* London, 1967.

Lehmann, J. H. *All Sir Garnet: A Life of Field Marshall Lord Wolseley.* London, 1964.

Lockhart, J. G. and C. M. Woodhouse. *Cecil Rhodes.* New York, 1963.

McCourt, E. *Remember Butler.* London, 1967.

Mallet, B. *British Budgets, 1887–88 to 1912–13.* London, 1913.

Manson-Bahr, P. H. *History of the School of Tropical Medicine in London.* London, 1956.

———. and A. Alcock. *The Life and Work of Sir Patrick Manson.* London, 1927.

Marais, J. S. *The Fall of Kruger's Republic.* Oxford, 1961.

Milne, A. H. *Sir Alfred Lewis Jones.* London, 1914.

Newton, Lord. *Lord Lansdowne.* London, 1929.

Oliver, R. *Sir Harry Johnston and the Scramble for Africa.* London, 1957.

Pakenham, Elizabeth. *Jameson's Raid.* London, 1960.

Pearson, H. *Labby: The Life of Henry Labouchere.* London, 1936.

Perham, Margery. *Lugard.* 2 vols. London, 1956–60.

Preston, R. A. *Canada and "Imperial Defense": A Study of the Origins of the British Commonwealth's Organization.* Durham, N.C., 1967.

Robinson, H. *Carrying British Mail Overseas.* London, 1964.

Robinson, R. and J. Gallagher. *Africa and the Victorians.* New York, 1961.

Saron, G. and L. Hotz, eds. *The Jews in South Africa, A History.* London, 1955.

Saul, S. B. *Studies in British Overseas Trade, 1870–1914.* Liverpool, 1960.

Semmel, B. *Imperialism and Social Reform.* Cambridge, Mass., 1960.

Thompson, L. M. *The Unification of South Africa, 1902–1910.* Oxford, 1960.

van der Poel, Jean. *The Jameson Raid.* Cape Town, 1951.

Wrench, J. E. *Geoffrey Dawson and Our Times.* London, 1955.

Articles

Blainey, G. "Lost Causes of the Jameson Raid," *Economic History Review*, XVIII (1965), 350–366.

Burton, Ann M. "Treasury Control and Colonial Policy in the Late Nineteenth Century," *Public Administration,* XLIV (Summer, 1966), 169–192.

Cell, J. W. "The Colonial Office in the 1850's," *Historical Studies: Australia and New Zealand,* XII (October, 1965), 43–56.

Checkland, S. G. "The Mind of the City, 1870–1914," *Oxford Economic Papers,* n.s., IX (October, 1957), 261–278.

Cromwell, Valerie. "Interpretations of Nineteenth-Century Administration: An Analysis," *Victorian Studies,* IX (March, 1966), 245–255.

Cross, J. A. "The Colonial Office and the Dominions Before 1914," *Journal of Commonwealth Political Studies,* IV (July, 1966), 138–148.

Drus, Ethel. "A Report on the Papers of Joseph Chamberlain Relating to the Jameson Raid and the Inquiry," *Bulletin of the Institute of Historical Research,* XXV (November, 1952), 33–67.

———. "Select Documents from the Chamberlain Papers Concerning Anglo-Transvaal Relations, 1896–1899," *Bulletin of the Institute of Historical Research,* XXVII (November, 1954), 156–189.

Dummett, R. E. "The Campaign Against Malaria and the Expansion of Scientific, Medical and Sanitary Services in British West Africa, 1898–1910," *African Historical Studies,* I (1968), 153–195.

Galbraith, J. S. "The 'Turbulent Frontier' As a Factor in British Expansion," *Comparative Studies in Society and History,* II (January, 1960), 150–168.

Hazelwood, A. "The Origin of the State Telephone Service in Great Britain," *Oxford Economic Papers,* n.s., V (March, 1953), 13–25.

Joyce, R. B. "Sir William MacGregor—A Colonial Governor," *Historical Studies: Australia and New Zealand,* XI (November, 1963), 18–31.

MacDonagh, O. "The Nineteenth-Century Revolution in Government: A Reappraisal," *Historical Journal,* I (1958), 52–67.

Madden, A. F. "Changing Attitudes and Widening Responsibilities [in the Empire-Commonwealth], 1895–1914," *Cambridge History of the British Empire*, III (1959), 339–405.

Pugh, R. B. "The Colonial Office, 1801–1925," *Cambridge History of the British Empire*, III (1959), 711–768.

Saul, S. B. "The Economic Significance of 'Constructive Imperialism,'" *Journal of Economic History*, XVII (June, 1957), 173–192.

Sayre, W. S. "Premises of Public Administration: Past and Emerging," *Public Administration Review*, XVIII (Spring, 1958), 102–105.

Steiner, Zara. "The Last Years of the Old Foreign Office, 1898–1905," *Historical Journal*, VI (1963), 59–60.

Stokes, E. "Milnerism," *Historical Journal*, V (1952), 47–60.

Waldo, D. "Organization Theory: An Elephantine Problem," *Public Administration Review*, XXI (Summer, 1961), 210–225.

Wilde, R. H. "Joseph Chamberlain and the South African Republic, 1895–1899," *Archives Year Book for South African History*, I (1956), i–158D.

Woodhouse, C. M. "The Missing Telegrams and the Jameson Raid," *History Today*, XII (June and July, 1962), 395–404, 506–514.

Dissertations

Blakeley, B. L. "The Colonial Office: 1870–1890." Ph.D. dissertation, Duke University, 1966.

Kubicek, R. V. "Joseph Chamberlain and the Colonial Office." Ph.D. dissertation, Duke University, 1964.

Index